Entertaining the Braganzas

Entertaining the Braganzas

When Queen Maria of Portugal visited William Stephens in 1788

Jenifer Roberts

PEN & SWORD HISTORY

AN IMPRINT OF PEN & SWORD BOOKS LTD.
YORKSHIRE – PHILADELPHIA

First published in Great Britain in 2018 by
Pen & Sword History
An imprint of
Pen & Sword Books Ltd
Yorkshire - Philadelphia

Hardback ISBN: 9781526715210
Paperback ISBN: 9781526751492

A CIP catalogue record for this book is available from the British Library.

Typeset in Ehrhardt MT 11/13 By SRJ Info Jnana System Pvt Ltd.

Printed and bound by TJ International Ltd.

Pen & Sword Books Ltd incorporates the Imprints of Pen & Sword Books
Archaeology, Atlas, Aviation, Battleground, Discovery, Family History,
History, Maritime, Military, Naval, Politics, Railways, Select, Transport, True
Crime, Fiction, Frontline Books, Leo Cooper, Praetorian Press, Seaforth
Publishing, Wharncliffe and White Owl.

For a complete list of Pen & Sword titles please contact

PEN & SWORD BOOKS LIMITED
47 Church Street, Barnsley, South Yorkshire, S70 2AS, England
E-mail: enquiries@pen-and-sword.co.uk
Website: www.pen-and-sword.co.uk

or

PEN AND SWORD BOOKS
1950 Lawrence Rd, Havertown, PA 19083, USA
E-mail: Uspen-and-sword@casematepublishers.com
Website: www.penandswordbooks.com

For Paul, with love

Contents

Illustrations

1. Church of St Sidwell, Laneast, Cornwall.
Photograph by Jenifer Roberts

2. Hornafast on the banks of the River Tamar, Pentillie estate, Cornwall.
Photograph by Hazel McHaffie

3. Pentillie Castle. Engraving by Thomas Allom, 1832.
Private collection

4–5. Two engravings by R. White of the Cathedral Church of St Peter in Exeter, 1744.
Published in Rocque's plan of the city of Exeter. Reproduced with the kind permission of North Devon Athenaeum and Devon Archives and Local Studies Service

6. Terreiro do Paço and Ribeira Palace before the earthquake (arrival of a new papal nuncio, 1693).
Coleção de Jorge de Brito, Cascais

7. Maria de Bragança at the age of four. Painting by Francisco Pavona, 1738/9.
Palácio Nacional de Queluz, Direção-Geral do Património Cultural / Arquivo de Documentação Fotográfica (DGPC/ADF), photographer: Paula Cintra/Laura Castro Caldas

8. William Stephens aged 21. Miniature painting set in gold brooch, Lisbon, 1752.
Private collection

9. Maria, crown princess of Portugal. Painting attributed to Francisco Vieira de Matos (Vieira Lusitano), c.1753.
Palácio Nacional de Queluz, Direção-Geral do Património Cultural / Arquivo de Documentação Fotográfica (DGPC/ADF), photographer: Manuel Palma

10. Maria's mother, Mariana Vitória de Bourbon, painted in early middle age.
Palácio Nacional de Queluz, Direção-Geral do Património Cultural / Arquivo de Documentação Fotográfica (DGPC/ADF), photographer: Luísa Oliveira

11. Maria's father, José I. Painting by Francisco José Aparício.
Museu Nacional dos Coches, Direção-Geral do Património Cultural / Arquivo de Documentação Fotográfica (DGPC/ADF), photographer: Henrique Ruas

12. The Lisbon earthquake, 1 November 1755. Engraving by Christoph Henrich Bohn after drawing by Reinier Vinkeles, late eighteenth century.
Rijksmuseum, Amsterdam, RP–P–OB–64.534

Museu Nacional dos Coches, Direção-Geral do Património Cultural / Arquivo de Documentação Fotográfica (DGPC/ADF), photographer: José Pessoa

29. The palace at Vila Viçosa.
Photograph by EDARF, 2007

30. Maria I. Engraving by Marie Anne Bourlier from original miniature portrait, probably by Daniel Valentine Rivière.
Published in London, October 1807. Private collection

31. Carlota Joaquina, painted in celebration of her marriage to Prince João, 1785.
Palácio Nacional de Queluz, Direção-Geral do Património Cultural / Arquivo de Documentação Fotográfica (DGPC/ADF), photographer: Paulo Cintra/Laura Castro Caldas

32. Prince João. Engraving from original miniature portrait by D. Pelegrim, 1808.
Fundação Biblioteca Nacional, Brazil

33. Maria I. Painting by Guiseppe Troni, 1783.
Palácio Nacional de Queluz, Direção-Geral do Património Cultural / Arquivo de Documentação Fotográfica (DGPC/ADF), photographer: José Pessoa

34. William Stephens aged 67. Engraving by A. Smith from drawing by Bouck, published in London, 1799.
Private collection

35. William's mansion house in Marinha Grande.
Photograph by Edwin Green

36. The factory courtyard in Marinha Grande.
Private collection

37. The Basilica da Estrela. Lithograph by Salema, c.1870.
Biblioteca Nacional de Portugal, Lisbon, E.983.A

38. Maria I, holding a miniature portrait of her husband, c.1786–91.
Palácio Nacional de Mafra, Direção-Geral do Património Cultural / Arquivo de Documentação Fotográfica (DGPC/ADF), photographer: José Paulo Ruas

39. Dr Francis Willis. Pastel by John Russell, c.1789.
© *National Portrait Gallery, London*

40. The Dona Maria Pavilion at Queluz.
Direção-Geral do Património Cultural / Arquivo de Documentação Fotográfica (DGPC/ADF), photographer: Luís Pavão

41. Largo do Paço, Rio de Janeiro. Engraving from original painting by J. Stainmann.
Published in Edmundo, Luíz, A Côrte de D. João no Rio de Janeiro (Rio de Janeiro, 1939)

Acknowledgements

I should like to thank everyone who assisted me in my research, particularly Professor José Pedro Barosa who inspired my interest in Marinha Grande and responded with generosity to my constant requests for information about the glass industry in Portugal, a subject on which he is an acknowledged authority. He guided my research, provided material, and made many helpful suggestions.

Luís de Abreu e Sousa looked after me in Marinha Grande, answered many questions, obtained images, and talked with enthusiasm about the history of his home town. The mayor of Câmara Municipal da Marinha Grande granted access to several thousand letters in his care and Paula Maia, archivist at Marinha Grande, undertook the lengthy task of reading the letters and sending me a précis of their contents. Ana Margarida Magalhães carried out research for me in Lisbon, and Dr Jorge Custódio provided information on two poems written by Marquesa de Alorna. I am grateful to them all.

In England, I should like to thank Ted and Sarah Coryton of Pentillie Castle for their interest and hospitality; and Yvonne Cova and Christine Robinson, who spent many hours helping with the translation of documents. Christine also translated two poems written by Marquesa de Alorna in honour of William Stephens.

I am grateful to Pen & Sword for having faith in this book, Claire Hopkins and Janet Brookes for their help and encouragement, and Eleri Pipien for her enthusiasm. Many thanks also to my generous and helpful readers – Lady Sarah Backhouse, Dr Hilary Custance Green, Dr Jean Shennan and Professor Gareth Williams – whose comments were invaluable. Finally, I am deeply grateful to my husband, Paul Beck, for his constant support, his company and help on most of my travels, and his tolerance as I spent so many hours immersed in the eighteenth century.

Permission to quote from original material has been granted by the Banks Project at the Natural History Museum, British Historical Society of Portugal (Lisbon branch), Câmara Municipal da Marinha Grande, Norfolk Record Office, and West Sussex Record Office. I am grateful to the late Mrs Timothy Mitchell Ellis for permission to quote from the Portugal diary of William Julius Mickle (published in *The Visit to Portugal in 1779–80 of William Julius Mickle* by S. George West, Lisbon, 1972), and to Donald D. Horward for permission to quote from *The French Campaign in Portugal 1810–1811* by Jean-Jacques Pelet (University of Minnesota Press, 1973).

My thanks to Edwin Green, Hazel McHaffie and João Reis Ribeiro for their generosity in allowing me to reproduce their photographs. Permission to reproduce images has also been granted by Deolinda Bonita, Câmara Municipal da Marinha Grande, Devon Archives and Local Studies Service, Direção-Geral do Património Cultural (Lisbon), Collection of the Museum of Lisbon/Lisbon City Council – EGEAC, National Portrait Gallery (London), and North Devon Athenaeum.

Every effort has been made to contact copyright holders. The publisher would be interested to hear from any copyright holders not here acknowledged.

STEPHENS FAMILY

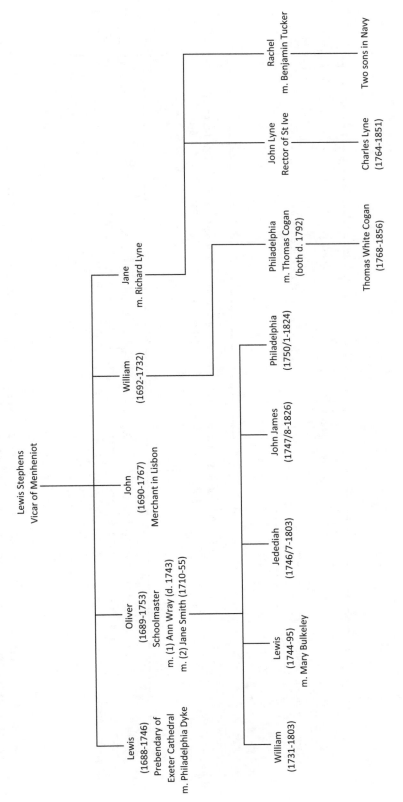

Lewis Stephens
Vicar of Menheniot

Lewis
(1688-1746)
Prebendary of
Exeter Cathedral
m. Philadelphia Dyke

John
(1690-1767)
Merchant in Lisbon

Oliver
(1689-1753)
Schoolmaster
m. (1) Ann Wray (d. 1743)
m. (2) Jane Smith (1710-55)

William
(1692-1732)

Jane
m. Richard Lyne

William
(1731-1803)

Lewis
(1744-95)
m. Mary Bulkeley

Jedediah
(1746/7-1803)

John James
(1747/8-1826)

Philadelphia
(1750/1-1824)

Philadelphia
m. Thomas Cogan
(both d. 1792)

John Lyne
Rector of St Ive

Rachel
m. Benjamin Tucker

Thomas White Cogan
(1768-1856)

Charles Lyne
(1764-1851)

Two sons in Navy

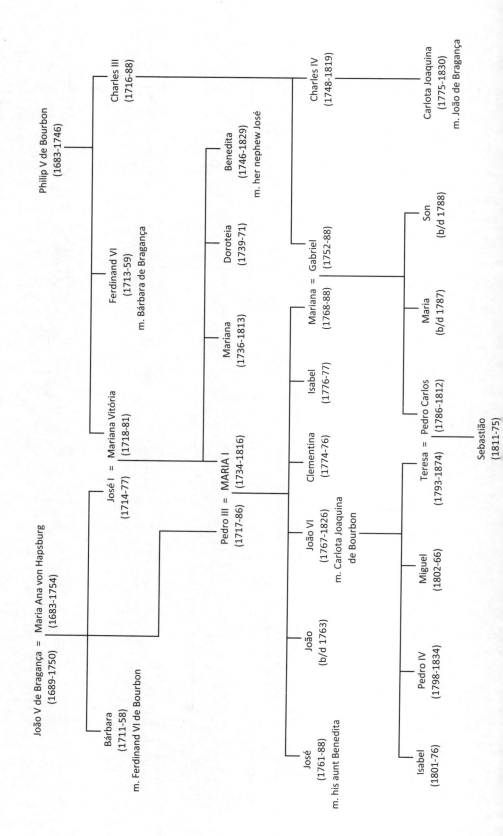

BRAGANÇA (Portugal)

BOURBON (Spain)

João V de Bragança = Maria Ana von Hapsburg
(1689-1750)   (1683-1754)

Philip V de Bourbon
(1683-1746)

Bárbara
(1711-58)
m. Ferdinand VI de Bourbon

José I = Mariana Vitória
(1714-77)   (1718-81)

Ferdinand VI
(1713-59)
m. Bárbara de Bragança

Charles III
(1716-88)

Pedro III = MARIA I
(1717-86)   (1734-1816)

Mariana
(1736-1813)

Doroteia
(1739-71)

Benedita
(1746-1829)
m. her nephew José

Charles IV
(1748-1819)

Carlota Joaquina
(1775-1830)
m. João de Bragança

José
(1761-88)
m. his aunt Benedita

João
(b/d 1763)

João VI
(1767-1826)
m. Carlota Joaquina
de Bourbon

Clementina
(1774-76)

Isabel
(1776-77)

Mariana = Gabriel
(1768-88)   (1752-88)

Isabel
(1801-76)

Pedro IV
(1798-1834)

Miguel
(1802-66)

Teresa = Pedro Carlos
(1793-1874)   (1786-1812)

Maria
(b/d 1787)

Son
(b/d 1788)

Sebastião
(1811-75)

Central Portugal

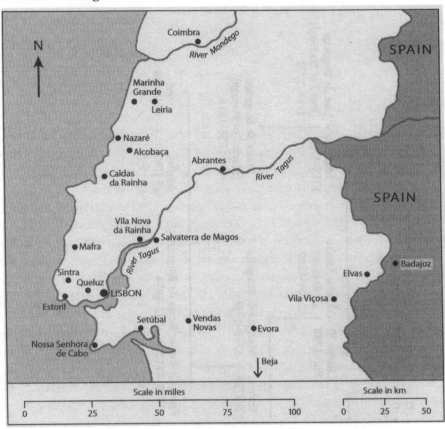

Lisbon area

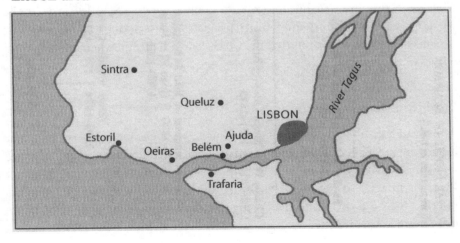

Notes to the Reader

Names and Titles

Portuguese names have been used for the Bragança family (João, José, Maria, Pedro). The names of Spanish kings have been anglicised as they are better known to English readers as Philip, Ferdinand and Charles.

A major figure in the story is Sebastião José de Carvalho e Melo, known to history as Marquis de Pombal. He used the name Carvalho until he was given the title of Count de Oeiras in 1759. Ten years later, he was created 1st Marquis de Pombal. With a few exceptions at the beginning of the story, the name Pombal has been used throughout. The same applies to Viscount de Ponte de Lima, the secretary of state whose previous title was Viscount de Vila Nova da Cerveira.

It was the custom in some noble families to have two concurrent titles. During the lifetime of the 3rd Marquis de Távora (1703–59), his eldest son used the title of 4th Marquis de Távora (1723–59). They were known respectively as the 'old marquis' and the 'young marquis'. Their wives were similarly known as the 'old marquesa' and the 'young marquesa.'

It was common practice for a man to attach his mother's maiden name to his paternal surname, linking the two with 'e' (Carvalho e Melo, Seabra e Silva, Melo e Castro). Such men were normally referred to by the first of these names (Carvalho, Seabra, Melo).

After 1748, Portuguese monarchs were known by the title of Most Faithful Majesty, a title granted by the pope to compete with the titles of Catholic Majesty (kings of Spain) and Most Christian Majesty (kings of France). For reasons of brevity, I have omitted the words 'Most Faithful' when quoting from letters of the period.

Diplomats and Consuls

Ambassadors, the highest-ranking diplomats, were exchanged between major monarchies. Smaller monarchies normally exchanged lower-ranking diplomats known as Envoys or Ministers (full title: Envoy Extraordinary and Minister Plenipotentiary). In the text, the British diplomat to the Court of Lisbon is referred to as the envoy and the Portuguese diplomat to the Court of St James in London as the minister.

During the second half of the eighteenth century, British envoys in Lisbon were: Abraham Castres (1749–57), Edward Hay (1757–67), William Henry Lyttelton (1767–70), and the Hon. Robert Walpole (1771–1800). Two envoys on special mission are mentioned in the text: Lord Tyrawley (1752) and Lord Kinnoull (1760).

Consuls were state-appointed officials who looked after British commercial affairs in foreign countries. A consul of the highest rank was known as Consul General, but the word consul has been used throughout except in quotations. Consuls mentioned in the text are: George Crowle (1752–4); Edward Hay (1754–7); and Sir John Hort (1767–96). Vice-consuls were consular officials of a lower grade.

Currency, exchange rates and monetary value

The Portuguese currency of the eighteenth and early nineteenth centuries was based on a decimal system. The basic unit was the *real* which had an insignificant value. A thousand *reis* (plural of real) formed a *milreis,* in which accounts were maintained and payments made. A thousand milreis formed a *conto* of reis (a million reis). Two other coins were in circulation: the *cruzado* was worth 400 reis; the *moydore* was worth ten times this amount, 4,000 reis or 4 milreis.

During the period of this story, the pound sterling was worth a little over three and a half milreis, so a conto of reis was worth about £286. Varying values of the pound sterling are not a reliable indicator of present-day values of Portuguese currency, but I have sometimes used such calculations to give an idea of scale. To obtain present-day values, I used Bank of England figures for 2016 taken from the consumer price index (CPI) compiled by the Office for National Statistics.

According to these figures, £1 sterling in 1750 would be worth about £200 today. Values decreased during the second half of the century and declined further during the Napoleonic Wars, before recovering after 1815. They reached a high in 1822, then declined to about £100 by the end of the story in 1826.

The Calendar

The Gregorian calendar was introduced into most European countries, including Portugal, in the late sixteenth century, but was not adopted in England until September 1752. The difference in time between the new Gregorian and the old Julian calendar was eleven days. For example, 1 January in the Julian calendar (referred to as 'Old Style') became 12 January in the Gregorian calendar ('New Style'). Therefore, during the first years of this story, dates in England were eleven days behind dates in Portugal.

In the Julian calendar, the new year started on 25 March. In September 1752, it was brought forward to 1 January. As a result, January, February and most of March changed from being the last months of the old year to the first months of the new. Although such dates are often referred to by using both Old and New Style (e.g. 1 January 1750/1), only New Style is used in the text to date events prior to September 1752.

The English Factory

The English Factory in Lisbon was a trade organisation for British merchants in the city, its name derived from the word 'factor' (as in broker or agent). During the period of this story, the word 'manufactory' was used to denote a manufacturing enterprise. In the text, the word 'Factory' with a capital letter is used to refer to the English Factory in Lisbon, the word 'factory' in lower case to an industrial concern.

Crystalline Glass

Crystal glass is made by the addition of lead oxide to the mix. Crystalline glass (also known as lead-free crystal) contains no lead and is generally cheaper to produce. The factory at Marinha Grande did not use lead in the production process, so 'crystalline glass' is used in the text to describe the production of tableware.

Appendix

The account by Philadelphia Stephens of the royal visit to Marinha Grande in the summer of 1788 is transcribed in full in the appendix. Her idiosyncratic use of capital letters has been retained, both in the appendix and in quotations used in the text. Some words (English and Portuguese) have been changed to modern spelling.

Glossary

A glossary of Portuguese and archaic English words is provided on pages 208–210.

Introduction

On 25 July 1788, Philadelphia Stephens sat by an open window in her brother's 'pretty little palace' in the village of Marinha Grande in Portugal. She was writing to a cousin in London and, as she reached the sixteenth page, she wrote the following words:

> 'My Brother has attained what nobody else in the Kingdom can boast of, which is the honour of entertaining the Royal Family and all the Court ... and given universal satisfaction to everybody from the Queen down to the Scullions and Stable Boys ... That she should come ... and sleep two Nights in the house of a private person, an Englishman and a Protestant, is a thing that never entered the Idea of the Portuguese and has struck all ... People with amazement.'[1]

Entertaining the Braganzas is the story of this unique event in royal history. Maria I of Portugal was a monarch with absolute power. William Stephens was an English industrialist; the illegitimate son of a Cornish servant girl, he travelled to Lisbon at the age of fifteen and survived many setbacks before achieving industrial success. The contrast between these two people could not have been greater – they were poles apart in every facet of their lives – yet they formed an unlikely friendship within the stifling formality of the Portuguese court.

Maria has been treated unkindly by history. Her reign is often relegated to a footnote, sandwiched between the more dramatic periods of the Marquis de Pombal and the Peninsular War. She deserves better than this, not only because she was a good woman whose misfortune was to inherit the crown, but also because her reign is a graphic example of the eighteenth-century battle between church and state, between the old superstitions and the age of reason. The queen embodied these contradictions. Pulled by her instincts towards the old religion, she understood at least some aspects of the Enlightenment and took a humanitarian approach to state affairs. A weak and fragile woman, she was unsuited for monarchy and the struggle for power between church and state helped to destroy her.

William Stephens achieved great things in a country which, at the time, was extremely backward by north European standards. He ran a thriving glass factory in a small village 70 miles north of Lisbon. He introduced a system of social welfare which was decades ahead of its time. He formed an orchestra composed entirely of factory workers. He built a theatre where men who had never learnt to read and write performed translations of Shakespeare and Voltaire. He transformed the rural economy, increasing life expectancy in the village beyond the national average. If his factory had been based in England, he would certainly have been one of the great names of the Industrial Revolution. The cotton mills of the Derwent Valley in Derbyshire and New Lanark on the Scottish borders are UNESCO World Heritage Sites, but William achieved at least as much in terms of worker welfare and did so thirty years earlier. And never has an industrial proprietor been more loved by his workers.

The friendship between William and Maria culminated on 30 June 1788 when she arrived in Marinha Grande with her family and all the court. William's house in the factory courtyard had been transformed into a miniature palace; servants had assembled the royal beds in rooms on the first floor and fastened curtains of crimson damask over the doors and windows. Maria stayed here for three days and, according to Philadelphia, she 'liked her Situation so well that she regretted leaving it and would have stayed longer had it not been for the unavoidable necessity of returning so soon to Lisbon'.

It is astonishing that all knowledge of this unique occasion was soon forgotten. There was no reference in the *Gazeta de Lisboa*; it was not mentioned in the dispatches of the British envoy (which normally described the queen's activities in some detail). When I researched the factory for my book *Glass: The Strange History of the Lyne Stephens Fortune*, I could only find four tantalising references.

The first was a list of items bought 'for the Queen's visit' in the one surviving accounts book at Marinha Grande; this made no reference to the length of her stay and it seems that no one fully understood its significance. The second was a brief mention of 'the Court's visit' in a footnote to the published journal of the poet Robert Southey who visited the factory in 1801.[2] The third was in the memoirs of Dr William Withering, a member of the Lunar Society of Birmingham, who spent several days in Marinha Grande in 1793:

> 'Mr Stephens had the honour to entertain the Queen and Royal Family of Portugal for ... three days in 1788. Her Majesty's attendants, with the vast influx of persons from the surrounding countryside, formed an assembly of many thousands.'[3]

Dr Withering has the reputation of a careful and thorough man. No one could accuse him of exaggeration but, in referring to a three-day visit, I did wonder whether his memory had served him correctly.

The final reference was in a book of memoirs published privately in 1871 by Charlotte Hawkey, a cousin of the Stephens family. After writing briefly (and inaccurately) about the glass factory, she explained that a letter describing the royal visit had been read aloud to Queen Charlotte in Windsor Castle, 'as being one containing some curious and interesting information'.[4] This was the only clue to the existence of a letter which, if it was not a figment of Miss Hawkey's imagination, I assumed had been lost down the centuries.

The Stephens family came from Cornwall. Geography had not led me to the West Sussex Record Office but, after the publication of *Glass*, the curator added some additional manuscripts to the Access to Archives website (a collation of catalogues of record offices throughout the country). One day, idly typing 'Marinha Grande' into the search box, I found the following reference: 'Account by Philadelphia Stephens of a Visit by the Queen and Royal Family of Portugal to Marinha Grande, 25 July 1788.'

Next morning, I was on my way to Sussex. As I sat in the record office reading Philadelphia's closely written pages, I realised that I might be the first person to read the letter for more than 200 years. It seemed miraculous that it had survived the centuries – and even more miraculous that it had fallen into my hands, possibly the only person in England who was aware of its true significance.

Philadelphia's handwriting is so easy to read, her prose so fluid, that it was easy to conjure the scene in my mind. Contemporary accounts of Portuguese royalty were normally written by men with an emphasis on politics and power. Philadelphia was interested in domestic detail: the clothes worn by the queen and her sisters; how the servants dressed the royal beds; how the family was served at table. Her account of the visit provides an intimate glimpse into the world of absolute monarchy, a snapshot of court life in the old Europe, just one year before the French Revolution began to change the face of the continent.

Having discovered the letter, I was able to trace its journey from Marinha Grande to the West Sussex Record Office. It must have been sent to Thomas Cogan in London, who had taken care of Philadelphia when she was orphaned at the age of five. He kept the letter and, when he died in 1792, it passed to his son, Thomas White Cogan, rector of East Dean in Sussex. It remained in the Cogan family for several more generations until it was presented to the record office as part of 'the residue of Mr W.P. Cogan's records as a solicitor', having been found in an empty house in Chichester in the early 1960s.

Part One

Marquis de Pombal

Prelude

The Catalyst

The morning of 1 November 1755 was unseasonably warm in Lisbon, the sun shining from a cloudless sky. Most people were in church to celebrate mass for All Saints' Day when, at half-past nine, they heard a noise which sounded like the king's heavy carriage rattling through the streets. The earth shuddered, then jerked upwards in a motion that felt like a wagon being driven violently over rough stones. The captain of a ship in the harbour watched the buildings of Lisbon rock to and fro like corn in the wind before they began to crumble in clouds of dust. 'In a quarter of an hour,' wrote the British consul, 'this great city was laid in ruins.'

The dust billowed through the lanes and alleyways, transforming sunlit morning into deepest night, and when the air began to clear, swarms of people emerged from the gloom, stumbling among the ruins. Later that day, a young merchant searched his pockets for pen and paper to describe what he saw:

> 'Old, Young, Male and Female, seeking their Parents, Children, Relations and Friends, many sick, many maimed and wounded from the fall of the Houses, some dead and most part especially Women half naked, so dismal a sight was never seen, neither can thought imagine or fancy describe the various scenes of misery … Everyone in Tears and knowing not whether to fly, or to remain …
>
> 'In the streets of Lisbon … saw many coaches, chaises, carts, Horses, Mules, Oxen etc, some entirely some half buried under Ground, many People under the Ruins begging for assistance and none able to get nigh them, many groaning under ground, many old and hardly able to walk, now without shoes and stockings and still hurrying to save life.'[1]

Survivors clambered over the ruins, heading for the river bank where they would be safe from falling houses. But soon the waters receded, pulled back towards the sea, before the first of three giant waves came surging up the river, travelling at immense speed. Ships in the harbour crashed into each other, while the waves tore through the low-lying areas of the city, sweeping away the people who had taken refuge on the riverside, destroying everything in their path. Meanwhile, the fall of curtains and woodwork onto candles lit for All Saints'

Day in every church and chapel led to the outbreak of innumerable fires; by the end of the day, they had joined into one vast conflagration.

That night, the western suburbs were filled with thousands of terrified refugees. Among them were two very different people whose lives would come together a quarter of a century later. William Stephens was a young English merchant; Maria de Bragança was crown princess of Portugal. The disaster of 1 November 1755 was the catalyst in the rise to power of the future Marquis de Pombal, the man who would change the lives of both William and Maria – for better and for worse.

1

A Young Merchant

He who never saw Lisbon never saw a fine thing.

Old Portuguese Proverb

William's story begins on 16 May 1731 in the hamlet of Laneast, on the fringes of Bodmin Moor in Cornwall. Four days later, he was carried to church and baptised in the granite font. The curate filled in the register: 'May 20, William, ye son of Jane Smith of Landulph, father unknown.'

Daughter of a tenant farmer in the parish of Landulph, Jane worked as a domestic servant in Pentillie Castle, a small stately home on the banks of the river Tamar. She was 19 years old. Her lover, Oliver Stephens, was a local schoolmaster, a married man more than twice her age. They had few opportunities to be alone together but, as the summer of 1730 brought hot sunny days to the Tamar valley, they arranged to meet in the countryside, in the secluded woods of the Pentillie estate.

At the end of the year, Jane was sent to stay with relatives in Laneast. It was a cold winter, described as a time of 'Great frost'. Snow lay in drifts around the village and ice covered the lanes and fields. The spring of 1731 came late to Bodmin Moor. The streams were still swollen with melted snow, the leaves still opening on the trees, when Jane gave birth to her son on 16 May and carried him to church four days later.

She was loyal to her lover. She refused to name him as father of her child but, 20 miles away in Landulph, Oliver felt uneasy. The ecclesiastical court ruled in such matters and, if reported for adultery, he could lose his position as schoolmaster in the diocese. The wisest course was to leave the area, so he and his wife packed up their belongings and crossed the river Tamar into Devon.

Son of the vicar of Menheniot (near Liskeard), Oliver had grown up in a learned household. Two of his brothers had followed their father into the church and Oliver, too, was destined for Oxford and holy orders until he scandalised his family at the age of 18 by eloping with a family servant. After his marriage, he found work as a teacher, but his positions were humble and poorly paid for all schoolmasters of any standing were men of the church. He moved to Exeter when his son was born and, with the help of his eldest brother

Lewis (a prebendary in the cathedral), he obtained a position in a charity school for boys. He took lodgings in Cathedral Close and kept in touch with Jane, who returned to domestic service in Pentillie Castle while her son lived with his grandparents in Hornafast, a smallholding on the Pentillie estate.

The land at Hornafast sloped steeply towards the Tamar, with areas of pasture and woodland, a marsh with tidal mudflats, and a quay where timber was shipped downriver to Plymouth. There were several limekilns on the river banks nearby which burned limestone for use as fertiliser. The stone was sourced from quarries near Plymouth and transported upriver on boats which sailed past the cottage where William spent his childhood. He attended the school where his father had taught but spent most of his time helping his grandfather on the land, tending the crops and looking after the animals. He expected nothing more of life than to become a tenant farmer himself but in early May 1743, two weeks before his twelfth birthday, his mother collected him from Hornafast. As they boarded the coach for Exeter, she told him that she was going marry his father and they would live together as a family near the cathedral.

As the coach travelled east towards Exeter, another coach was travelling in the opposite direction, from London to the packet boat service in Falmouth. On board was the Portuguese minister to the Court of St James in London, the future Marquis de Pombal, on a journey home to Lisbon. The two coaches may even have crossed on the road for Pombal arrived in Lisbon on 19 May, eight days after William watched his parents exchange their vows in the church of St Mary Major.

Oliver had waited for twelve years before he could meet his son. As soon as his wife died in March 1743 (after thirty-six years of childless matrimony), he obtained a marriage licence, sent money for the journey, and asked his brother the prebendary to obtain a place for William in the Exeter Free Grammar School which provided a classical education for middle-class boys, preparing them for entry to university or the professions.

William was older than the boys with whom he took lessons, for he was untutored in Latin and had much work to do to catch up with pupils of his own age. Every morning, he walked along Cathedral Close to the lane which led to the High Street, then turned his steps towards the East Gate and the old building of St John's Hospital to spend his days reading Latin primers and struggling with ancient grammar.

In the spring of 1744, a new headmaster arrived at the Grammar School, straight from Eton and Cambridge. He brought fresh ideas of education. He emphasised the study of English and contemporary culture; he introduced arithmetic which allowed William to master book-keeping and accountancy;

and he arranged for the boys to perform plays before the mayor and city dignitaries, sometimes by classical authors but more often by modern writers such as Richard Steele.

In November 1744, when Jane gave birth to her second child, the prebendary came to Cathedral Close to baptise the boy with his own name (Lewis). Eighteen months later, as William was approaching his fifteenth birthday, his days as a schoolboy were coming to an end. Oliver could not afford to send him to university, so it was time to find employment.

Exeter had a thriving trade in woollens and several boys at the Grammar School were sons of merchants. Over to France, Holland, Portugal and Spain went the woollen cloth and back came wine, a lucrative trade which enriched the merchants who congregated around Cathedral Close to discuss the latest business and mercantile news. Oliver's second brother was a merchant in Lisbon and it was soon arranged that William should be apprenticed to his uncle John for seven years, sailing to Portugal on one of the fortnightly packet boats from Falmouth. On a hot day in July 1746, Oliver accompanied his son to Cornwall. As the ship prepared for departure, he delivered him into the care of the captain, then watched from the shore as the packet slipped its moorings and set sail for the open sea.

...

The packet service used brigantines, the smallest of the square-rigged sailing ships. Less than 100 feet long and 23 feet wide, they were tossed about on the rough waters of the Bay of Biscay and most travellers complained of sea-sickness. William suffered too, spending the first two days in a tiny cabin with a bed described as 'a thing placed in a dark closet, and clapp'd betwixt two planks ... so that it looks something like a trunk without a lid'.[1]

He felt better on the third morning at sea. Leaving the cabin, he spent his days on deck, watching the sailors at work and scanning the horizon for enemy vessels; England was at war with France and merchants in Lisbon complained of the large number of privateers which preyed on shipping. But the voyage passed uneventfully, the days became warmer, and when the coast of Portugal came into view, he saw a range of brown hills fringed with sandy beaches. Soon the ship moved into a bay lined with villas and gardens and reached Belém where the bay narrowed into the river Tagus. All vessels had to drop anchor here and wait for customs and health officials to come on board and inspect the passengers and their luggage.

William looked around him. The fortified tower of Belém occupied a small island near the shore; behind it stood the great monastery of Jerónimos, constructed during the Age of Discovery when Portugal was a great maritime power. And when the ship set sail again and rounded a bend in the river, he saw the city of Lisbon rising up its seven hills, its domes and towers gleaming in the sunshine. The river widened into the harbour and the packet came to a halt near the Terreiro do Paço, the great square on the waterfront where the Ribeira palace of the Bragança family stood grandiose and proud.

After landing formalities had been completed, William stepped ashore, unsteady on his feet after so many days at sea. He was met by his uncle at the quayside and taken through the streets of Lisbon to his new home. Bathed in the bright light of summer, the city rambled over steep slopes, its narrow streets lined with four- and five-storey houses. Merchants and the upper classes travelled on horseback or in two-wheeled chaises drawn by mules, and the streets and squares were crowded with beggars and feral dogs which roamed the city at night, scavenging and fighting.

John Stephens lived in his counting house near the river and William was put to work as a clerk, copying correspondence, working on invoices and accounts, and learning the lucrative business of Anglo-Portuguese trade. With more than 10 per cent of the population in holy orders, Portugal was unable to feed or clothe its people from its own resources. It relied on imports of clothing and textiles, wheat, fish and other foodstuffs, which it paid for in gold from the mines of Brazil. Because of the advantages conferred by treaty, it was English merchants who handled the bulk of this highly profitable trade. They were exempt from domestic taxes, from the jurisdiction of Portuguese courts, and from most commercial regulations. In the words of the British envoy: 'A great host of his Majesty's subjects reside at Lisbon, rich, opulent, and every day increasing their fortunes and enlarging their dealings'.

A few weeks after William arrived in Lisbon, the English Factory (a trade organisation for British merchants in the city) hosted a 'magnificent feast' in honour of the Duke of Cumberland and his recent victory over the Scottish rebels at Culloden. This was, explained the consul, 'so elegant an entertainment to which … the Secretaries of State, the Presidents of the tribunals, and all the grandees in town have been invited and have promised to honour the nation with their company'.

On a warm September evening, dressed in silk clothes and powdered wig, William accompanied his uncle to the British envoy's garden where a pavilion had been erected in the form of a Roman temple with a portrait of the Duke of Cumberland on a gilded throne in the portico. There was music and dancing, followed by a banquet shortly before midnight, twenty-nine courses served on silver dishes and accompanied by different wines. Then the tables were cleared away and the merchants of Lisbon danced until the sun rose in the morning.[2]

...

William worked in his uncle's trading house for four years, but he soon realised that John Stephens was not a successful merchant. Despite the advantages conferred by treaty, he was bankrupted – 'broken' as it was known – in the summer of 1750, a time when Lisbon was mourning the death of one king and celebrating the accession of another. William was 19 years old, little more than halfway through his apprenticeship, and it was an anxious time for him and for his parents in Exeter.

Oliver appealed to his sister-in-law Philadelphia (wife of the prebendary) who had spent her childhood near the Buxted Park estate in Sussex, home of Thomas Medley and his family. At the time of John Stephens's bankruptcy, the estate was in the possession of Thomas's unmarried grandson, Edward Medley, whose younger brother George was a wine merchant in Lisbon. At Philadelphia's request, George employed William as a clerk and gave him accommodation in his counting house.

Less than a year later, in August 1751, George Medley inherited the Buxted Park estate (on the death of his elder brother) and made plans to return to England to take his place as a member of the landed gentry. Intending his trading house to remain in business, he appointed William and another young merchant, John Churchill, to act as his agents in Lisbon. They would handle all aspects of book-keeping and bills of exchange, send copies of correspondence to Medley in England, and keep him informed of the latest developments in trade and diplomatic relations. In return, they would receive commission on the sale of goods shipped to and from the Tagus.

This new role in Medley's trading house gave William greater prestige in the merchant community and, in July 1752, he was elected to membership of the English Factory. This depended mainly on an ability to pay the contributions required but it was still a coveted achievement; applicants had to prove that they were making money from trade, that they had paid their dues and tariffs on time, and were earning sufficient profits to pay their contributions.

To celebrate the occasion, he sat for a miniature portrait (not much more than an inch in both dimensions) wearing a powdered wig, blue silk jacket with lace ruffles at the neck, and a large diamond-headed pin. This tiny portrait was set in a gold brooch which he sent to his mother in Exeter, an image of a fresh-faced, successful young merchant who had come a long way since his childhood on the banks of the river Tamar.

2

The Most Opulent City

This king's gaieties were religious processions. When he took to building, he built
monasteries. When he wanted a mistress, he chose a nun.

Saying about João V of Portugal, attributed to Voltaire

On 17 December 1752, six months after William was elected to the
English Factory, he took his usual late-afternoon stroll along the banks
of the Tagus, meeting his Factory colleagues in the Terreiro do Paço
and walking with them on the new marble-faced quay near the custom house.
As day faded into evening, he watched servants in the Ribeira palace put lighted
candles in the windows in honour of the crown princess, Maria de Bragança,
who was celebrating her eighteenth birthday.

Maria was born on a cold wet evening in the winter of 1734 when squalls blew
in from the river and the rain lay in puddles in the great square by the waterside.
According to custom, she emerged from her mother's body in a room filled with
priests, courtiers, ministers, doctors and attendants. Gathered into the arms
of her grandmother, she was taken into an adjacent room and presented to her
grandfather (João V) and her father (Crown Prince José) who fell onto their
knees to give thanks to God for a safe delivery.

The announcement was greeted by cheering crowds. Bells pealed, the artillery
fired 21-gun salutes, and soon the carriages of foreign diplomats arrived at the
palace. The British envoy wrote to London later that night:

> 'I immediately went to Court and had audiences of the King, Queen and
> Royal Family to congratulate them on this occasion ... I recommend that the
> King's letter of congratulation may not be deferred a moment but sent by
> the next packet ... as this Court is very punctilious in these sorts of affairs.'

The celebrations continued for three days. The Te Deum was sung in the
churches, bells continued to peal, and as darkness fell, the people of Lisbon
placed lighted candles in their windows to illuminate the city at night. On
9 January 1735, the infant was carried into the palace chapel and baptised, 'with
great pomp and ceremony', Maria Francisca Isabel Josefa Antónia Gertrudes
Rita Joana de Bragança.

Her mother, Mariana de Bourbon (daughter of Philip V of Spain), sent regular despatches to her parents in Madrid. 'I am well by the Grace of God,' she wrote on 3 January, 'and the little one also … She was very small when she was born but has put on a lot of weight.' Five days later: 'every day my little one becomes fatter and prettier.' On the 17th: 'The little one is even more beautiful. The King adores her.'[1]

Maria was born in the richest and most opulent city in Europe, a Lisbon enriched by the gold and diamond mines of Brazil. Every year, treasure fleets arrived from Rio de Janeiro with cargoes of precious stones and metals, one fifth of which (the 'royal fifth') belonged to the king personally. João V was a man of great religiosity and he bestowed this wealth on the Portuguese church until it rivalled the Vatican in pomp and splendour.

The Archbishop of Lisbon, known as the patriarch, was elevated to the rank of pontiff; he wore similar vestments to the pope and was attended by a sacred college of prelates dressed in scarlet robes. 'There is no ecclesiastic in the world,' wrote a visitor to Lisbon, 'that is … surrounded with so great a pomp as this Patriarch. But his revenue, they say, amounts to thirty thousand pounds, and so he may well afford it.'[2]

The king built convents and churches, lined them with rare marbles and stuffed them with treasure: gold and silver altars studded with precious stones; paintings and sculpture from Italy; libraries with tens of thousands of books. His entertainments were religious processions; his mistresses were nuns. His favourite convent was the nunnery of Odivelas where he kept an apartment lined with mirrors and carpets. Two of his many bastard children were conceived here.

Meanwhile, his wife, Maria Ana of Austria, bore him six legitimate children, three of whom survived to adulthood: Bárbara, José and Pedro. In a double ceremony at the Spanish border in 1729, Bárbara married Ferdinand de Bourbon (crown prince of Spain), and José married Ferdinand's 10-year-old sister, Mariana. It was one of the most glittering occasions in Portuguese history. As a British diplomat wrote more than thirty years later, 'Everybody knows that the immense cost of clothes and equipage when the double marriages were celebrated at the frontier of Spain depressed for many years the noble families, and some have not yet recovered from that wound.'

Mariana reached puberty around the time of her fourteenth birthday in March 1732. José joined her in the marriage bed and the court began to wait for news of a pregnancy. The succession depended on her fertility, so there was great rejoicing in the summer of 1734 when it was announced that she was at last expecting a child. During the next twelve years, she gave birth to four daughters: Maria, Mariana, Doroteia, and Benedita (who was born in July 1746, about the time that William Stephens arrived in Lisbon). She continued to long for a boy and, when she was pregnant with Benedita, she wrote to her parents of 'my hopes for a son … if God wishes to give me this favour, it will be a great consolation'.

These were years of gloom in the palace. In letters to her parents, Mariana complained of the lack of entertainments at court and the continual mourning after deaths in the extended royal family. 'There's never anything new here,' she wrote in January 1735. Sixteen months later: 'I do what I can to relieve my melancholy but it's very difficult in a country where there are no amusements. My only joy is singing because of my passionate love for music. Lately we've gone out a lot, but only to churches.'

By May 1738, she was 'feeling the lack of freedom more and more every day. I don't know how I could live without music. I'm afraid they will take a dislike to this too and deprive me of it, for then I'd be quite desperate.' Three years later: 'We're very sad as the mourning goes on with the same severity, which everyone finds rather ridiculous, and we cannot have music on gala days.'

Mariana's daughters grew up together at court, spending most of their time in the Ribeira palace in Lisbon. The south façade overlooked the harbour, three miles wide and always full of shipping. To the east lay the Terreiro do Paço, the meeting place of the city. Religious processions passed through the square, the people of Lisbon strolled by the waterfront, and bullfights were held here on Sunday afternoons.

Every night during Holy Week, processions of hooded penitents gathered in the square, bare-footed with 'long heavy chains fastened to their ankles which … made a dismal rattling'. Carrying heavy crosses on their shoulders, they whipped themselves with knotted cords until their backs were covered in blood.[3] And twice a year, in *autos-da-fé* attended 'with great diligence' by the king and members of the court, the square was filled with torches and flaming pyres as victims of the Inquisition were punished beneath the palace windows.

Religious imagery, the violent and the beautiful, filled the days of Maria's childhood. She spent long hours at her devotions, attended morning mass and evening prayers in the palace chapel, and celebrated a saint's day or religious festival at least once a week. There were festivals in the countryside too, where palaces with hunting parks allowed the family to indulge their passion for blood sports.

The immense convent-palace in Mafra, which housed royal apartments as well as several hundred Franciscan friars, was built by João V to fulfil a vow made on his wedding night, that he would build a convent dedicated to St Francis if his bride gave birth to a son. The palace in Belém, three miles west of Lisbon, had an indoor riding school where the royal horses were trained and Maria learned her skills on horseback. The Moorish palace in the hills of Sintra offered escape from the summer heat, and the hunting parks at Salvaterra de Magos and Vila Viçosa provided excellent sport.

As the family travelled from one palace to another, their furniture and furnishings travelled with them: beds, tables and chairs, tapestries, rugs, mirrors, dinner services, silver and glassware. 'The Court cannot move a step without taking its furniture along with it,' wrote a Frenchman who lived in Lisbon, 'for the Kings of Portugal have none in more than one palace at a time and cannot change their abode without carrying it all along with them, even down to their beds and bedding.' Carriages, chaises and carts ('a prodigious number of vehicles … a medley of carriages old and new') had to be requisitioned for each journey, as well as large numbers of horses and mules for the stages on the road.[4]

When Maria was 7 years old, her grandfather suffered a massive stroke which paralysed the entire left side of his body. Prayers were read in the churches and convents, state affairs came to a standstill, and 'religious processions filled the streets night and day from the instant he was taken ill'. The doctors advised him to take the baths at Caldas da Rainha, in the hope that immersion in hot sulphurous waters would help to restore his health. The king set out on the ten-hour journey on 9 July 1742, travelling upriver by royal barge to Vila Nova da Rainha where a carriage was waiting to take him overland to Caldas. His family joined him a few days later.

They returned to Lisbon on 17 August. Six weeks later, João had another attack, 'a fainting fit which deprived him of his senses for quarter to half an hour'. All public appearances were cancelled, although he insisted on attending an auto-da-fé on 4 November, an event which lasted for fourteen hours and was 'a source of fatigue to several in better health who were obliged to attend'. The king had a third stroke on 12 November and, for the rest of his life, he suffered 'violent seizures' every few weeks, sometimes for days at a time.

There were no more visits to country palaces but the doctors still believed in the efficacy of the baths, and João and his family travelled to Caldas thirteen times in eight years. Each time they made the journey, their furniture and furnishings travelled with them – and when the king had a stroke on the road, the entire entourage had to turn around and head back to Lisbon.

Life in the palace became even more dismal during João's illness. As Mariana wrote to her parents in March 1745:

> 'Everything is in a most miserable state … My ladies-in-waiting organised some small private balls but the Queen sent orders that there must be no more dancing … My ladies are desperate with boredom but there is nothing for us to do but be patient.'

The queen acted as regent whenever João was too ill to meet his ministers but mostly he kept matters of state to himself. There were complaints about

Maria Ana's inexperience and the nobility hoped the crown prince would take a more active role in government. The king refused to consider it. According to the British consul, 'His Majesty has become so very infirm, as at best to only doze, being mighty peevish, dispatching nothing, and yet will have everything go through his hands.'

As João's health continued to decline, he spent his days attending divine service in the patriarchal church. Paralysed by the stroke, his arm and leg began to 'swell considerably' and he was often 'seized with raving fits'. He made his final journey to Caldas in September 1749. When he returned to Lisbon, he was, in the words of the British envoy, Abraham Castres, 'in a deeper melancholy now than he ever was at any other period of his distemper, which no doubt proceeded ... from the notion he has long entertained of his dying before his sixtieth year complete, no prince of the house of Bragança having ever reached that age'.

Despite this foreboding, the king survived his sixtieth birthday in October. He lingered on for another nine months and, as the hot weather arrived in the summer of 1750, he lay in his bedchamber, bloated with oedema and barely able to move. The room was filled with priests and friars, among them a Jesuit, Gabriel Malagrida, a man treated with reverence by the royal couple who believed him to be a saint and a prophet.

João V died on 31 July 1750, 'after a lingering distemper ... accompanied with various and extraordinary symptoms'. As his body was taken to the royal mausoleum in the church of São Vicente de Fora, his two sons, José and Pedro, accompanied the coffin to the palace doors but did not follow the cortège. According to custom, the family confined themselves to their apartments for eight days after the death and saw no one but their servants.

...

João had been a long time dying, but no plans had been made for the transfer of power and the court was 'thrown into disarray'. The new king, José I, was described by Abraham Castres as 'naturally irresolute ... extremely diffident of himself and is conscious that his education has been greatly neglected'. By mistake, he doubled the length of court mourning – ordering two years instead of one – and was horrified to learn that his mother had plans to retire to a convent. He pleaded with her until she agreed to stay in the palace and advise him on matters of government.

José was 36 years old when he came to the throne, 'of a good stature ... his features regular, his eye quick and lively, if a habit of holding his mouth somewhat open had not diminished the expression of intelligence which his countenance would otherwise have conveyed'.[5]

His wife Mariana was 'very agreeable in her person', with 'dark, lively and piercing' eyes. Castres found her 'lively and affable' at official audiences; she replied cheerfully to his compliments and engaged him in long conversations.

The new king was enthroned during the afternoon of 7 September in a ceremony known as an acclamation (the ritual of coronation was discontinued in the sixteenth century when a king lost his life – and the diadem – on a battlefield in Morocco). A pavilion had been erected in the Terreiro do Paço and the square was a heaving mass of people, the harbour filled with boats. As José took the oath, the crowds roared '*Viva Rei*', trumpets sounded, bells pealed, and the artillery fired 21-gun salutes.

Maria sat in a box to one side of the pavilion with her grandmother and sisters. Over the years, her parents had produced four daughters (and four miscarriages), but there had been no pregnancies since 1746 and hopes for a son had faded. She was 15 years old and, as she watched José and Mariana take centre stage, she was acutely aware of her future role in life. There was no Salic law in Portugal to exclude women from the throne, so she too would inherit the crown, the first female monarch in Portuguese history.

Having grown up in a court described as 'very dull and ceremonious' (even the British envoy referred to the 'excessive tediousness' of royal etiquette), Maria was accustomed to the many formalities of palace life. Her first official audience as crown princess – with the hereditary title of Princess of Brazil – was on 10 August. This was a *beija-mão*, a kissing of hands, an intricate procedure of bows and curtseys as members of the court kissed the outstretched hands of royalty.

There were more ceremonies during the next few weeks, but José was unsettled by his new responsibilities. He felt the need for fresh air and exercise, so he and his family travelled to Mafra in early October, 'partly on account of St Francis's festival and partly for the sake of hunting the stag and the wild boar in the King's park near that place'.

The new king and queen soon developed a passionate love for hunting. In January, the royal barges took them upriver to Salvaterra where they hunted for several weeks and 'led a very jovial life'. In the spring of 1751, they set out on the three-day journey to Vila Viçosa, close to the border with Spain. The summer months were spent in Belém where they indulged in shooting and falconry, with excursions to Mafra for more hunting.

Mariana was a spirited, fun-loving woman whose life had been constrained by the tedium of her father-in-law's court. Now she was free to enjoy herself. An excellent horsewoman, her face was soon burnt dark from long hours in the saddle:

'No woman in Europe rode bolder, or with more skill … She sat astride …
and wore English leather breeches, frequently black, over which she threw
a petticoat, which did not always conceal her legs. A jacket of cloth and
a cocked hat … completed the masculine singularity of her appearance.
When, after having let loose the falcon, she followed him with her eye in
his flight, she always threw the reins on her horse's neck, allowing him to
carry her wherever he pleased, fearless of accidents. She was admitted to
be an excellent shot, seldom missing the bird at which she fired, even when
flying.'[6]

There were accidents from time to time – broken fingers, a dislocated shoulder,
an occasion when her shot missed a partridge and grazed her husband's temple
– but nothing could restrain the royal couple from their favourite pursuit. At
Salvaterra, they 'hardly passed a day … without being on horseback five, six,
and often eight and ten hours, especially on the days appointed for the wild boar
which occurred very frequently'.

Their other passion was music, particularly Italian opera. João V had used
the 'royal fifth' to enrich the Portuguese church. His son used it to transform
the royal opera into 'the most pre-eminent in Europe'. His first project was
a magnificent theatre in the Ribeira palace, 'built at an immense expense …
the finest theatre of the size in Europe'. The opening performance was on
12 September 1752, by which time José had commissioned an Italian architect
to build another opera house in the city, the even grander Casa da Ópera.

He built theatres in his country palaces too, including the hunting lodge at
Salvaterra. The royal singers and musicians accompanied the family as they
moved from one palace to another, and productions were staged several times
a week. All female roles were sung by castrati, for José – like his father – was a
libertine and Mariana was 'excessively jealous'. She not only banned all women
from the royal opera, she also banned her attendants from appearing in the
king's presence and was said to have chosen the oldest and ugliest women at
court to be her ladies-in-waiting.

Despite her efforts, José had several mistresses, including the wife of the
young Marquis de Távora. One evening at court, an English visitor 'perceived
the Marquesa de Távora was very well with the King; they did nothing but eye
each other as much as they dared in the Queen's presence'.[7]

…

In September 1752, José celebrated the second anniversary of his acclamation
with a series of bullfights and operas in Lisbon. 'The Court,' wrote Abraham
Castres, 'is entirely taken up with bull-feasts, concerts and opera, almost every
day of the week.'

Three months later, Maria's eighteenth birthday was celebrated with a *beija-mão* in the palace. She had grown tall and slender, with sharply defined features and a warm smile, and she accepted compliments at official audiences with a gracious elegance. Despite a limited education, taught by Jesuit priests with no emphasis on state affairs, she was an accomplished young woman. She was fluent in French, the diplomatic language of the courts of Europe. She read Latin and studied religion and theology. She was taught to draw and paint by the best artists in the country. She studied singing with the Italian music master, David Perez, and she and her sisters 'all were proficient ... on different instruments'. Kind and affectionate, timid and shy, she suffered from depression (described at the time as 'melancholy') and nervous agitation. She had inherited her grandfather's religiosity and her bedroom was 'strewed over with books of devotion and saintly dolls of all sorts and sizes'.[8]

Her faith was strengthened in the summer of 1753 when she nearly died of a 'violent inflammatory fever'. She was taken ill on 29 June during an opera in the Ribeira palace. By 4 July, she was 'in such immediate danger as to require the sacraments, which that day were administered to her, and the next day the Papal Nuncio was sent for in great haste to give her the apostolic blessing in articulo mortis'. At the same time, her mother ordered that a wooden statue of Jesus be brought from the Convent da Graça.

The statue, believed to have miraculous powers, was known as Senhor dos Passos (Lord of the Passion). It depicted Jesus in purple robes with an enormous cross on his shoulders, 'under the weight of which he was represented as stooping, till his body bent almost double'. The statue was carried to the palace 'in great pomp' and placed in Maria's bedroom. Early next morning, 'some of the worst symptoms had begun to remit'.

By 9 July, Maria was 'considerably better'. As the statue was carried back to the convent 'with the greatest pomp and solemnity', Castres attributed her recovery to a German doctor who, 'discovering the nature of the distemper ... proposed remedies as were proper for malignant fevers and saved the life of this most amiable princess'.

A few days later, the family moved to Belém. And while Maria regained her strength during the hot weeks of summer, one of her father's ministers was tightening his grip on power.

3

The Rise of Pombal

A little genius who has a mind to be a great one in a little country is a very uneasy animal.

Sir Benjamin Keene on Sebastião de Carvalho e Melo (Marquis de Pombal), October 1745

Sebastião de Carvalho e Melo, the future Marquis de Pombal, was an imposing man, six feet tall with a long face and handsome features. Born in 1699 into a family of minor gentry, he achieved little during his early life until, at the age of 40, he was appointed Portuguese minister to the Court of St James in London. Four years later, he moved to the Court of Vienna as special envoy, a position he held until he returned to Lisbon in 1749.

Abraham Castres referred to his 'difficult, chicaning temper', but marriage in Vienna to an Austrian aristocrat led him into the favour of João V's Austrian-born queen. João himself had never trusted Pombal – he called him 'a man with a hairy heart' – but his widow had great influence over her son. When José pleaded with her to remain in the palace and advise him on matters of state, she persuaded him to appoint Pombal as secretary of state for foreign affairs, the most junior of his three ministers.

The new king had no taste or capacity for public affairs. He was also nervous and easily led, traits which Pombal soon began to exploit. As the French chargé d'affaires wrote in the autumn of 1750:

> 'Carvalho may be looked upon as the principal minister. He is indefatigable, active and expeditious; he has won the confidence of the King ... and in all political matters, none has it more than he.'[1]

Six months later, Castres wrote that Pombal was 'gaining ground in the King's good graces', and by the summer of 1751, there had been a subtle change in the balance of power:

> '[The king] showed at the beginning of his reign a ... suspicion of ... his ministers in the despatch of business, but when ... Monsieur de Carvalho had found means to establish ... credit with him, matters have been carried on with uncommon expedition, his Majesty having shown in some remarkable instances a docility and patience in despatching what was laid before him, much greater than could be expected from a prince so little used to business.'

During the next two years, the balance of power continued to shift. 'Since Monsieur de Carvalho has had his foot in the stirrup,' wrote Castres in June 1753, 'matters are greatly changed to his advantage.' By February 1754, the envoy was referring to:

> 'the haughty airs this minister knows how to assume ... He is universally disliked, not to give it a harsher name. This he cannot but be informed of, and is what makes him jealous of every man, whether native or foreigner ... The Queen Mother has lost a great part of her influence over her son, and it is said, greatly repents her having saddled him with Monsieur de Carvalho.'

The old queen did not live to repent for long. Over 70 years old and in poor health, she asked the Jesuit priest, Gabriel Malagrida, to help her prepare for death. When she died on 14 August, her body was interred in a convent in Lisbon but her heart was sent home to Austria, 'where everyone that knows the Princess is convinced it has always been'.

Pombal's years as Portuguese minister in London had given him a jaundiced view of British attitudes to commerce. He admired the success of the English middle classes but was angry that the British government granted no reciprocal privileges to Portuguese merchants, although bound to do so by treaty. He also had many complaints about the treatment of the small Portuguese community in London; even the sailors suffered as people threw stones at them, telling them to go back to their own country and stop taking bread and beer from the mouths of honest Englishmen.

Such behaviour rankled with a man who was aware that English merchants in Portugal had appropriated a large part of his country's trade and commerce. As he wrote home to Lisbon:

> 'I found on coming to this Court that the most interesting duty of a Portuguese Minister in London is to investigate the causes which have resulted in the decadence of Portuguese commerce, at a time when the commerce of England is in expansion.'[2]

He nursed his anti-British sentiments during his years in Vienna and, now he was rising to power in his own country, he set out to curb the privileges of the English Factory. As the merchants explained in a petition to the secretary of state in London:

> 'The government is inclineable to discourage us in all branches, for it plainly appears they attack us whenever they can and study every artifice to burden and embarrass our commerce. Almost every day produces somewhat new

and, tho' it be in trifles that at first are disregarded, still so many creep
upon us that if we are not relieved, the trade must in the end sink under
the weight of them.'

Meetings of the English Factory were rowdy occasions. As Pombal complained
to Lord Tyrawley, a British envoy on special mission, 'You have many merchants
here of worth and prudence, but you also have many young people in the
Factory who affect to lead and govern others and whose conduct … is by no
means prudent.' On 9 July 1752, eight days before William Stephens attended
his first Factory meeting, Tyrawley hoped these younger merchants would 'take
my advice and act with more caution, tho' I am far from being the guarantee of
either'. A few weeks later, he received a letter from an older merchant referring
to an altercation at a meeting:

'which caused such a clamour as I never saw till then, and a great deal
of foul language and unmannerly reflections were thrown out on various
subjects … and many other shocking things, all proceeding from spleen
and passion.'

There was a postscript: 'I beg your Lordship to keep this letter to yourself,
being unwilling to bring on my head this nest of wasps.'[3]

In September, a new British consul arrived in Lisbon to take the chair at
Factory meetings. A former member of parliament, George Crowle was
inexperienced in mercantile matters and found it difficult to control the
merchants. As he wrote to London on 5 November:

'Since I have been here, I have received great civility from the gentlemen
of the Factory, but still a very unpleasant spirit prevaileth and nothing but
grievances are talked of … I hope soon this violent spirit will cease, but it
will be some time before things are brought into their proper channel.'

William attended meetings and signed letters and petitions, but he felt uneasy
during these early months of his membership. The merchants of Exeter had
never behaved so boisterously and his uncle John was an even-tempered man
who had learnt his manners in a Cornish vicarage. But William was young and
enthusiastic, and the next time Pombal tampered with the trading privileges of
British merchants, he was ready to add his voice to the clamour of complaint.

Harvests in the Iberian Peninsula had been poor for several years and, by
the autumn of 1753, Spain was threatened with famine. Cargoes of British
corn were arriving in the Tagus but, with higher prices across the border,
Pombal was concerned that merchants would re-export their cargoes to Spain,

leaving Portugal with insufficient grain. He drew up regulations forbidding the re-exportation of corn and ordered that all grain entering the city should be delivered to a central entrepôt for distribution to Lisbon market traders.

The English Factory was alarmed at these orders which were in breach of privileges granted by treaty under which British traders could import all types of merchandise and sell it as they pleased without impediment. Grain which they hoped to re-export was sitting in ships in the harbour, in danger of deterioration, while the vessels were unable to be reloaded with produce for England. Castres arranged a meeting with Pombal and, when he explained the situation, the minister's face hardened. 'What! said he with a mixture of passion and seeming surprise, would you pretend to be entitled to greater privileges than the Portuguese themselves?' to which Castres replied, 'Yes, Sir, in point of corn and the free disposal of it', and quoted the words of the treaty.

Meanwhile, George Crowle had refused to sign a petition from Factory members to the secretary of state in London. He considered the wording to be biased and exaggerated, the new regulations being imposed, according to the merchants:

> 'in an unreasonable manner and on the most trifling pretences … to the great prejudice and even peril of ruin to many of his Majesty's subjects and to the entire endangering of the British corn trade to this Kingdom.'

Dated 10 September, the petition was delivered to Castres after the consul refused to sign it, after which Crowle – who had suffered abuse on several occasions – chose not to attend the next two meetings of the Factory. Angered at his absence, the members persuaded him to chair a meeting on 25 September, at which he restated his opinion that the Factory had no justifiable complaint. Shouts of 'Sir, that is false' erupted from the floor. When he explained that the wording of a treaty 'should not prevent the King of Portugal from making what laws he pleases to prevent famine in his country', a young merchant jumped to his feet. 'Sir,' he yelled, 'if you will fully sacrifice the rights of the nation, you *will* be a traitor to your King and an enemy to your country' – at which point Crowle muttered to himself, hitched up his breeches, and left the room.[4]

He refused to attend any further meetings and, on 19 October, the merchants wrote a letter of complaint to London. Addressed to the secretary of state, it referred to the 'mortification' felt by Factory members at Crowle's persistent refusal 'to join with us in proper measures to procure redress of our many heavy grievances'. Previous consuls had always agreed to measures resolved by a majority of members, whereas Crowle:

'appears activated … by so strange a spirit that he seems to set himself in constant opposition to all proposals that might possibly have eased … ourselves of the calamities we suffer … We really find he stands more and more in need of counsel in mercantile matters than anyone remembered by us in that office.'

The merchants nursed their anger for another eight months before the new regulations were suspended and they could once more import corn freely into Lisbon. Factory members rejoiced in the reinstatement of their privileges but George Crowle was less fortunate. He was dismissed from office in May 1754 and died from a massive stroke a few weeks later, having never recovered from his treatment by the merchants. As he wrote to London the previous October:

'Their behaviour to me … is without precedent, and such treatment as obliged me sometimes to leave the assembly rather than be insulted … I have had a most difficult part to act for two months in the corn affair … I did everything in my power to conciliate and gain all I could, perhaps I should have obtained more if their behaviour had been more decent.'

Crowle was replaced as consul by Edward Hay, who arrived in Lisbon in October. Two months later, the secretary of state in London congratulated him on his 'satisfactory co-operation' with members of the Factory, and hoped that his more conciliatory approach would establish 'the commercial affairs of his Majesty's subjects on a quiet and durable footing'.

4

Catastrophe

A courier despatched by ... the Spanish Embassy in Lisbon ... has brought an account of such a desolation as I do not remember to have heard of in any age in these parts of Europe.

Sir Benjamin Keene, Madrid, 10 November 1755

The king's magnificent new opera house, the Casa da Ópera, was finally completed in early 1755. The opening performance was on 31 March, the queen's birthday, an opera composed and directed by David Perez, Maria's music teacher, in which a troop of trained horses appeared on stage, prancing in time with the music.

In September, the annual treasure fleet arrived in Lisbon: twenty-six ships from Rio de Janeiro with cargoes of gold and diamonds; a ship from Macao carrying twenty million cruzados in gold; nineteen ships from Bahia with treasure worth two million cruzados; and three ships from Goa, one of which brought the old Marquis de Távora home from a posting as viceroy of India. The marquis had sailed for Goa in February 1750, taking his wife and elder son with him – and leaving his daughter-in-law in Lisbon to catch the eye of Crown Prince José.

In early October, a letter was sent to Falmouth to await the Lisbon packet. William's father had died during the height of the corn affair, leaving his mother with four children, the youngest just 3 years old. Now Jane too had died. In normal circumstances and with favourable winds, William should have received news of his mother's death between three and five weeks after the letter was posted. So he may – or may not – have received the letter by the morning of Saturday, 1 November, when Lisbon was hit by one of the most powerful earthquakes ever recorded.

At half-past nine that morning, he heard the noise which sounded like the king's heavy carriage rattling through the street. His experiences during the next twelve hours would have been similar to those of another young merchant who rescued his commonplace book from the ruins of his house and used the charred and empty pages to record the events of that calamitous day:

'I was … just finishing a letter, when the papers and table I was writing on began to tremble with a gentle motion which surprised me, as I could not perceive a breath of wind stirring. Whilst I was reflecting with myself what this could be owing to … the whole house began to shake from the very foundation, which at first I imputed to the rattling of several coaches in the main street, that usually passed that way at this time, from Belém to the Palace. But on harkening more attentively I was soon undeceived as I found it was owing to a strange frightful kind of noise underground, resembling the hollow, distant rumbling of thunder. All this passed in less than a minute, and I must confess, I now began to be alarmed …

'I threw down the pen and started on my feet, remaining a moment in suspense, whether I should stay in the apartment or run into the street … But in a moment I was … stunned with a most horrid crash; as if every edifice had tumbled down at once. The house … shook with such violence that the upper stories immediately fell and altho' my apartment, which was the first floor, did not then share the same fate, yet everything thrown out of its place … I kept on my feet, and expected nothing less than to be soon crushed to death, as the walls continued rocking to and fro in the frightfullest manner; opening in several places; large stones falling down on every side from the cracks, and the ends of most of the rafters starting out from the roof.

'To add to this terrifying scene the sky, in a moment, became so gloomy that I could now distinguish no particular object. 'Twas an Egyptian Darkness indeed … owing no doubt to the prodigious clouds of dust and lime raised from so violent a concussion … I found myself almost choked for near ten minutes …

'I shall always look upon it as a particular providence that I happened … to be undressed; for had I dressed myself … I should in all probability have run into the street at the beginning of the shock, as the rest of the people in the house did, and consequently have had my brains knocked out, as every one of them did … I still had presence of mind enough to put on a pair of shoes and a coat, the first that came to hand (which was everything I saved), and in this dress I hurried down stairs … and made directly to that end of the street which opens to the Tagus, but finding the passage this way entirely blocked up with the fallen houses, to the height of the second storey, I turned back to the other end …

'I had now a long narrow street to pass, with the houses on each side four or five stories high, all very old, the greater part tumbled down or continually falling and threat'ning the passengers with inevitable death at every step; numbers of whom lay killed before me, or … so bruised and wounded that they could not stir to help themselves. For my own part … I only wished that I might be made an end of at once and not have my limbs broken; in which case I could expect nothing else but to be left on the spot, lingering in misery, like these poor unhappy wretches without receiving the least succour from anyone …

'I proceeded on as fast as I could, tho' with the utmost caution and, having at length got clear of this horrid passage, found myself safe and unhurt in the large open space before the church of São Paulo, which had been thrown down a few minutes before and buried a great part of the congregation … Not thinking myself safe in this situation I came to the resolution of climbing over the ruins of the west end of the church in order to get to the river-side, that I might be as far as possible from the danger of the tottering houses, in case of a second shock.

'This with some difficulty I accomplished, and here found a prodigious concourse of people of both sexes and all ranks of conditions … I could not avoid taking notice of an old venerable Priest, in a Stole and Surplice, who I apprehend had escaped from São Paulo's. He was continually moving to and fro among the people exhorting them to repentance, and endeavouring to comfort them. He told them with a flood of tears that God was grievously provoked for their sins, but if they would call on the Blessed Virgin she would intercede for them … A more affecting spectacle was never seen. Their tears, their bitter sighs and lamentations would have touched the flintiest heart. I knelt down amongst them and prayed as fervently as the rest …

'In the midst of our devotions came on the second great shock, little less violent than the first, which completed the ruin of those buildings that had been already much shattered … You may judge of the force of this shock when I inform you that 'twas so violent I could scarce keep on my knees, but it was attended with some circumstances still dreadfuller …

'On a sudden I heard a general outcry. The sea is coming in, we shall all be lost … Turning my eyes towards the river, which in that place is near four miles broad, I could perceive it heaving and swelling in a most unaccountable manner, as no wind was stirring. In an instant there appeared at some small distance a vast body of water, rising as it were like a mountain, it came on foaming and roaring, and rushed towards the shore with such impetuosity that altho' we all immediately ran for our lives … many were swept away. The rest were above their middles in water, a good distance from the banks. For my own part I had the narrowest escape, and should certainly have been lost … had I not grasped a large beam which lay on the ground, until the water returned to its channel, which it did almost in the same instant, with equal rapidity.

'As there now appeared at least as much danger from the sea as the land, and I scarce knew where to retire for shelter, I took a sudden resolution of returning back, with all my clothes dripping, to the area of São Paulo. Here I stood some time, and observed the ships tumbling and tossing about, as in a violent storm. Some had broken their cables and were carried to the other side of the Tagus. Others were whirled round with incredible swiftness, several large boats were turned keel upwards and all this without any wind … The fine new quay, all built of rough marble at an immense charge, was entirely swallowed up with all the people on it who had fled thither for safety … At the same time a great number of boats and small vessels anchored near it, all likewise full of people … were swallowed up, as in a whirlpool, and never more appeared …

'I had not been long in the area of São Paulo when … the sea rushed in again and retired with the same rapidity, so that I remained up to my knees in water, tho' I had got on a small eminence at some distance from the river, with the ruins of several intervening houses to break its force. At this time … the waters retired so impetuously that some vessels were left quite dry which had rode in seven fathom water, thus it continued alternatively; rushing in and retiring several times together …

'I was now in such a situation that I knew not which way to turn … If I remained there, I was in danger from the sea; if I retired farther from the shore, the houses threatened certain destruction. At last I resolved to go to … my friend's lodgings, thro' a long, steep and narrow street. The new scenes of terror I met with here exceed all description, nothing could be heard but sighs and groans. I did not meet with a soul … who was not bewailing the death of his nearest relations and dearest friends, or the loss of all his substance. I could hardly take a step without treading on the dead or dying. In some places lay coaches with their masters, horses and riders *almost* crushed in pieces; here mothers with infants in their arms; there ladies richly dressed. Priests, friars, gentlemen, mechanics, either in the same condition or just expiring; some had their backs or thighs broken; others vast stones on their breasts. Some lay almost buried in the rubbish and crying in vain to the passengers for succour, left to perish with the rest.'

By the end of the day, the young merchant had made his way to safety in the western suburbs where he joined the thousands of refugees who were gathering in the open spaces. Lisbon was now in flames and as it grew dark:

'the whole city appeared in a blaze … so bright that I could easily see to read by it … 'twas on fire at least in an hundred different places … Everyone had his eyes turned towards the flames, and stood looking on with silent grief, which was only interrupted by the cries and shrieks of women and children, calling on the saints and angels for succour, whenever the earth began to tremble; which was so often this night … that the tremors … did not cease for a quarter of an hour together.'[1]

'If you happened to forget yourself with sleep,' wrote another merchant:

'you were awakened by the tremblings of the earth and the howlings of the people. Yet the moon shone and the stars with unusual brightness. Long wish'd for day at last appeared, and the sun rose with great splendour on the desolated city in the morning.'[2]

It was another bright sunny day. The merchants roamed the suburbs, seeking out their friends and colleagues. 'It is almost inconceivable,' wrote one young man:

'the vast joy it gave us to meet our friends again; each looked upon the other as in a manner risen from the dead; and all having a wonderful escape to relate, all were equally satisfied to have preserved their lives only, without desiring anything further. But, in a short time, the prospect of living brought back along with it the cares of life; the melancholy consequences making them almost regret that the same stroke had not deprived them at once of existence as well as fortune.'[3]

The fires in the city burned for another five days, watched by the refugees in the suburbs. And when the flames died down, they ventured into the ruins and moved with difficulty through the rubble. 'It is not to be expressed by human tongue,' wrote the captain of a ship in the harbour:

'how dreadful and how awful it was to enter the city after the fire was abated, and looking upwards one was struck with terror in beholding frightful pyramids of ruined fronts, some inclining one way, some another … then one was struck with horror in beholding dead bodies by six or seven in a heap, crushed to death, half buried and half burnt; and if one went through the broad places or squares, nothing to be met with but people bewailing their misfortunes, wringing their hands, crying the world is at an end.'[4]

The area where William lived and worked was the worst affected. As Edward Hay, the new British consul, explained, 'The part of the town near the water where most of the merchants dwelt for the convenience of transacting their business, is so totally destroyed by the earthquake and the fire that it is nothing but a heap of rubbish.'

'I was so far from being able to distinguish the … spot where my house stood,' wrote the young merchant in his commonplace book, 'that I could not even distinguish the *street* amidst such mountains of stones and rubbish that rose on every side.'

'Oh! dreadful sight,' wrote another merchant who searched the ruins in a nearby street, 'dead bodies, some upon the rubbish, others halfway up their bodies in the rubbish, standing like statues … and the stench … so great that it was impossible to stay long among the ruins.'[5]

William clambered over the fallen masonry until he found the heaps of blackened stonework that had been his home and counting house. Digging around in the rubble, he may have rescued a few items which had survived the fire: metal boxes; piles of coins fused together by heat. He may also have found the body of his partner – the name of John Churchill would soon be listed among the British dead – but if so, he had to leave it there, lying in the rubble, until a team of workmen threw it onto a cart and took it away for dumping at sea.

…

An estimated 30–40,000 people died in the earthquake, crushed by falling masonry, drowned in the tsunami, burnt in the flames. Huge numbers of buildings were destroyed: the opulent Casa da Ópera (opened just seven months earlier), the patriarchal church, convents and nunneries, churches and chapels, libraries and shops, thousands of private houses.

The Ribeira palace was destroyed too, shattered by the jolting of the earth, pounded by the waves that swept over the Terreiro do Paço. The royal family owed their survival to a last-minute decision to travel to the palace in Belém after celebrating early morning mass. An hour or so after they arrived in Belém, as Mariana wrote to her mother in Spain:

> 'We felt a most terrible tremor of the earth. We fled outside with immense difficulty since we could barely remain standing. I ran for the staircase where, without the help of God, I would certainly have broken my head or my legs for I could hardly proceed and was consumed by fear … The King joined me soon after, having fled from the other side of the house. My daughters had been in the oratory and were able to join us later.'[6]

As servants bustled about the palace gardens erecting tents for the family's accommodation, Maria gazed eastwards to the dust cloud that hung over the ruins of Lisbon; she watched the waters rising and receding as the giant waves surged up the river. Pombal arrived a few hours later, having set out for Belém as soon as he could make his way through the ruins. He found the king surrounded by priests and in a state of total bewilderment. 'What is to be done?' José asked him, to which his minister made the famous reply, 'Bury the dead and feed the living.'

Given full powers to restore order, Pombal lived in his carriage for the next eight days. He wrote more than 200 proclamations and encouraged people to dig for survivors and provide food and shelter for the homeless. For one period of twenty-four hours, he ate nothing but a bowl of soup brought by his wife, who picked her way over the ruins to his carriage.

He ordered that corpses be disposed of as a matter of urgency; those close to the river were collected in barges, towed out to sea and thrown overboard, others were buried in mass graves. He ordered that looters be hanged, their bodies left exposed as a deterrent to others. Incoming vessels with shipments of food were compelled to sell their cargoes; outgoing vessels were searched for stolen treasure. Troops converged on the city from the provinces, driving back the refugees required for relief operations. Prices of foodstuffs and building materials were fixed at those prevailing on 31 October.

Shelters were erected in the open spaces, depots requisitioned, food centres organised, camp-kitchens and ovens built, latrines dug, and temporary hospitals set up for the wounded and destitute. Thousands of homeless people were constructing makeshift huts of wood and canvas. Business was at a standstill, food was in short supply, and because so many churches had been destroyed, priests were hearing confessions and conducting services in the open air.

On 5 November, Abraham Castres (accompanied by the Dutch envoy) arrived in Belém to offer their condolences to the king. As Castres wrote the following day:

> 'Though the loss his Majesty has sustained on this occasion is immense, and his capital city is utterly destroyed, he received us with more serenity than we expected … The Queen in her own name and all the young Princesses sent us word that they were obliged to us for our attention, but that being under their tents, and in a dress not fit to appear in, they desired that for the present we would excuse their admitting our compliments in person.'

Maria re-emerged in public on 16 November when she and her family walked in a 'solemn penitential procession' through the western suburbs. Aftershocks continued to jolt the earth, sometimes with violence, and her twenty-first birthday on 17 December went largely unheeded. Five days later, she attended an official audience in what had become known as the 'royal tent' as her father thanked Castres for the British government's swift response to the disaster. The Treasury in London had allocated £100,000 for the relief of Lisbon; ships would be sent to the Tagus carrying gold coins, foodstuffs, shoes and clothing, picks, shovels and crowbars. According to Castres, José and Mariana received the news with 'tenderness both in their looks and tone of voice, as plainly showed the emotion of their hearts'.

The royal sisters prepared lint and bandages for the wounded, while servants raked through the debris of the Ribeira palace. By early January, they had found most of the royal diamonds, together with twenty-two tons of melted silver plate, and Maria was happy to learn that Senhor dos Passos had been rescued unharmed from the ruins of the Convent da Graça.

The palace at Belém, built on a seam of hard volcanic rock, remained structurally sound but José was so distressed, so frightened of further movements of the earth, that he refused to re-enter the building. He insisted that his family continue to live in tents until a new palace built of timber was constructed on the nearby hill of Ajuda, 'preferring to reside in a wooden building, however mean or inconvenient, rather than encounter the perils annexed to a stone edifice'.[7]

The royal tents were cold during the winter months and rain leaked through the canvas seams. Maria was unaccustomed to such discomfort, although the servants did their best to provide warmth and luxury. They lined her tent with rugs and tapestries, piled up her bed with coverings, and kept the braziers burning. Troubled by the deaths of so many people while celebrating mass for All Saints' Day, she was comforted by her Jesuit confessor, Timoteo de Oliveira, who assured her that the disaster was God's punishment for their sins.

...

Meanwhile, members of the English Factory were doing their best to rescue their trading houses. At first, the future looked bleak:

> 'Our poor Factory, from a very opulent one, is totally ruined, at least for the major part, and as this calamity fell with the greatest fury upon the trading quarters of this city, there is hardly one merchant in a hundred … that has saved anything, excepting some few part of their cash, which they have been raking for among the ruins. As to their goods, their houses having being burned to ashes … not one of them that I hear of has been able to save a rag, nor can the Portuguese, who are all greatly indebted to our merchants, pay one single shilling of what they owe them.'

On 8 November, the merchants wrote a letter to José in which Pombal had no difficulty in detecting self-interest. They offered their condolences to the king and assured him of:

> 'their cheerful and determined resolution to prosecute … a commerce so particularly necessary at this time, and always so advantageous to the Kingdoms of Great Britain and Portugal. They think it … their duty to express the strong reliance they have on your Majesty's princely care for making such wise regulations for the security of commerce and re-establishment of mercantile credit as may fix them on the justest and firmest foundations.'

Ships were arriving in the Tagus but, with all warehouses destroyed, it was impossible to offload the cargoes. Edward Hay had a word with Pombal:

> 'I represented to him the deplorable condition of the merchants and how necessary it were to take some steps towards the re-establishment of the commerce … His answer was that it could not be yet, that I could but see the distressed situation they were in … that the Kingdom was threatened with a plague and a famine.'

These matters had to be dealt with first, Pombal told him, only then would commerce 'be taken care of'.

In December, Pombal accepted an offer by Portuguese merchants to pay an additional 4 per cent duty on imports, a contribution towards the cost of rebuilding the city. The English Factory objected (on the grounds that total duties on British goods would now be higher than the maximum agreed by treaty) and Castres asked Pombal to suspend the duty on imports from England. The minister refused with some irritation. He would have thought, he said, that British merchants, who were 'so greatly concerned in the commerce of Portugal, ought to be full as anxious as the natives to see [the city] restored to its ancient lustre'. He had never expected opposition to a scheme aimed at the revival of trade, 'were it even to be attended with some little inconvenience'.

The outlook had improved by the turn of the year. Most Factory members had found alternative accommodation and resumed at least some of their trading activities As Edward Hay explained on 14 January:

> 'Some few have met with houses, others … are building wooden houses in gardens, and thus by degrees everybody will get settled in a tolerably commodious manner … The loss our trade has sustained is very great but I am far from thinking it total … As no house of business can have their whole capital at one time in one place, so we are reasonably to suppose that what was in Lisbon was but part of the fortunes of most of our merchants.'

William Stephens was not so fortunate. In his country house in Sussex, George Medley decided to retire from business. He closed his trading house and William was left without income or employment. He and his uncle John were living in a makeshift shelter in the western suburbs, enduring the cold night air and the winter rains, while beneath them the earth continued to tremble. His parents were dead; his house was destroyed; he had lost his agency, his partner and all his possessions; and apart from his uncle who relied on him for sustenance, he was alone in a devastated city.

5

Retribution

*There is not the least outward demonstration of discontent but much inward
murmurings and heart-burnings at the measures of a certain great Minister.*

Edward Hay, 28 April 1759

Pombal's house in Rua do Século (in the upper town) had suffered little
damage in the earthquake, a sign – in the king's opinion – of divine
guidance, proof that his minister had been sent by God to help him in
his hour of need. His influence with José was greatly enhanced by this stroke of
luck, as well as his efficient handling of the disaster, and in May 1756, he was
appointed the most senior secretary of state, with the portfolio for home affairs.
As Edward Hay put it, 'Monsieur de Carvalho is the leading man, and is in
effect prime minister … for nothing is done without him.'

Pombal regarded the earthquake as a natural event, but his plans to restore
order were hampered by the clergy who insisted that the disaster was a
punishment from God. As the first anniversary approached, the Jesuit priest
Gabriel Malagrida published a pamphlet attacking Pombal's policies and
thundering on about divine retribution:

> 'Learn, O Lisbon, that the destroyers of our houses, palaces, churches, and
> convents, the cause of the death of so many people and of the flames that
> devoured such vast treasures, are your abominable sins, and not comets,
> stars, vapours and exhalations, and similar natural phenomena … It is
> scandalous to pretend the earthquake was just a natural event, for if that be
> true, there is no need to repent and try to avert the wrath of God, and not
> even the Devil himself could invent a false idea more likely to lead us all to
> irreparable ruin … It is necessary to devote all our strength and purpose to
> the task of repentance … God is watching us, scourge in hand.'[1]

Pombal was furious. He accused the Jesuits of using the disaster to 'frighten feeble
and superstitious minds', persuaded the papal nuncio to banish Malagrida from
the city, and drafted an edict denouncing the pamphlet as 'fanatical, malicious
and heretical'. Meanwhile, several Jesuits had begun to plot against him, their
intrigues mirrored at court where the nobles also simmered with resentment,
having lost much of their power and influence over the king.

The minister showed his teeth for the first time in the summer of 1756 when he arranged the disgrace of Diogo de Mendonça, one of his fellow secretaries of state. Mendonça was jealous of Pombal; he was indiscreet enough to criticise him in public and there was talk of a conspiracy. On 31 August, he was banished from Lisbon and given three hours to leave the city. During the next few months, he was arrested, imprisoned and exiled to Angola where, like so many of those banished to the African colony, he died from the effects of climate, disease and malnutrition.

Having convinced himself that Jesuits were involved in the conspiracy, Pombal persuaded José to dismiss all Jesuit confessors from court. Ordered to return to the colleges of their order, they left their positions on 19 September and Maria lost the support of Timoteo de Oliveira, a man she held in great respect. Less than two years later, in June 1758, the Society of Jesus was ordered to cease all business affairs and the priests banned from preaching and taking confessions. Pombal's excuse this time was that Jesuits were plotting against the government in South America, but as Edward Hay (who had recently succeeded Castres as envoy) explained, 'the order of Jesuits is very powerful in this country, so their disgrace is the more remarkable'.

José was complicit in these proceedings against the Jesuits – he signed the edicts which Pombal placed before him – but he may have had a sense of foreboding. A few weeks later, the French envoy reported that the king appeared 'weak and anxious, as if anticipating some dreadful calamity'.[2]

The royal family were now housed more comfortably. They had left their tents in Belém in July 1757 and moved into their new wooden palace on the hill of Ajuda. Known as the *Real Barraca* (the royal hut), it was a long single-storey building described by one jaundiced observer as 'a very mean structure, with no kind of magnificence', by another as 'a prodigious long stable building ... nothing but a low wood-built house, with an extensive row of windows'.

On 31 August 1758, a letter arrived from Spain informing José of the death of his sister Bárbara (wife of Ferdinand VI). According to custom, he ordered his family to confine themselves to their apartments for eight days and imposed a court mourning of six months. However, as Edward Hay reported on 13 September:

> 'Unhappily, the execution of this order has been interrupted by his Majesty's indisposition, it being the custom of this Court to put on gala when any of the Royal Family is blooded.'

The king had been bled by the doctors. It was announced that he had fallen in the Real Barraca on the night of 3 September and bruised his arm, and the queen was acting as regent during his indisposition.

José should have been confined to his rooms during the evening of 3 September, grieving for his sister, but the truth was that he had slipped out of the palace to visit his mistress, the young Marquesa de Távora. It was a dark night – the second night of a new moon – and on his return journey, shortly before midnight when his chaise was travelling down a narrow lane, three masked horsemen emerged from the darkness and opened fire. The first shot misfired, the second and third ripped into the back of the chaise.

The king was not seriously wounded; shot merely grazed his shoulder and arm. As the horsemen fled the scene, he told his coachman to drive direct to the royal surgeon's house in Rua da Junqueira. His wounds dressed, he returned to the Real Barraca and sent a message to Pombal ordering him to come at once to the palace. Next morning, on Pombal's advice, the story about the fall was given out. As Edward Hay explained:

> 'When I went to Court to enquire of his Majesty's health, I was there informed that the King ... passing the gallery to go to the Queen's apartment, had the misfortune to fall and bruise his right arm. He has been blooded eight different times, and as his Majesty is a fat bulky man ... his physicians have advised that he should not use his arm, but refrain from business for some time.'

Pombal sensed an opportunity – and he needed time to think. His ambitions were to increase the commercial prosperity of his country and (as he told Edward Hay) to 'emancipate this nation from subjection ... to the Court of Rome and ... eradicate old prejudices from the minds of a superstitious people'. He also had a despotic side to his nature and was certainly a man to hold grudges.

In his youth, he had proposed marriage to a daughter of the Távora family and the Távoras, calling him a common adventurer, had ordered him out of their house. The Duke de Aveiro, too, had become an enemy. The most important nobleman in Portugal, he had never concealed his dislike of Pombal. It was he who headed the opposition to the indolent manner in which José ran his country – and to Pombal as the king's first minister.

During the next three months, Pombal used his spies to collect 'evidence' against the nobles and their Jesuit confessors. The suspects were arrested on 13 December. They included the Duke de Aveiro and all the Távora family: the old marquis; his wife the old marquesa; his four brothers; his two sons (the elder of whom was married to the king's mistress); and his two sons-in-law (Count de Atouguia and Marquis de Alorna). Also arrested were thirteen Jesuit priests, including Gabriel Malagrida and Timoteo de Oliveira.

Pombal persuaded José to allow the use of torture and took charge in person as the prisoners were interrogated on the rack. Servants were tortured to extract information about their employers, nobles tortured into betraying their friends. Charged with attempted assassination, the trials began on 9 January 1759 and the verdicts (a foregone conclusion) announced three days later. All the defendants were found guilty of treason, ten of them to be executed the following day in Belém.

Six of the condemned were aristocrats and Maria knew them well. It was said that she pleaded with her father when the sentences were announced, but José was unmoved by her tears. Carpenters worked all night on the scaffold and they fixed six wheels onto the platform, one for each of the nobles. In her bedroom on the hill of Ajuda, Maria heard the distant sounds as they sawed and hammered through the night.

Next morning, a light rain was falling as the condemned arrived at the scaffold one by one. The following day, an English visitor described the proceedings:

> 'The flower of the nobility was executed yesterday. The old Marquesa de Távora died first. She was beheaded. Her husband and two sons, together with the Duke de Aveiro, were broken upon the wheel, and an assassin burnt alive. All the dead bodies were consumed along with him and their ashes swept into the Tagus.'[3]

As a final disgrace, the houses of the Távora and Aveiro families were demolished and the land on which they stood sprinkled with salt so that nothing more would grow there.

On the morning after the executions, Maria attended an official audience to receive compliments on her father's escape from death. The following day, the family attended a Te Deum in the church of Nossa Senhora do Livramento in the nearby suburb of Alcântara. It was the first time José had appeared in public since the assassination attempt and he waved his handkerchief in the air with both hands, one after the other, to show the crowd that he had suffered no lasting injury.

During the next three days, the family attended a religious festival, the Devotion of Santa Engrácia. On the 19th, they left the Real Barraca to spend six weeks in Salvaterra – and during their absence, Edward Hay wrote a confidential despatch to London. It was written in code:

> 'There is a circumstance that seems to have been industriously concealed … the King's intimacy with the young Marquis's wife, which began during the time the old Marquis was Viceroy of India and has been continued ever since … When the rest of the relations were confined, this lady was sent

to a convent, not a very strict one, where it is said that she lives very much at her ease.'

On 15 July, José granted Pombal his first title, Count de Oeiras. He also granted him an escort of forty bodyguards who, according to an unimpressed Englishman:

'ride after his chaise with their swords drawn … An officer with a drummer attending him and beating at their head render him a very pompous figure. The reason assigned for this is lest any of the family of the poor nobles should choose to revenge their death upon him, whom every person esteems the author of it.'[4]

Seven weeks later, on the first anniversary of the assassination attempt, the king signed a decree condemning the Jesuits as:

'notorious rebels, traitors, enemies and aggressors against the Royal Person of the King, against the public peace of these Kingdoms and Dominions, and against the common good of his subjects … [to be] outlawed, proscribed and exterminated for ever out of the Kingdom and Dominions of Portugal.'

During the month of September 1759, processions of Jesuit priests moved along the roads to Lisbon, accompanied by armed soldiers on horseback, forbidden to carry anything with them except the clothes on their backs. They embarked on ships destined for the papal states, after which the only Jesuits remaining in the country were those imprisoned for complicity in plots against the king or against Pombal – including Gabriel Malagrida.

Nine years earlier, when José came to the throne, Portugal was ruled by the monarch, the church and the aristocracy. Now the nobility and the church had both been crushed and Pombal was – in effect – dictator of the country. The king attended few meetings of state, rarely gave audiences to foreign ministers, and giving full authority to Pombal, simply signed the documents that were placed before him, often in the early hours of the morning after he had spent his days on horseback and his evenings at the opera.

Meanwhile, the dungeons were filled with people suspected of further intrigues, men and women arrested and imprisoned without trial. Nobody dared discuss politics or criticise Pombal's actions; it was illegal even to speak of the Távora conspiracy. 'So many have already been thrown into jail on this account,' wrote Joseph Baretti (a friend of Dr Johnson) when he visited Lisbon in 1760, 'that the poor souls are quite frighted at the mere mention of some names.'[5]

6

A Quiet Wedding

*A marriage so essential to the tranquillity and prosperity of Portugal, and to
the stability of the succession in the present Royal Family.*

William Pitt, 24 June 1760

L isbon was still in ruins when Maria celebrated her twenty-fifth birthday
in December 1759. Five weeks later, as the royal barges passed the
waterfront of the city on their way to Salvaterra, she gazed at the toppled
churches and convents, the ruins of the Ribeira palace, the rubble heaped up
in the Terreiro do Paço. 'Nothing is to be seen,' wrote Joseph Baretti, 'but vast
heaps of rubbish, out of which arise ... the miserable remains of shattered walls
and broken pillars.'[1]

Pombal had prepared detailed plans for rebuilding the city but the work was
delayed, partly because the mines of Brazil were producing less gold than in
previous years, but mostly because the Seven Years' War was threatening to
become a wider conflict. France was putting pressure on José to renounce the
Anglo-Portuguese alliance, while Pombal, foreseeing an alliance between France
and Spain, feared invasion by Spanish forces. He had to upgrade the defences
of the country (described as 'totally neglected, sunk into the most wretched
condition') with the result that men, money and materials were diverted from
the task of reconstruction.

Writers of the time refer to Maria's expression of melancholy and it was public
knowledge that her mind was 'deeply impressed with the tragical catastrophe of
the Duke de Aveiro, and his associates, whose fate she was believed to lament, as
having been unmerited, or unjust'.[2] She loathed Pombal for his tyranny, as well
as his persecution of the church. She tried to believe that José had acted fairly
but her instincts told her that the minister – and by default her father also – had
persecuted God's representatives on earth.

Twenty-five was a late age for a princess in the marriage market. Maria's
mother had married at the age of 10, her aunt Bárbara at 17, but this was the first
time that a woman was heir to the throne of Portugal. Under the fundamental
laws of the country (the twelfth-century Laws of Lamego), she was forbidden
to marry a foreign prince:

'If the King have no male issue and have a daughter, she shall be Queen
after the death of the King provided that she marry a Portuguese nobleman.
The law shall always be observed that the eldest daughter of the King shall
have no other husband than a Portuguese lord in order that foreign princes
may not become masters of the Kingdom. If the King's daughter marries a
foreign prince or noble, she shall not be recognised as Queen.'

Despite these laws, there had been several half-hearted attempts to arrange a
betrothal with a foreign prince, including the Duke of Cumberland (third son
of George II) and one of Maria's uncles in Spain. These came to nothing, as
did an early attraction between Maria and João de Bragança, her father's first
cousin. The laws about the marriage of a crown princess had never been tested
and it was feared that, if Maria married into the Portuguese aristocracy, the
succession would be disputed by male members of the Bragança family.

Her grandfather proposed a solution as early as 1749. He suggested that she
marry her uncle Pedro, José's younger brother, but Mariana opposed the idea.
Pedro was 'suspected to have a great sway' over his brother and, fearing that he
was ambitious for power, she brought her husband round to her point of view.
At the same time, Pedro's enemies spread rumours that he was impotent, that
he suffered from 'some natural defect ... which will not allow him to become
the Princess of Brazil's husband and will oblige him in all likelihood to enter
into Holy Orders'.

Pombal also viewed Pedro with suspicion. On one occasion, he persuaded
José to banish him to his country house at Queluz (ten miles west of Lisbon) on
the pretext that he was planning a coup against him, but Maria persuaded her
father to revoke the order. It was true that Pedro disliked Pombal, but he soon
lost his more youthful ambition. The rumours of impotence died away, people
continued to talk of the marriage (in 1754, it was 'impatiently expected by
people of all ranks') and, by the spring of 1760, José and Mariana had changed
their minds.

On the morning of 6 June 1760, Lord Kinnoull (a British envoy on special
mission) attended an official audience in the Real Barraca in honour of the
king's birthday:

'which happened upon so extraordinary a day, when the Court was so agreeably
surprised with a most welcome declaration of his Majesty's intentions, that a
marriage should be *that* evening celebrated between his brother, the Infante
Dom Pedro, and the Princess of Brazil. I need not mention how long and
how ardently the nobility, the whole people of this Kingdom, have sighed for
this interesting event, or the great and universal joy with which the almost
unexpected accomplishment of their wishes was received.'

This marriage between uncle and niece was a quiet one by royal standards, celebrated privately in the chapel of the Real Barraca. Five years after the losses sustained in the earthquake, José had ensured that 'the nobility and gentry are put to no expense and an example is set for all future marriages which used to be the occasion of great expense and profusion'. He was aware of the cost of his own marriage in 1729 and now, 'thro' his Majesty's paternal attention ... things have been so managed that there will not be so much as the additional expense of a suit of clothes'.

Three days of public rejoicing began as soon as the ceremony was over, with the usual pealing of bells, cannon-fire and illuminations. And that night, according to custom, Maria's mother and sisters prepared her for the marriage bed. They undressed her, perfumed her body, laid her between fine linen sheets, and waited until Pedro entered the room and climbed into bed beside her.

Maria delighted in marriage. She enjoyed her husband's warm body and on her wedding night, following her grandfather's example, she vowed to build a church and convent dedicated to the Heart of Jesus (to which she was 'especially devoted') if she was blessed with the birth of a son. Members of the court commented on her radiant smile – but Pombal soon cast his shadow over her first weeks of conjugal bliss.

First, he banished the papal nuncio from the country. He had been hoping to sever relations with the Vatican for some time, accusing the nuncio of 'intermeddling with his Majesty's government and fermenting a dangerous sedition amongst the King's subjects'. Now he had an excuse. The nuncio had failed to illuminate his house in celebration of the marriage and Pombal chose to perceive this as an insult to the royal family. On 14 June, in the nuncio's own words:

> 'An order was brought to me in writing to quit Lisbon in an hour; but the fifty soldiers who brought that order did not allow me a minute. Their commander hurried me into a boat without giving me time to shut my writing-desk, made me cross the Tagus, and saw me to the [river] Caya in four days. On the road I had no bed, and scarce anything to eat; and all this without my knowing why.'[3]

'This step,' wrote Lord Kinnoull, 'has stunned and astonished many who never thought to have seen such a measure taken in Portugal.'

Six days after the nuncio's departure, Pombal imprisoned two senior members of the aristocracy. The Count de São Lourenço and Viscount de Vila Nova da Cerveira were accused of intriguing with the nuncio and having 'conversed much with priests', although their real crime was being a little too free in their conversation. São Lourenço was known as a wit. When it was said that Pombal's house in Rua do Século had been saved by divine providence, he made the point that God had also saved Rua Suja – the street of brothels – a joke the minister failed to appreciate.

Finally, on 21 July, Pombal banished two of Maria's half-uncles (bastard sons of João V) to a convent in the hills of Busaco, accusing them of corresponding with the nuncio and being 'deeply engaged in all his intrigues'. It was said that one of them, hoping to marry Maria and disappointed at her marriage to Pedro, had taken to 'caballing' with the Jesuits. A more likely explanation is the story of an argument with Pombal, during which 'they lost their temper … pulled off the Marquis de Pombal's wig, beat it about his face, and turned him out of the apartment'.[4]

...

Pedro was eighteen years older than Maria and shared her religiosity. 'Fanatically devout, reserved, gloomy, constantly engaged in prayers and processions', he was a simple man with no interest in state affairs. At the time of his marriage, he was rebuilding his house in Queluz, converting it into a rococo palace surrounded by formal gardens, citrus groves, water cascades and fountains. During the summer months, he staged lavish entertainments, private parties restricted to members of the royal family and their gentlemen-in-waiting. The fêtes on 24 and 29 June (the feast days of São João and São Pedro) were particularly elaborate, with horse races, bullfights, banquets, fireworks, and concerts in the music room where Mariana and her daughters sang cantatas and arias from Italian opera.

These summer fêtes were even more magnificent in 1760 and, on 29 June, as a special honour, Lord Kinnoull was taken through the gardens to enjoy the festivities on São Pedro's day. He watched the bullfight and a concert by the royal musicians, enjoyed a 'sumptuous supper' in a marquee, and was led into the music room to hear the queen and princesses sing. He was overwhelmed by the brilliance of the occasion:

> 'I had heard much of the musical performances of her Majesty and the Infantas … my expectations raised high by report were truly exceeded by the performance. The Queen, who is a superior mistress of music, sings with that perfect skill and knowledge which conceals every defect of the voice and always gives delight. The Princesses, taught by David Perez, the best master in Europe, all discover a most excellent taste … The whole of this entertainment was the most princely and magnificent that I ever saw and the serenity of the night did justice to the splendour of it.'

Every Sunday afternoon in summer, the family attended bullfights in the wooden bullring at Campo Pequeno a few miles north of the city. Joseph Baretti was in the audience on 31 August and wrote that the king 'was dress'd in a plain sky-blue with some diamonds about him'; the queen and her daughters were 'all sparkling with jewels'. Having watched several bulls slaughtered in a variety of ways, Baretti recounted 'an incident that suspended for about half an hour this horrible entertainment':

> 'The seventh or eighth bull had been just slain and dragg'd out, and the man at the bull's-gate was going to let in another, when the people in the ground-floor boxes …rose at once and all with the most hideous shrieks, leapt precipitously into the area, and ran about the place like madmen.
>
> 'This sudden disorder terrified the assembly, and few were those who had any sang-froid left. All wanted to know what was the matter, but the noise of a cataract could not have been traced through the cries of such a multitude. The King and the Queen, the Princesses and Dom Pedro raised their hands, fans, and voices, as I could see by the opening of their mouths, but it was a considerable while before a word could be heard about the cause of so violent a commotion. Yet at last … a report went round that some people, where the uproar began, had cried out *Earthquake! Earthquake!*
>
> 'In a country where people have still fresh in their minds the effects of an earthquake, it is no wonder if such a cry, that came at once from several quarters, proved terrifying; and if those who heard it, without giving themselves an instant to reflect, sprung over the barriers into the area, to escape being crush'd by the fall of the edifice.
>
> 'However, the fact is that not the least shock of an earthquake had been felt by anybody. The cry had been raised by a gang of pick-pockets in order to throw the people into confusion, and gain an opportunity of stealing. The scheme took to a wonder. Many men lost their handkerchiefs and many women their caps, not to speak of swords and watches, necklaces and ear-rings.'[5]

Three days later, Baretti was in Belém to watch José lay the foundation stone of a memorial church to commemorate his escape from the gunmen. It was the second anniversary of the assassination attempt and a pavilion had been built on the exact spot. The interior was 'hung with a kind of red serge striped and fringed with a tinsel-lace'; an altar in the centre was 'gloriously adorned'.

Pombal arrived first, 'preceded by many gentlemen, many servants, a drummer and a trumpeter, all on horseback. He was alone in a coach drawn by six grey horses, attended by two grooms on foot, one on each side of the coach, and by five and twenty of the King's horse-guards.' Then came the patriarch and his establishment in a train of forty coaches, followed by the royal family and their ladies- and gentlemen-in-waiting. José and Pedro arrived in a carriage drawn by six piebald horses, Mariana and her daughters in another coach and six:

'She and the Princesses were most magnificently dress'd, wearing most ample hoops, their heads, necks, breasts, arms, waists, and feet glittering with jewels. The Princesses have very fine shapes, fine complexions, and the finest eyes that can be seen. One of them (I think the third, but am not sure) ... is a striking beauty. I was pleased to see them so lively and hopping out of the coach with so much nimbleness.'

It was a hot day and the windows of the pavilion were thrown open, giving Baretti a clear view of the proceedings. The Te Deum was sung ('with much noise of music'), after which José, Pombal and 'some other gentlemen':

'descended into a kind of hole about breast-high, where silver-shovels, silver-hammers, and other implements of masonry had been placed before hand with stones, bricks and mortar. His Majesty put some gold and silver medals at the bottom of that hole and cover'd them with a quadrangular stone; then both he and his attendants took up their shovels, and fell a-covering that stone with bricks and mortar, beating the bricks with the hammers from time to time, as they were directed by a gentleman, who I suppose is the King's architect ...

'In a few minutes the business of laying the stone was over, during which I could not help wondering at some vulgar women who, looking through one of the windows, laugh'd immoderately at the masons, probably because they were somewhat awkward at their new trade, and this discomposed a little the gravity of the bye-standers. Yet no body took any particular notice of their impertinence.

'The King and his company returned to their places, and as soon as they were seated, the Patriarch ... celebrated a high mass assisted by his dignitaries and canons ... During the mass the musicians play'd and sang most gloriously ... The mass lasted a full hour, and was followed by the patriarchal benediction, after which the company broke up and everybody went home tired and fatigued. The heat without was great, as the sun shone very bright, but within was quite intolerable.'[6]

After their marriage, Maria and Pedro appeared side-by-side at official audiences but took no part in state affairs. 'In all the duties and departments of private life she was exemplary,' wrote an English visitor to Lisbon. 'Married to her uncle, only brother to the King, they exhibited a model of nuptial felicity.'[7] Their first child was conceived in November. 'I am not publicly authorised to inform you of the pregnancy of the Princess of Brazil,' wrote Edward Hay in March 1761. 'Her Royal Highness is said to have gone four months of her term and is in perfect health.'

This was the son Maria had prayed for, a prince born in the Real Barraca shortly before midnight on 20 August. Seven days later, the infant was baptised in the palace chapel and named José after his grandfather. By the time Maria reappeared in public on 24 September, attending a bullfight in Campo Pequeno in honour of her new-born son, Pombal had once again cast a shadow over her marital bliss.

Gabriel Malagrida, the priest revered by her grandparents as a saint and a prophet, had been a thorn in Pombal's side for many years. The best-known Jesuit in Portugal, his pamphlet about the earthquake had hampered efforts to restore order and he was suspected of involvement in the Távora conspiracy. Old, tired and almost certainly out of his mind, the 70-year-old priest had languished in dungeons for more than two years until Pombal found a way to be rid of him. He handed him over to the Inquisition and personally drew up the indictment: heresy, blasphemy, false prophecy, and 'having abused the Word of God.'

The auto-da-fé was held in Lisbon on the night of 20 September, attended by Maria's husband and father. Thousands of people had gathered in the square and, as they watched the garrotte tighten around the old man's throat, as they watched the faggots burning, press-gangs moved among them to seize young men for service in the army. Pombal's fears of a wider conflict had become a reality: an alliance signed on 15 August between France and Spain had opened the door to invasion.

In May 1762, after José refused to renounce the Anglo-Portuguese alliance, a Franco-Spanish army crossed the northern border. Pombal called on the old alliance and Britain sent 8,000 troops to Portugal. They disembarked in Lisbon on 16 June and, before marching north to engage the enemy, the commander and senior officers were invited – at Pombal's request – to the entertainments at Queluz on 24 and 29 June.

They were led through the gardens (as Lord Kinnoull had been two years earlier) and after the bullfight and 'an elegant supper':

> 'they had the honour to be admitted into the Concert Room to hear her Majesty and the Princesses sing ... Nothing could exceed the attention that was paid that evening to the English gentlemen by the King and Queen personally and by the ministers and nobility.'

Skirmishes were fought during the next few months but the Seven Years' War was coming to an end. The invading army retreated across the border in October, shortly after Maria miscarried her second child in the sixth month of pregnancy. The following September, she gave birth to a boy who lived for just two weeks. The infant was interred in the royal mausoleum in São Vicente de Fora, and Edward Hay wrote to London that 'the Princess of Brazil has borne the loss of her son with surprising fortitude and resignation, and recovers daily from her lying-in'.

7

Alcântara

Is it not surprising ... to hear the Portuguese constantly repeat ... that their city is soon to be built over again, quite regular, quite fine, finer than it ever was? ... Then where are the materials ... where is the lime?
Joseph Baretti, 2 September 1760

While Portugal celebrated the end of the Seven Years' War and Maria mourned the loss of her new-born son, William Stephens was living through the worst years of his life. His resilience and optimism had survived the bankruptcy of his uncle in 1750; they had been crushed for a time after the earthquake of 1755; and now his third business venture had collapsed, leaving him in penury.

He and his uncle had lived in a shack for almost a year after the disaster. Provisions were in short supply, aftershocks continued to jolt the city, and there were torrential rains during the spring of 1756. The outlook was grim, but William was resourceful and soon put his mind to business opportunities.

Pombal had discussed his ideas for a modern city to rise from the ruins only a few weeks after the earthquake, a city with wide streets built on a grid system. To enable the work to be carried out quickly and cheaply, the design was a simple one, a style of plain-fronted buildings with wrought-iron balconies which became known as Pombaline. As the architects drew up the plans, William realised that there would soon be great demand for building materials. The supply of stone and timber presented few opportunities, but large volumes of lime mortar would be required and he remembered the kilns on the banks of the river Tamar. He had seen them in operation during his childhood on the Pentillie estate and had some understanding of the technology involved.

Limestone was plentiful to the west of the city. There were several lime-makers in the Lisbon area, but they used an ancient method of production, an open platform built above a furnace which burned intermittently (the fire being extinguished while finished lime was removed from the platform and replaced by piles of freshly quarried stone). Their output was low, their lime of poor quality, and their furnaces fuelled by firewood which was now in short supply, timber having been used in great quantities to build shelters for the homeless people of Lisbon.

The kilns on the Tamar were fuelled by culm, waste powder from the mining of anthracite, a type of coal found mainly in the collieries of south Wales. A cheap and inferior form of coal, culm was an inadequate fuel for other purposes, but its great advantage in lime production was its small particle size which allowed it to burn at consistently high temperatures. Coal-fired kilns were far more productive than the open platforms still in use in Portugal; the limestone and culm were loaded into the kiln in layers, so the furnace burned continuously, new materials being loaded at the top and the finished lime extracted from the base.

Convinced that a series of coal-fired kilns could provide sufficient lime for the reconstruction of the city without the need to burn valuable timber, William prepared a proposal. As an unknown foreigner, he was not in a position to approach Pombal directly but, with the help of an intermediary, he was soon summoned into the minister's presence to describe the operation of coal-fired kilns.

Pombal intended the reconstruction to start as soon as possible, an undertaking which required large amounts of mortar, so he was easily convinced of the value of William's proposal. In a decree signed by the king on 3 November 1756, William was granted a loan to build the kilns in Alcântara, a mile from Belém on the Lisbon road, close to a quay on the river Tagus. Cargoes of imported culm would be exempt from customs duties; the limestone would be transported from quarries in the Alcântara valley; and the finished lime had to be sold at or below the price fixed by Pombal at the time of the earthquake.

William rented a house in Alcântara and engaged an English engineer, William Elsden, to draw up plans for the factory complex. He employed twenty workmen to clear the site and construct four batteries of deep cylindrical chambers, each with four furnaces, providing a total of sixteen kilns. He wrote to Charles Dingley (a merchant who had returned to London after the earthquake), asking him to source the culm and despatch it to Lisbon. Lime production required at least a third of its volume in fuel. Large quantities would be required for sixteen kilns to operate continuously, so he instructed Dingley 'to send him any quantity, to charter and load ships with culm'.

When the first cargo arrived at the Alcântara quay in April 1757, he was horrified to discover that Dingley had shipped low-grade coal instead of culm, coal which was useless for burning lime. Four more ships containing low-grade coal arrived during the next few weeks and, after an urgent exchange of letters, William learnt that Dingley had been daunted by the high cost of chartering vessels at the Welsh ports. He had therefore ordered his agent in the north of England:

'to ship an inferior sort of coals, which he was told would burn lime as well as culm, [but] the sending of these coals has proved a very great loss and disappointment to Mr Stephens as … he cannot burn lime with them and they lay on his hands useless.'

In June, with more than 700 tons of unusable coal occupying space in the warehouse (a problem solved by paying import duties and selling it on to third parties), Elsden sailed for England 'to examine such collieries as had the best culm … at the cheapest rate, that the price might not be rose on them as the quantity would be very considerable'. He carried with him a letter of introduction from the British consul (Edward Hay) to Sir Thomas Stepney, a coal merchant in south Wales. Hay had been asked to write the letter, but he had recently applied for the post of British envoy in place of Abraham Castres (who had died in May) and felt the need for caution. A few days later, he wrote a second letter to Thomas Stepney:

> 'I wrote you a letter some days ago by one Mr William Elsden [of] some kilns belonging to a lime contract. He goes over to treat about a correspondence for importing hither coal and culm. I beg leave to observe to you that I understand nothing of the nature of their contract. They give lime upon very cheap terms; whether they can afford it or not I do not pretend to know, nor do I know anything about the circumstances of Mr William Stephens, the person who has formed the contract. I think myself obliged to tell you this much … that you may not blame me in case any correspondence you may enter into with them should not succeed … I have thought it … proper to explain myself, that you may not pay too great a regard to my recommendation and repent of it afterwards … I beg leave to answer for nothing, nor nobody.'[1]

Meanwhile, Dingley was doing his best to remedy his mistake. Between May and July, he loaded nine ships with a total of 2,000 tons of culm from south Wales – but almost half of these vessels failed to arrive in Lisbon. One was burnt at sea and, because England was again at war with France, three were captured by French privateers and sunk. As a result, only 1,200 tons had arrived by August 1757, the time when the kilns were ready to enter production.

The three cargoes sunk by the French were carried in British craft, so William asked Dingley to charter foreign ships which would receive less attention from enemy vessels. A few more cargoes arrived in the autumn, but customs officials in Wales were charging such high export duties (particularly on cargoes carried in foreign ships) that William was unable to sell lime at the price fixed by Pombal. In December, he was forced to instruct Dingley to send no more culm to Lisbon. He also asked him to take up the matter with the Treasury in London.

Dingley wrote to the Treasury in January 1758, explaining that William had built the kilns to provide lime for the rebuilding of Lisbon. The king of Portugal had agreed to exempt the culm from import duties and promised to use William's lime in all rebuilding works in the city on condition that it was sold at the price fixed after the earthquake. He explained that British customs officials had been treating the culm as coal (the value of which was four times higher) and made the point that the high level of duties prevented William from selling lime except at a loss, 'thereby the kilns erected at a very great expense are become useless and his intention of aid in rebuilding the city of Lisbon abortive'.

When the Treasury considered the matter in February, it was decided that any reduction in export duties might lead to fraud, giving 'an opportunity to officers to pass coals as culm, the one not being in many cases distinguishable from the other, and thereby enable foreigners to supply their forges at a cheaper rate'. Dingley replied, in a strongly worded letter, that it was easy to distinguish culm from coal and explaining that neither he nor William were 'by no temptation whatever capable of fraud or collusion'.

A few weeks later, he wrote again, explaining that continuing delays in the matter were likely to 'put a final end to the undertaking' and asking for permission to present his case to parliament. After a few anxious days, he 'waited on his Grace the Duke of Newcastle, First Lord of the Treasury, and his Grace was pleased to tell him that he had their leave to apply to Parliament for a Bill to empower him to export culm to Lisbon … paying only a trivial duty'.

Parliament debated the matter in April and, when the bill passed to the House of Lords, several members accompanied it there, including William Pitt who spoke 'very warm on the occasion, how glad the nation was to oblige the Portuguese, and he declared that he was on his part willing to let culm be sent to Lisbon even without any duty'. The Culm Act was passed on 26 April 1758. With immediate effect, and for a period of fifteen years, exports of culm to Lisbon would incur only a token duty.

The news reached Lisbon in May, four months after William had been summoned into Pombal's presence to discuss the supply of lime for the reconstruction. Praying that Dingley's negotiations would be successful, that his kilns would be working at full capacity by the time the work began, he asked for a loan to cover his operating costs. Pombal agreed, authorising an advance payment of 8 contos of reis to be repaid in consignments of lime for rebuilding the arsenal and the custom house.

Most of this money was sent to London to pay for cargoes of culm which were despatched as soon as the Culm Act came into force. The first cargo incurring the token duty arrived in June, after which ships began to arrive in increasing numbers. By September, eleven cargoes had arrived in the Tagus and William was ready to supply the state with large quantities of lime. But the elation he experienced in the summer soon evaporated when the building work did not go ahead as planned.

With no lime required for the reconstruction, he had to sell to individuals, as he had done a year earlier when his furnaces were lit for the first time. He now had greater quantities to sell, so he produced an advertising leaflet with instructions for preparing lime for different purposes: mortar for walls, rough mortar for flat roofs, fine plaster for decoration. He explained that, although good quality mortar was made in the past, lime-making in Portugal had deteriorated since then and was now believed to be the most inferior in Europe. However, 'with lime from the new factory, a firm bonding will be achieved, similar to that obtained by the old methods'.[2]

Lime produced in traditional kilns was brought into the city and sold at the price fixed by Pombal. Because of reduced transport costs, William was able to undercut this price by 15 per cent and this, together with his critical remarks about their product, enraged the local lime-makers. They made derogatory comments about his lime; they said it was discoloured and contaminated by ashes. Lime from continuous coal-fired kilns was often a more brownish colour than that produced in traditional kilns and the lime-makers were telling no more than the truth, but when their comments reached the ears of William's private buyers, most of them took their custom elsewhere. As a result, he had no choice but to close some of his kilns. By the autumn of 1760, only three kilns remained in operation.

…

The lime factory was just over a mile from Belém and, during his first months in Alcântara, William watched the wooden palace being constructed on the nearby hill of Ajuda. Activity increased in July 1757 when the Real Barraca was ready for occupation and the servants brought the furniture and furnishings up the hill from Belém. The royal carriages clattered through Alcântara on their way to and from Lisbon; and from the carriage windows, Maria could see the smoke rising from the factory chimneys.

In September 1758, there was much discussion about the king's supposed fall and the injury to his arm. Three months later, everyone in Alcântara was talking about the Távora conspiracy. On the night of 12 January 1759, while Maria lay awake in the wooden palace, William lay in his bed at the lime kilns, listening to the carpenters at work on the scaffold. The following morning, he heard the distant sounds from Belém. Later that day, the crowds who had watched the executions passed through Alcântara on their way home to Lisbon:

'Their pace was slow, their eyes fixed on the ground. There was a perfect silence. Except some sighs and the pattering of their feet, nothing was heard. Their countenances without exception were filled with the deepest melancholy.'[3]

Two days later, the royal family came to the church of Nossa Senhora do Livramento and William saw the king wave his handkerchief in the air with both hands as the crowd roared its approval. In June 1760, he illuminated his house in celebration of Maria's marriage. On 3 September, his lime was used to lay the foundation stone of the memorial church in Belém. As he mingled with the crowds to watch the proceedings, he saw Maria and her sisters 'wearing most ample hoops … hopping out of the coach with so much nimbleness'.

By this time, work had begun on rebuilding the arsenal but the city remained in ruins. In a petition to the king, William explained that the demand for lime was much less than previously estimated. It had been assumed that sixteen kilns would be needed to supply lime for the reconstruction, but with only three kilns in operation, he was still producing greater quantities than he could sell. He was deeply in debt and he begged José to have pity on him and suspend repayments of his loan.

He received no reply and, on 21 July 1761, he offered the factory to the state in payment of his debts. Pombal declined the offer although, on 19 August, he agreed to make an advance payment of 1,650 milreis for further consignments of lime for the arsenal. The following night, William heard the bells and cannon-fire announcing the birth of Maria's first child. He put lighted candles in the windows of his house – but he was not in a mood to celebrate. The advance payment would pay off some of his creditors but he remained deeply in debt, mainly to Charles Dingley to whom he owed 1,977 milreis (more than £106,000 in today's values) for consignments of culm.

In January 1762, William was forced to extinguish the last three furnaces. He was 'broken' – and to make matters worse, his four orphaned siblings (ranging in age from 11 to 17) would soon arrive in Lisbon to join him. After their mother died in 1755, William's brothers and sister had been cared for by friends in Exeter while appeals were made to the extended Stephens family. Thomas Cogan, a cousin in London, was a governor of Christ's Hospital (a school for children of good family whose parents were unable to maintain them). He arranged for the youngest boy, John James, to be admitted to the Hospital in May 1756, 'to be there educated and brought up among other poor children'.[4]

Only one child from a family could enter the Hospital, so the eldest boy, Lewis, was taken in by another cousin (John Lyne, rector of St Ive in Cornwall) and the next boy, Jedediah, by John's sister Rachel (wife of Benjamin Tucker, a warrant officer in the navy). The youngest child, Philadelphia, travelled with John James to London where she would live with Thomas Cogan above his haberdashery in Cornhill.

In his letters to England, William never mentioned his difficulties at the limekilns or his accumulating debts, and the family still believed him to be a successful and wealthy merchant. In December 1761, just a few weeks before he closed the factory, he received a letter from Thomas Cogan. John James would be 14 years old in January, the age when boys not destined for university were apprenticed to a trade or merchant house, and Cogan thought it appropriate that he should work for his brother in Lisbon. Perhaps because he was too proud to admit the truth, William accepted John James as an apprentice and, deciding that it was time to take responsibility for all his siblings, he suggested that the other three children should accompany their brother to Portugal.

John James was discharged from Christ's Hospital on 17 March 1762, 'the boy being to serve Mr William Stephens of Lisbon, merchant, for seven years'.[5] Six weeks later, the children sailed on the packet boat which left Falmouth on 30 April and arrived in Lisbon on 13 May. William met them at the quay and, in his mule-drawn chaise, he took them through the ruined streets of the city. When they reached Alcântara, he had to explain why no furnaces were burning, why the factory was deserted, why John James had been apprenticed to a business which had ceased to exist.

It was a bad time for the children to arrive for political reasons too. The Franco-Spanish invasion had begun eight days earlier and the city was living in fear of enemy occupation. British troops arrived in Lisbon on 16 June but their commander, Lord Loudoun, soon found it difficult to obtain sufficient supplies. He spoke no Portuguese, government officials spoke little or no English, and William sensed an opportunity. He wrote to Loudoun towards the end of June, about the time that the British officers were entertained at Queluz:

> 'It is humbly submitted to Lord Loudoun's consideration whether the inconveniencing to which the English troops are exposed for want of the Portuguese language might not be remedied, and impositions, delays and ill-blood prevented, by the establishment of an Intendant for the army. Should such an employment be thought necessary, William Stephens begs leave to offer his services and to state his qualifications.
>
> 'He is an Englishman, a master of the Portuguese language, well versed in the laws and customs of the country and in the different sorts of address necessary to do business with all ranks of people in Portugal. He is well known to the Count de Oeiras [Pombal] and has reason to believe he should be supported by him with the authority requisite to carry all branches of this employment into execution.

'He will not presume to point out to his Lordship the various parts of business within the province of a Military Intendant, but those in which he flatters himself he might [be] particularly serviceable are in inspecting minutely into the goodness of all forage and provisions and to superintend the regularity of the delivery; and when the whole or any part of the army should march, to see that supply of all sorts be ready before the troops arrive at their destination.'[6]

Loudoun did not take up the offer. And when Pombal ordered that all baggage animals in Lisbon be requisitioned to transport equipment to the front, William lost most of the mules from his stables.

Four months later, he reached the lowest point of his time in Alcântara. Bailiffs came to the house on 21 October, to enforce an order instigated by Dingley, and William watched from the yard as the men carried away his possessions. First came the drop-leaf dining table, another table with panels of ebony embossed with gold, twelve brazilwood chairs with leather seats, two sofas, and a side table. From the kitchen came the pine table, the dinner service, twelve pewter dishes and three copper casseroles. Finally, from the stables, came the chaise, the one-remaining mule, the donkey, and the tack.

William was defeated. The ceasefire in November failed to lift his spirits and it was not until early 1763 that he raised the energy to write again to Pombal. He was, he explained, 'without the means to support my person or my family and without possessions of any value. I beg your Excellency to allow me to attend to the extreme misery in which I find myself.' There was a quantity of lime at the factory; if the government could send money for this, it would help to sustain his family who, 'since October of last year, have experienced the most terrible misfortunes'.

He received no reply so he tried again a few weeks later, this time addressing his petition to the king:

'I have been reduced to the most abject poverty because of the great loss I sustained in the lime factory which I built in good faith for the reconstruction of the city. Because of the war that stopped the rebuilding works, the factory is useless and dead, and I have had the distress of selling the furniture of my house to feed my family of three brothers and a sister, orphans.'

This was stretching the truth (the furniture had been taken to repay his debt to Dingley) but William was hoping to soften the king's heart by referring to his orphaned siblings. He had no other recourse than to ask for clemency – and reverting to the request he had made almost two years earlier, he begged José to accept the limekilns in payment of his debt.

The government was unwilling to take on such an unprofitable factory and William continued to live in poverty for the next two years. It was not until the summer of 1764 that his fortunes began to change. With state finances improving, Pombal at last turned his attention to the rebuilding of Lisbon. He gave thought to William's situation at Alcântara and, now the work was about to begin, he authorised another advance payment for lime.

The reconstruction finally began during the summer of 1764. Builders set to work in the low-lying area behind the Terreiro do Paço and William reopened his factory. He re-employed his workmen, ordered shipments of fuel, purchased mules and carts, re-furnished his house, and re-lit the furnaces. Three thousand tons of culm were discharged at the Alcântara quay in 1765 and a further 6,000 tons arrived during the next three years as work on the reconstruction surged ahead and William's kilns worked at full capacity to provide lime for the builders.

Three years after smoke rose again from the factory chimneys, William's uncle John died at the advanced age of 77. He had lived with William at the lime kilns for ten years, helping with the paperwork and the housekeeping. A few hours after his death, the body was taken on a mule cart to the Protestant cemetery in the western suburb of Estrela, a peaceful square of ground surrounded by cypress trees (ordered by the Inquisition 'to hide the burial ground of heretics from the sight of the faithful'). He was buried in the south-east corner of the cemetery and the chaplain filled in the register: '26 June 1767, John Stephens of the Lime Kilns.'

A few days later, William wrote to Pombal. His exemption from duties on imported culm had less than three years to run and he asked for an extension of this privilege. He had, he explained, been of considerable service to the state. He had built the kilns at his own expense and supplied lime for the reconstruction promptly and efficiently, but his costs had been excessive and his debts could not be repaid without a significant increase in time.

On 27 July, the king signed an order extending the exemption for a further twenty years – and by this time Pombal had other plans for William. As a visitor to Lisbon would remark many years later, 'his first speculation was not ... of any great pecuniary advantage to him; his next was of a far more profitable nature'.[7]

8

An Unfortunate Muleteer

How formidable an ecclesiastical faction is to the peace of any country ... The King's favour ... perhaps will enable him entirely to subdue the ecclesiastical hydra, although new heads should spring up as others are lopped off.
William Henry Lyttelton on Marquis de Pombal, 24 January 1769

On 13 May 1767, six weeks before William's uncle died in the lime factory, Maria gave birth to her second surviving child, a son named João after her grandfather. As Lisbon celebrated, 'the joyful event made public by firing of guns from all the castles and forts ... and the ringing of bells in churches and convents', William placed lighted candles in the windows of his house in Alcântara.

On 5 July, to celebrate his fiftieth birthday, Pedro hosted an entertainment at Queluz similar to those held on the feast days of São Joao and São Pedro. Edward Hay attended the occasion, accompanied by a visitor to Lisbon, Henry Hobart (brother of the Earl of Buckinghamshire), who described the evening in his journal. After the bullfight and a banquet, 'the table extremely well served, the wine good, and well waited upon', the guests were taken to the concert room to hear the queen and two of her daughters sing. Maria did not take part, 'being just recovered from laying in'; neither did Doroteia, who 'has bad health and never attempts it'.[1]

Maria conceived for the fifth time the following March. Her pregnancy had almost reached full term on 8 December 1768 when she attended a performance of Molière's *Tartuffe* in a theatre in Lisbon. The play was about religious hypocrisy. The role of Tartuffe, the arch-hypocrite who fakes a display of piety to ingratiate himself with a wealthy bourgeois before swindling him out of his money and his wife, was played in Jesuit costume. It was easy to recognise the subtext of this production and three people were 'committed to prison for speaking their sentiments too freely on the subject of this new play'.

The following day, Pombal ordered the arrest of one of Maria's favourite clerics. The elderly Miguel da Anunciação, Bishop of Coimbra, was related to the Távora family. His crime was to write a pastoral letter condemning several books which had been specifically sanctioned by the Real Mesa Censória, a secular body set up by Pombal to take over matters of censorship from the

Inquisition. The bishop was sentenced to death for treason, 'for a long train of projects tending to counteract and subvert the present system of his Majesty's government', but he was spared execution because of his advanced age. Instead, he was imprisoned in a fort at the mouth of the Tagus.

Six days after the bishop's arrest, Maria was 'brought to bed of a daughter at quarter past seven o'clock in the morning'. On 21 December, the infant was carried to the royal chapel and baptised Mariana after her grandmother. On the 23rd, copies of the bishop's offending letter (which according to Pombal 'had certainly been dictated from Rome') were burnt by the public executioner 'as false, seditious and treasonable', and Pombal told the new British envoy, William Henry Lyttelton, that the king 'had been much disturbed by the machinations of ecclesiastics and therefore he required him to take such measures as might effectively silence these turbulent spirits'.

...

Two weeks later, the royal family travelled to Salvaterra, leaving Doroteia (who 'continues very indisposed') in the Real Barraca. The daily hunts were accompanied by trumpeters and drummers, guards, equerries, and falconers dressed in scarlet livery trimmed with gold. José and Mariana and the men of the court hunted hares and rabbits, deer and wild boar, while 'the ladies, from the comfort of their carriages, have the amusement of watching rabbits being killed, deer being caught with ropes, hares and rabbits running and birds flying'.

At Salvaterra, José entertained 'all foreigners who are properly introduced … and furnishes every one with horses for the chase'. Henry Hobart spent a week here in April 1769 and described the hunts and operas in his journal:

> 'Sunday went a-shooting with their Majesties. It is usual for them to go in chaises a league or two distant, where they mount their horses and ride to some open place in the woods or covers, which is cut on purpose, whilst some hundreds of peoples surround a certain quantity of ground, and drive all the game towards these open glades, where they shoot at them as they pass …
>
> 'Monday went a-hawking … Tuesday attended their Majesties a-shooting. Killed some deer, and stags, and a wild boar which the Queen shot herself and made us a present of … Wednesday went a-hawking, the Princesses of the party, a very royal sight when the Falconers go out full drest, as their coats are richly laced, their hawks are of different species and all very good …
>
> 'The Operas here are as magnificent as those at the Ajuda, and not inferior to them in scenes and decoration … Nobody goes drest, every person as they like with or without boots. Their Majesties generally stay

long in the field, are about half an hour eating a late dinner or early supper, and go to the Opera towards the dusk of the evening in the same dresses as they have had on all the day. The King generally wears a coloured silk handkerchief about his neck.'[2]

In June, Hobart was invited to the celebrations at Queluz. He was about to leave Lisbon and the entries in his diary had become a little jaded. He was particularly taken by Benedita ('a very fine young woman ... a desirable piece'), but made the comment that 'the Queen has lost her teeth and should leave off singing'.

...

José was now 55 years old. He was troubled by the breach with Rome, aware that his father had suffered a near-fatal stroke at the earlier age of 52. He had no wish to die without papal absolution so, to humour him, Pombal re-established relations with the Vatican. The breach had lasted ten years, long enough for Pombal to remove the church's dominance over state affairs; he had placed the church under government control and reduced the powers of the Inquisition. As Lyttelton explained, 'although it was resolved to admit the lion, it was with his nails cut and his teeth drawn'.

A new papal nuncio was appointed in August and, on 16 September, the king thanked his minister by giving him the title by which he is known to history, Marquis de Pombal. Five weeks later, the royal family left Lisbon for an extended stay in the palace at Vila Viçosa.

On the morning of 3 December, the king set out for the chase ahead of his attendants. He was passing through a gate into the walled hunting park when a 'tall strong man in the habit of a peasant' attacked him with a wooden pole, 'a long staff with one end knottier and heavier than the other end which formed the handle'. He was a muleteer named João de Sousa and he aimed three blows at the king; the first landed on his shoulder, the second on his left hand, the third on his horse's rump. Attendants galloped to the rescue but Sousa fought with great strength before he was overpowered. José, who had only suffered bruises to his hand and shoulder, continued the hunt; Sousa was taken off to the dungeons.

That afternoon, the palace was in turmoil. Mariana had come close to losing her husband for a second time; Maria had faced the prospect of inheriting the throne, a position for which she was painfully unprepared. An urgent message was sent to Pombal in Lisbon who dispatched two magistrates to interrogate the prisoner.

Sousa had a grievance against the king. His mules had been requisitioned for the journey of the court to Vila Viçosa and one of them was driven so hard that it died on the road. He had petitioned José for compensation, but his request was ignored. He was ill-treated, angry, and 'not in his right wits', but Pombal perceived the attack as a Jesuit conspiracy, a suicide mission: Sousa had fought so valiantly with his captors because he hoped to die at their hands. He was, said Pombal, 'neither out of his wits, nor drunk, but the most insolent of all men living and calm as fanatics usually are'.

While Sousa was brought to Lisbon 'loaded with irons', tortured in the presence of Pombal and two judges, and died in the dungeons, José feared for his personal safety. He stopped attending councils of state. He failed to attend public audiences – and when he did appear, he sat on a particularly high throne behind a balustrade. A detachment of cavalry accompanied him when he went out hunting and soldiers escorted him whenever he left the palace. 'He does not walk five yards from his coach but thro' the lines of his guards,' wrote Lyttelton on 13 January, 'and when he goes on Saturdays to hear Mass at a chapel of a convent in Lisbon, the guards are drawn up from the coach to the high altar.'

Aware of his lack of education – and no doubt encouraged by Pombal – the king gave orders that his elder grandson should receive a more appropriate schooling. Several months earlier, Pombal had appointed Manuel do Cenáculo Vilas Boas, one of his most intelligent advisers, to be Prince José's confessor. Now, Cenáculo was appointed Bishop of Beja and given the role of the prince's preceptor. Described by the British envoy as having 'a very liberal understanding ... esteemed for eloquence and freedom of thought', he taught the prince political history, geography, geometry and law; he provided books for him to read, including works by Erasmus and Racine; and he instilled in his mind a more secular approach to state affairs.

The new papal nuncio arrived in Lisbon on 28 May 1770, welcomed by the people of the city who knelt on the river banks in their thousands as he was rowed across the Tagus. On 4 July, he was received in the Real Barraca for his first audience with the king. Seven months later, he hosted a banquet in honour of Maria's birthday, a diplomatic gesture given unusual significance because of the failure of the previous nuncio to celebrate her marriage. This should have been a happy occasion for Maria, blending her religious faith with the return of a nuncio and her happy conjugal life. Instead it was tinged with anxiety.

Her sister Doroteia had been mentally ill for more than seven years. Her condition appears to have been anorexic in nature, described as 'in part hysteric and accompanied with an almost total lack of appetite which has reduced her to a state of extreme weakness'. By the time of the nuncio's banquet on 17 December, her condition was considered to be 'very dangerous' and she died four weeks later, aged just 31. According to custom, the family confined themselves to the palace for eight days, after which they made their usual journey to Salvaterra. In April 1771, Maria conceived for the sixth time. In the summer, she enjoyed the entertainments at Queluz and, on 22 September, she 'miscarried of a prince'.

Meanwhile, she and Pedro continued to appear side-by-side at official audiences but still took no part in state affairs. No attempt was made to educate the crown princess (or her husband) for her future role as monarch. Only Pombal gave the matter thought – and he was biding his time.

9

Marinha Grande

Had much talk of Portugall ... That there are there no glass windows,
nor will they have any.
Samuel Pepys, 17 October 1661

uilt is not an emotion normally associated with Marquis de Pombal, dictator of Portugal, but perhaps he felt a little responsible for William's difficulties at Alcântara. It was he who had encouraged him to build the kilns on an industrial scale, to provide large quantities of lime for the rebuilding of Lisbon. He had intended to begin the reconstruction in the spring of 1757, but events conspired against him and work did not start until seven years later.

As soon as the rebuilding began, William proved to be an efficient supplier, providing large quantities of lime to order and on time. The factory at Alcântara could never be truly profitable while it relied on imported fuel and the end-product had to be sold at fixed prices, but maybe an opportunity would arise when he could put the Englishman's ideas and experience to better use.

In an effort to reduce the country's reliance on imports, he had set up a number of new industries, granting loans to men of business who could compete with products from overseas. Several of the men chosen to run these industries were foreigners; there was so little commercial activity in Portugal, and the country was so heavily in thrall to the church, that it was difficult to find competent Portuguese with business experience.

One of the few industries to pre-date these initiatives was the royal glass factory established in 1719 at Coina, near the southern shore of the Tagus, with furnaces fuelled by coal imported from England. This angered the British glass merchants, one of whom (using the pseudonym 'a Lisbon Glass Man – *formerly*') complained of 'the fatal consequences attending such practices', particularly as the factory was operating 'under *English* management'.[1]

In 1747 (under the directorship of John Beare), the factory was relocated to Marinha Grande, a small village close to the sawmill in the royal pine forest of Leiria. Beare drank heavily in Marinha Grande. He fell into debt and in 1767, when he declared himself 'broken', Pombal included the factory in his programme of new industries. The glassworks would be reopened and enlarged to provide increased levels of production and, more important in the short term, to manufacture window glass for the rebuilding of Lisbon.

William was on friendly terms with Beare's partner, Edward Campion, who had handled the sale of glass in Lisbon. Seeking an entrepreneur to reopen the glassworks, Pombal's advisers discussed the matter with Campion and he put forward the name of his friend, a man for whom Pombal felt some degree of responsibility. The minister felt confident that William would be successful at Marinha Grande. The factory would burn firewood from the royal pine forest and, apart from window glass (categorised as a building material), its finished products would not be subject to fixed prices.

Pombal delegated the matter to his brother, Francisco Xavier de Mendonça Furtado (secretary of state of marine and the colonies), and it was he who invited William to reopen the glassworks. But William was reluctant to leave his family and move to a small village 70 miles north of Lisbon. The limekilns were operating at full capacity and he feared that this new project would bankrupt him for a third time. As he would later explain:

'during the years 1767 and 1768, I was often asked by the Secretary of State ... to rebuild the decaying glass factory near the pine forest of Leiria. I refused the invitation for fear of the ruination experienced by those who had previously attempted the project.'

In 1769, Mendonça Furtado approached William again, 'severely reprimanding him for his reluctance and adding that the request was made by express command of the King'. José had seen the kilns from his carriage windows and, aware that the lime factory was operating successfully, hoped that the Englishman could achieve similar success at the glassworks.

William now had little alternative; it would have been difficult to disobey the king and Pombal was not a man to cross. He was capable of imprisoning (or worse) anyone whose loyalty he suspected, Portuguese or foreigner, and perhaps it was courageous of William to have held out for as long as he did. When he agreed to the request:

'The Secretary of State ordered me to leave directly for the palace to inform the King of my compliance, for which I was granted a private audience. I kissed his Majesty's hand, thanked him for the honour of his request, and explained the difficulty of the enterprise. The King was greatly pleased by my acceptance and promised his immediate Royal protection.'

He followed the usual ceremonial at the palace, bowing three times to the king as he advanced up the room and three times more as he retreated backwards towards the door. During their conversation, José told him to list his requirements and said that, if he needed help in the future, he should 'make representations, either to the Secretary of State or to his Royal Person, as the establishment and progress of the glassworks were very much in his Royal interest'.

Next day William drew up a list of his demands. He agreed them with Mendonça Furtado and submitted a formal petition to Pombal and the king. He entered into partnership with his youngest brother, John James, who would remain in Alcântara to manage the limekilns as well as handling the sale of glass from Marinha Grande.

On 7 July, the king signed a decree authorising the re-opening of the glassworks and ordering that William be given 'all the help and favour that is necessary'. The decree set out fifteen conditions under which the business would operate, including an interest-free loan of 32 contos of reis (about £1.5 million in today's values). To fuel the furnaces, he was given free use of decayed wood and branches from the royal pine forest, a significant benefit for such an energy-intensive industry. And for an initial period of fifteen years, he would be exempt from payment of all taxes on the sale of finished glass.

The loan from the Junta do Comércio (Board of Trade) would be paid in four instalments of 8 contos of reis, the first to be handed over immediately and the balance paid in three six-monthly instalments. It was to be fully repaid after thirteen years, the first repayment falling due four years after the factory re-opened, followed by annual payments over the next nine years. William received the first instalment on 20 July. The following morning, while his baggage was loaded onto a string of mules, his family gathered in the courtyard to say their farewells. It was a painful parting and, as he rode out of the factory gates, he was convinced that he was heading for yet another financial disaster.

For three days, he travelled along roads which were little more than tracks strewn with boulders. He spent the nights in country inns and reached Marinha Grande during the afternoon of Sunday, 23 July. The village was set in flat, sandy countryside and Beare's wooden workshops stood abandoned and derelict. The glassworkers, unemployed for two years now, were awaiting his arrival and, as news of his coming spread through the village, many of them turned up at the inn to present themselves to the new proprietor of the factory.

The following morning, he introduced himself to the villagers and surveyed the buildings. On Tuesday, he set to work, recording details of his expenditure in a notebook. He worked at a furious pace, spending long hours on paperwork and proving that – as Pombal had suspected – he was an administrator of great ability. He had been given power to acquire land by compulsory purchase but he preferred to work by negotiation. He wrote many letters about legal and religious matters for the transfer of land had its complications: one plot was owned by the Knights of Malta; another required regular masses to be read for a previous owner who had died several years earlier.

Most of Beare's craftsmen had remained in Marinha Grande and William soon employed seven glass-masters, five assistants and three apprentices, together with twenty-five workers for other duties and twenty-eight men to work as carters in the pine forest, transporting firewood to the factory in bullock carts. Work began on the restoration of the workshops on 7 August, an occasion celebrated with a feast for the craftsmen and labourers. Potters made crucibles, tools and equipment were cleaned and restored, and William organised the collection of raw materials for the production of window glass: sand (freely available in the soil around Marinha Grande) and soda alkali (imported from Spain).

By early October, the workshop for window glass was ready to enter production. Supplies of sand and soda had arrived at the factory and a furnace was lit to heat the crucibles. Two weeks later, William sent his first consignment of window glass to Lisbon. As he wrote to Mendonça Furtado on 19 October:

> 'I started to make glass on the 16th of this month and the first order is on its way for use in your Excellency's houses. I hope the establishment I have made here will be approved by your Excellency and by his Majesty, and that this approval will be even greater in the future when the glass-masters have perfected their work. To this end, I shall apply all my vigilance.'

At the same time, he was making arrangements for the production of tableware. Glass made with soda alkali was only suitable for window panes; it had a sea-green tint and hardened quickly on cooling. Crystalline glass required a slower-cooling mixture, achieved mainly by substituting the soda with potash. Production began in early 1770 in a second restored workshop, initially using John Beare's catalogue of designs (the moulds for which had remained at the factory). Meanwhile, work proceeded on the construction of a new stone-built workshop for crystalline glass, as well as buildings for the preparation of raw materials.

In February, William received a visit from the British envoy, William Henry Lyttelton, who was making a journey north from Lisbon 'after an indisposition which confined me to my house for above a month'. Pombal had told him of his plans to revive the glassworks and he was interested to see how the work was proceeding. Before leaving the city, he had received a letter from London asking him to inform Pombal of George III's 'most sincere congratulations upon the fortunate escape of his Majesty from the hands of that atrocious villain at Vila Viçosa'. This he did on 12 February, in a letter written from Marinha Grande.

At the end of the year, William sent his first annual report to the government. During the previous fifteen months, the factory had made 12,000 sheets of window glass and sent more than 100 crates of crystalline glass to Lisbon.

The glassworks now employed 150 men, with an additional seventy carters transporting firewood from the pine forest. The new stone-built workshop had entered production a few weeks earlier and William's next project was to demolish the wooden workshop in which he was making window glass and replace it with a second stone building.

Two months later, he made the journey to Alcântara to celebrate his sister's twentieth birthday in March 1771, travelling south across streams still swollen by winter rains. Needing a warehouse to stock his finished glass and provide storage for imported raw materials which arrived by ship in the Tagus, he found a plot of steeply rising ground on Rua de São Paulo, close to the river a little to the west of the major work of reconstruction. He bought the land at auction and, at a meeting with Pombal to discuss the glassworks, the minister gave him plans for a mansion house, warehouse and courtyard to be built on the site in Pombaline style, a little square still known today as the Largo do Stephens.

Leaving John James in charge of the building work, William returned to Marinha Grande. He had impressed Pombal with the speed of his progress and, in January 1772, he was congratulated by the Junta do Comércio: 'Although the workshops are still incomplete, the great success of this factory is very pleasing.' Two months later, when the Junta authorised the final instalment of his loan, he was informed that the government was 'extremely satisfied with the factory and had high hopes for its future progress'.

...

The compound at Marinha Grande covered an area of forty-four acres, enclosed by a wall. Inside the gates and beyond the porter's lodge lay a large courtyard which William planted with trees to provide shade. By the summer of 1772, elegant stone buildings in neo-classical style had taken the place of John Beare's wooden structures. The main workshops occupied two sides of the courtyard; behind them were ancillary structures for carpentry and pot-making, and for engraving, cutting and painting the glass. There was a large warehouse and several covered areas where the stocks of firewood were stored.

On the third side of the courtyard, William had built a small but well-proportioned mansion house, described by a Portuguese aristocrat as 'a pretty little palace with an exterior both grandiose and simple'.[2] The rooms were partially tiled in blue and white *azulejo* tiles, the ceilings decorated with mouldings incorporating the Stephens coat of arms, and a minstrel's gallery on the staircase adorned with musical motifs: two trumpets, a lute and a violin. The windows at the rear of the house overlooked a private garden planted with herbs, shrubs and low box hedges; this was bordered by a lake, beyond which lay vegetable plots and orchards.

The front of the house faced the courtyard where bullock carts arrived from the pine forest, their wooden axles creaking and grinding. As the craftsmen laboured in the heat of the furnaces, ancillary workers prepared the raw materials, washing and sifting the sand before adding the alkali and other ingredients. The mixture was placed in crucibles in the furnace and remained there for several days, after which it was cooled a little – to the consistency of treacle – before being taken up on the blowing irons. It was hot in the workshops where the craftsmen transformed these blobs of molten glass into a great variety of shapes and sizes. They rolled the glass into round or cylindrical masses, blew them into bubbles which they shaped by swinging the blowing rods, then cut them with shears, tongs and pincers. Meanwhile, they reheated the glowing blobs through apertures in the furnace, the whole process requiring precision, dexterity and a fine sense of rhythm.

Crystalline glass was prepared plain or coloured by metallic oxides. It was either hand-blown and spun into shape or blown into clay moulds. After cooling, it was cut using wheels of iron and sandstone; engraved with diamond tools or copper wheels; polished, gilded, enamelled, and painted. Finally, it was checked, sorted and packed in straw. Crates of finished glass were sent to Lisbon containing a wide variety of products (wine glasses and tumblers, decanters and vases, dishes and bowls, oil and vinegar dispensers, salt cellars and ink-wells, candlesticks and scent bottles), as well as sheets of pale sea-green glass for use as window panes.

Output continued to increase as new workshops entered production, but it soon became clear that sales were struggling. Glass from Marinha Grande faced competition from glass imported from Bohemia and, by the time the factory complex was complete, William's warehouse was stocked with more than 300 boxes of unsold glass. Fifteen years earlier, the lime-makers of Lisbon had spread rumours about the poor quality of his lime; now the merchants were spreading rumours that his glass was of lower quality than imported glass. They had also reduced their prices, undercutting the price of glass from Marinha Grande. Shops in the cities were controlled by the merchants and stocked only imported glass, so it was easy for the people of Lisbon to avoid buying the more expensive domestic product.

As a young man, William had been defeated by the lime-makers. Now, with royal protection, he was in a stronger position. Determined to put the merchants out of business, he drafted a long and well-argued petition, and travelled to Lisbon in June 1772 to present it personally to the government. He complained of the 'malice and subterfuge' of the merchants and their attempts to destroy his factory which had been reopened at the king's request 'for the good of the public'. He listed several reasons why glass production was cheaper in Bohemia (climate, cost of living, availability of skilled labour and raw materials) and made the point that the three-day journey from Marinha Grande to Lisbon, on roads consisting mainly of rocks and stones, cost twice as much as the merchants paid to ship Bohemian glass from Hamburg to the Tagus. And when his glass arrived in Lisbon, he was unable to show it to the public because the merchants controlling the shops had no intention of offering shelf-space to products from Marinha Grande. All his sales were made from the newly completed warehouse in Rua de São Paulo, where crystalline glass had to be sold in bulk, by the box rather than by piece.

His factory was capable of meeting the total demand for glass in Portugal and its colonies, with an excess available for export abroad. Annual capacity would soon be over 2,000 crates of glass, valued at 40 contos of reis. To ensure that his achievements at Marinha Grande should not be in vain, he asked that several measures be taken to reduce competition from imported glass.

First, he asked for an increase in import duties. Second, to compete more directly with imported glass, he asked for permission to display his glass in shops where his products could be sold in small quantities. Third, to make his prices more competitive, he asked that the factory be exempt from duties on imported raw materials. Finally, he asked for a prohibition on window glass arriving from Bohemia in pre-cut panes. Only whole sheets should be imported into the country, while the factory at Marinha Grande should be permitted to cut window glass into sections.

William had been exceeding his authority and selling pre-cut window panes for some time. Seven days after he submitted his petition, the glaziers of Lisbon made an official complaint against him. It was, they explained, their exclusive privilege to cut window glass which, until recently, had always been sent from Marinha Grande in whole sheets. However, as William pointed out, 'the public cannot be obliged, through a mere spirit of patriotism, to buy a whole sheet of glass from my warehouse to replace one window pane'. He compared the restriction to 'a tailor prohibiting people from mending their own clothes'.

Production at Marinha Grande was reduced during the hot summer months (only the strongest workers could continue their daily routine in the additional heat of the furnaces), so William remained with his family in Lisbon for several weeks. The mansion house on Rua de São Paulo was nearly complete and, because foreigners were not entitled to own lands or buildings in perpetuity, he applied to have the law set aside in his case, both for the Largo do Stephens and for the factory in Marinha Grande. In August, on Pombal's recommendation, the king signed two decrees permitting William to 'own, retain and convey his properties to his heirs and successors, even if foreigners, notwithstanding any law or custom to the contrary which are all dispensed with on this occasion'.

William met with Pombal several times during his stay in Lisbon. The minister was making plans to travel to Coimbra in September and he told William that he would visit Marinha Grande on his way north. He was interested to see the restored factory and he would stay the night in William's mansion house. This was a singular honour for the journey to Coimbra and the only time that Pombal travelled independently of the court.

When William returned to Marinha Grande in August, he brought his sister with him to act as hostess for the occasion. The courtyard and factory buildings were cleaned and tidied; the house was swept, dusted and polished; and William employed additional men in the kitchen to prepare a banquet for the first minister of the country.

10

A Miniature Welfare State

I see such marvels in the fields of Marinha ...
If gratefulness can presume the future,
William, your name will live for all eternity,
Equal to that of the Maker of my Country.

Leonor de Almeida Lorena (Marquesa de Alorna), c.1777–80[1]

Pombal was now at the zenith of his power. 'Age,' wrote an Englishman after meeting him in 1772, 'appeared neither to have diminished the vigour, freshness, nor activity of his faculties. In his person he was very tall and slender; his face long, pale, meagre, and full of intelligence.'[2]

The British envoy admired 'the vast variety of business, from those of the greatest importance to the most minute details of the least consequence, in every department of this government, which he was accustomed to go thro' at all hours, early and late, with an application astonishing in a man of his age'.

The French ambassador found it 'difficult to get a word in edgeways ... one would not have guessed from his appearance that his character was strong and relentless ... He gave me every reason to like him.'[3]

Pombal was, to use a cliché, a man of contradictions. While Maria was repelled by his cruelty, William was attracted by his enlightened thinking, his interest in reason and progress. Despite an age difference of more than thirty years, he and Pombal had much in common and William soon formed part of the small group which advised the minister on his reforms. This included members of Pombal's family, a few aristocrats and liberal-minded clergy (including Cénaculo Vilas Boas), and two foreign entrepreneurs: William Stephens and Jacome Ratton, a Frenchman with several manufacturing interests in Portugal.

One of Pombal's most cherished projects was reform of the system of education, which previously had been controlled by Jesuits. He founded a College of Nobles with an enlightened curriculum (foreign languages, mathematics and the sciences); he opened a commercial college to teach book-keeping and commerce; and in 1772, he reformed the University of Coimbra, establishing faculties of mathematics and natural sciences. He introduced the study of physics and ordered the construction of laboratories, an observatory and a museum of natural history. He created a botanical garden (for the 'instruction of boys, not for the ostentation of princes') and updated the faculty of medicine, allowing the dissection of corpses (previously banned on religious grounds) and the study of hygiene ('because it is easier to conserve health than to recuperate it once lost').

He made the journey to Coimbra to inaugurate the new faculties in person. He left Lisbon on 15 September, travelling up the Tagus in a royal barge before continuing the journey overland. He reached Marinha Grande two days later, arriving in time for the banquet at midday. After the meal, he 'spent the afternoon agreeably' as William showed him around the factory, explaining the process of glass manufacture and introducing him to the craftsmen who demonstrated methods of blowing the glass and cutting, engraving and gilding the finished pieces. Later that afternoon, he visited the sawmill in the royal pine forest before returning to the glassworks – 'and there he spent the night'.[4]

Philadelphia stayed in Marinha Grande after Pombal's visit, preferring the peace of the village to the noise and bustle of Lisbon. She took over the housekeeping and befriended the glassworkers and their families. She visited them in their homes, brought food and blankets when they were sick, and wrote letters for those unable to write their own. A strong, courageous woman, she was an intelligent companion to her brother, taking an interest in the financial aspects of the factory as well as the welfare of its employees. And she celebrated with him when news arrived from Lisbon that most of his recommendations had been accepted.

The king had signed two decrees. The first, dated 5 January 1773, allowed William to pre-cut window panes in the factory and display his products in the shops of Lisbon. The second, signed on 27 January, authorised a new customs tariff. Import duties would be doubled on crystal and crystalline glass, and increased by varying amounts on window glass according to quality. At the same time, Pombal approved a new price list for all types of glass from Marinha Grande.

The factory was the only glassworks of any significance in the country, so the high level of import duties and the ability to set his own prices gave William an effective monopoly of supply in Portugal and its colonies. He could now sell as much glass as his factory could produce and this, combined with his exemption from taxes and free use of fuel, would transform him into one of the richest industrialists in Europe.

...

Aware that a happy and motivated workforce was the key to high productivity, William introduced a programme of social welfare to Marinha Grande which was three decades ahead of similar developments in Britain. He paid good wages; opened a school where his apprentices received an education (learning to read, write and draw, and studying geometry and music); provided a first aid post where sick or injured workers were treated free of charge; organised a relief fund for illness; and set up a generous pension scheme.

His first three years in Marinha Grande had been marred by 'intoxication and disorder' in the factory as new taverns were opened to serve the growing population. Drunken behaviour during working hours often stopped production for many hours at a time, as well as posing a fire risk. After complaining to the government, William was given permission to close all taverns in the area except for one near the factory gates which limited its opening hours, restricted its sales to good-quality wine, and accepted cash payment only.

Another problem was a shortage of meat. Local butchers were unable to meet the increased demand so the glassworkers ('who because of their hard physical labour require substantial and vigorous foodstuffs') had to travel eight miles to the town of Leiria. These journeys had to be made in their working hours, reducing their productivity, while the meat in Leiria was expensive and of poor quality. William's solution was to provide a slaughterhouse and butcher shop in the factory complex, using animals obtained from farmers in the area, many of whom worked part-time as carters in the pine forest.

At the same time, he provided a greater variety of fruit and vegetables. Using the aqueduct which piped water to the factory compound, he created the lake behind his house and built conduits leading from the lake to an orchard and vegetable garden. He planted the orchard with fruit trees grown from seed imported from England and cultivated a wide variety of vegetables, including salad vegetables new to the country: lettuce, radishes, watercress, and chicory. As he wrote to Pombal in 1778:

> 'When your Excellency first sent me to this place, I found it difficult to find a lettuce to eat. Now, in imitation of my vegetable garden, and with plants and seeds taken from it, Leiria, Batalha and Alcobaça are all well provisioned with the most delicate greens. I rather flatter myself for having been of such public benefit.'[5]

He transformed agriculture too. His estates in Marinha Grande totalled 15,000 acres of unproductive land, mostly areas of scrub and heath which he used to extract sand for use in the factory. Having seen the poor harvests obtained by local farmers and the backward methods used to cultivate the soil, he reclaimed some of this land and used it to teach more up-to-date techniques of cultivation. Initially, he introduced methods of agriculture that were in general use in England, but the land was so sandy and sterile that the volume of crops harvested remained low.

Then he heard of the achievements of Thomas Coke, who inherited estates in Holkham, close to the sea in Norfolk where soil conditions were similar to those in Marinha Grande (barren sandy soil with little vegetation). Within a few years, Coke turned this unpromising ground into land which grew wheat, barley and corn, as well as pasturing the latest breeds of sheep and cattle. He planted pine trees to anchor the shifting sands. He adopted a new rotation of crops which enriched the soil. He dug deep pits to find seams of marl, a soft impure limestone which adds body to the soil and lowers acidity. He introduced clover and forage grasses, so that livestock could graze in the fields, and he reclaimed large areas of salt marsh and shingle from daily flooding by the tides and prepared them for cultivation.

Coke organised annual gatherings of his tenant farmers, events which expanded to include agriculturists and scientists from elsewhere in England, as well as from Europe and North America. When news of these gatherings travelled to Portugal, William set up a large farm three miles south of the glassworks, together with two smallholdings immediately outside the factory complex. As Coke had done in Norfolk, he planted pine trees to stabilise the soil and he wrote to England to ask for an agriculturist with knowledge of the methods used at Holkham to come to Marinha Grande to advise him.

A few months later, an agriculturist sailed up the Tagus and made the journey to the glassworks. He and William rode over the land and discussed its similarities to Holkham. They dug exploratory holes until they discovered seams of marl which could be added to the topsoil. He advised William to raise windbreaks planted with bushes to shelter the growing crops; he told him about the new four-course rotation of crops (which eliminated the need for a fallow year); and suggested that he order mechanical seed drills and iron ploughs from England.

William followed this advice and soon his farms were growing wheat, corn, barley and oats, as well as clover, grasses and alfalfa (lucern) for pasturage and cattle feed. The marl-enriched land nurtured the growing crops, producing greater volumes at harvest time, and local farmers learnt to use the ploughs and seed drills. The alfalfa fields, the first in Portugal, produced 'seven or eight abundant crops of lucern every year, although for ages past [they] did not yield a blade of grass'. This allowed more livestock to be kept on the land, increasing the supply of meat in the factory shop, and because alfalfa is pollinated by bees, William kept hives on his land which provided honey for the people of the village.

As a result of his efforts, his workers were stronger and better fed than in other parts of the country. He set a pattern for their daily lives – eight hours of work, eight hours of sleep, eight hours of leisure – and having closed the taverns, he provided cultural activities to occupy their hours of leisure. He employed tutors of music and dance, and built a theatre to one side of the factory courtyard.

Every Sunday, his workmen acted in plays of his choosing, including translations from Shakespeare. When the playwright Nicolau Luís da Silva directed a performance of his own translation of Voltaire's *Olimpia*, he was 'filled with admiration for workmen who had never seen theatre before, but who had the will and energy to commit themselves to this great and difficult tragedy'. In his opinion, the production in William's theatre fell only a little short of those staged at court by professional actors.[6]

The workers also formed an orchestra, performing concerts on Saturday afternoons in the music room in William's house. 'We have concerts every week,' wrote the merchant Antony Gibbs on a visit to the glassworks:

> 'never less than a player on the harpsichord, a bass, two violoncellos, two horns, and four fiddles; no one but a labourer in the fabrick being admitted into the holy band, or ever suffered to play a part at the theatre. Talk to a man in England of making his workmen good performers in the theatre or good musicians, and *he* will talk of sending *you* to Bedlam ... but in this fabrick you have among the labourers some excellent performers.'[7]

William saw himself as the patron and protector of his workmen and he acted more like a squire of an English village than a proprietor of an industrial concern. Every year on his birthday, after his workers had gathered in the factory courtyard, he emerged through the front door of his house. He gave a speech, then walked amongst them, clasping their hands, putting his arm around their shoulders, and engaging each one of them in conversation about their work and their families.

...

By 1774, the quality of finished glass had improved with the employment of a Bohemian master engraver and three of William's apprentices had learnt their craft so quickly that he employed them as assistant glassworkers before their apprenticeships were finished. Sales were keeping pace with production (imports had now declined to minimal levels) but, as an Englishman and a Protestant, he was viewed with suspicion by officials in the pine forest and he sometimes found it difficult to obtain sufficient fuel for the furnaces.

His contract allowed him to use wood which was of no value for construction, but the keeper of the forest refused to grant him a licence to cut branches. He had to make formal declarations that he had made full use of chippings from the sawmill and dead wood on the ground before his carters were allowed to cut from the trees. Even then, he had to declare that the branches were affected by fungal infestation and therefore useless for building purposes. At the same time, his carters were frequently removed from the forest on the pretence that they had infringed regulations.

William complained about this in his report to Pombal in December. During the previous three years, the minister had intervened in a number of his local difficulties and now he came to his aid once again. An enquiry was opened into the conduct of the forest administrators, and in June 1775, the officials were instructed by royal order to do everything in their power to assist the transport of firewood to the factory. The keeper of the forest was ordered to enlist 100 carters to work solely for the glassworks and an area of forest was set aside for their exclusive use.

Later that summer, William succeeded in changing the terms of his loan. In July, the Junta do Comércio reminded him about the first repayment of 800 milreis which was now 'long overdue'. He replied that it would be difficult to make payment in cash because the money was tied up in the factory and in stocks of finished glass. Instead, he suggested that payments be made in consignments of lime and window glass for the reconstruction of Lisbon. The Junta agreed, informing the king that this was 'the best means possible to obtain repayment of the loan without prejudice to the royal coffers, as well as encouraging the continuation of two factories which are so useful to the State'.

The glassworks were thriving. Six years after William's arrival in Marinha Grande, the factory was exempt from domestic taxes, competition had been removed by high import duties, his local difficulties were promptly dealt with, and his loan was repayable in kind. The only clouds on the horizon were Pombal's advanced age and the deteriorating health of the king.

11

The Succession

In her, a gloomy and severe spirit of superstition formed the predominant feature ...
She was taller than her sisters, as well as thinner; of a pale and wan complexion that
seemed to indicate melancholy.

Nathaniel Wraxall on Maria de Bragança, 1772

Pombal was 74 years old in the late summer of 1773 when news arrived from Rome which put him in great good humour. He had banished the Jesuits from Portuguese territories in 1759, France and Spain had followed his example (in 1764 and 1767), and now the Vatican had abolished the Society of Jesus. As Robert Walpole, the new British envoy, explained:

> 'the Marquis de Pombal ... is highly gratified in this last step to the extinction of a body with whom he has been contesting so many years ... especially as he must be allowed the merit of being the first in this country who has ventured openly to attack this Society.'

Perhaps it was this achievement which inspired him to think about changing the succession. Maria's elder son had been educated by Cenáculo Vilas Boas for four years now and was absorbing a liberal approach to state affairs. Alarmed by Maria's subservience to the church, Pombal formed the idea of bypassing her right to the throne and appointing Prince José as heir apparent. He worked on this plan in great secret during the autumn and winter of 1773 and only three people had any knowledge of it: Pombal, the king and José de Seabra e Silva.

José de Seabra was described by Robert Walpole as 'a man of talents, great application and pretty extensive knowledge'. He had endeared himself to Pombal in 1767 when he edited a book of anti-Jesuit propaganda, a book in which every ill in recent Portuguese history was laid firmly at the door of the Society of Jesus. Four years later, he was appointed secretary of state and soon became Pombal's unofficial second-in-command. He was in Pombal's confidence and it was assumed that he would, in time, take over the role of first minister. He was also on good terms with Mariana, and with Maria and Pedro, and he was unhappy about the plan to change the succession.

Pombal had not travelled with the king to his country palaces for several years, preferring to remain in Lisbon to deal with matters of government. Other ministers followed the court and, in early January 1774, Seabra accompanied the royal family to Salvaterra where Pombal's absence gave him an opportunity to speak to the queen in confidence.

Mariana was a woman of spirit and ability, 'with a sound understanding and a cultivated mind'. She never interfered in state affairs, but she was suspicious of Pombal and this latest intrigue was too important to ignore. She told her daughter of the plot and Maria, now four months into a seventh pregnancy, stood up for herself, one of the few times she had the courage to do so.

She remembered the time she had almost died from a fever and the statue of Senhor dos Passos was brought to her bedroom. She believed that God had saved her life so that she could inherit the crown and re-establish the power of the church. Confident that she was acting in the interests of divine providence, she begged her father to reconsider. Speaking with 'unusual energy and conviction', she told him that she would refuse to sign any paper renouncing her God-given right to the throne. José soothed her and, now the secret was out, he realised that life in the palace would be impossible if he allowed Pombal to continue with his plan.

On 15 January, when he returned to Lisbon to attend the Devotion of Santa Engrácia, José informed Pombal that there was a traitor in his service. He did not name the man or the nature of the treason, but because he had changed his mind about the succession, Pombal realised that it could only have been José de Seabra. In Walpole's words, Pombal 'expects a great deal from those whom he has favoured and is of an unforgiving temper whenever he finds his views are opposed'. He wrote a decree dismissing Seabra from his offices of state, exiling him to the country, and giving him twenty-four hours to leave the city. The king signed the decree on 16 January and, when Seabra arrived in Belém for the return journey to Salvaterra, he was ordered to go immediately to Pombal's house.

He left Lisbon early next morning. In April, he was arrested and imprisoned in a fort near Oporto. 'The poor gentleman's fate,' wrote Walpole, 'is growing every day worse and worse.' In October, he sailed for Rio de Janeiro where he was held prisoner on an island until he was put on board another ship bound for Angola. When he arrived in Luanda, he was incarcerated in the fort at Pedras Negras, 'where he would have fallen a victim to the climate had not an old negro woman taken care of him'.[1]

...

This dramatic episode had severe repercussions for the royal family, as well as for José de Seabra. He was a favourite with Mariana and her daughter, and it is easy to imagine their shock when they learnt of his fate. It is also easy to imagine the family arguments that ensued. A few days later, Mariana fell ill, supposedly with rheumatism, and remained 'indisposed' for several months. At the same time, José stopped hunting – indeed, he stopped taking any exercise at all. He was 'a fat, bulky man' and, four weeks after Maria gave birth to a daughter on 9 June, he suffered his first stroke, with 'a giddiness in his head' and weakness on one side of his body. As Walpole explained:

> 'This alteration in his state of health may have been brought upon him by a quick transition from a very active life to a more sedentary one which his Majesty has given himself up to ever since the beginning of the Queen's illness at Salvaterra. Previous to this, their Majesties used to be out shooting six or eight hours every day, in all weathers and at all seasons …
>
> 'His Majesty is of a sanguine complexion and has been very careless as to what he eats at his meals, which have been in general of the most savoury and unwholesome kind. [He] has for a number of years had swelled legs which are certain marks of a bad habit of body. These circumstances, added to that of his Majesty being arrived at an age which has been fatal to his family, makes his present state of health the more critical.'

José never recovered his spirits. He was 'blooded frequently' and ordered to take the baths at Alcaçarias near Lisbon, but he remained 'in a weak and dejected state and … very much out of humour'. He refused to take exercise and an ulcer broke out on one of his legs. Mariana, too, remained weak. They did not go into the country as usual in November, although they did (against doctors' advice) travel to Salvaterra in January 1775 where José suffered a number of strokes during the few months.

Four weeks after their return to Lisbon, on the king's sixty-first birthday, an enormous bronze statue was inaugurated in the Praça do Comércio, the great square by the riverside where the Ribeira palace used to stand. Lined with commercial and military buildings, the renamed square was the centrepiece of Pombal's reconstruction of the city, although one side remained incomplete and this was hung with a replica painted on canvas.

The great statue depicted José on horseback, wearing a breast-plate and plumed helmet, his horse trampling on writhing serpents, the pedestal decorated with allegorical figures and a bas-relief of the Marquis de Pombal. Made from thirty tons of bronze, the statue was, according to Walpole, 'larger than any modern work of the kind, is cast entire and has a great deal of merit'.

On the morning of 6 June, the artillery fired 21-gun salutes to signal the start of a three-day celebration. The great square had been swept and sanded, and the stands began to fill with members of the court, secretaries of state, foreign ministers, magistrates, and city dignitaries. The royal family arrived last and took their seats in a pavilion. At three o'clock, to the sound of rockets and cannon-fire, Pombal stepped forward to unveil the statue from its shroud of crimson silk. It was a ceremony of great pomp but José, partially paralysed by the strokes, was unable to 'resist fatigue and the heat of the sun as he used to do'. He showed no signs of pleasure when the great statue was unveiled.

A few days later, Pombal presented the king with a report on the inauguration of the statue, in which he listed his achievements as first minister of the country. Highly exaggerated, a masterpiece of self-congratulation, it began with his manufacturing enterprises, including the glassworks at Marinha Grande:

'Formerly, every manufactured article was imported, whereas now the native manufacturers furnish everything necessary for the dress and ornament of both sexes, and for the rich and numerous carriages used on this most brilliant occasion; even the looking-glasses, candlesticks and drinking glasses are made by his Majesty's subjects.'

After listing several other achievements, he ended with these words:

'The ninth example of our prosperity is the wealth of the people. Observant foreigners did not fail to remark the many millions that ... were spent on public and private buildings after the earthquake. They saw a most magnificent square surpassing all others in Europe in size and beauty. They saw a costly and unexampled equestrian statue erected in that square. They saw the city corporation giving the most splendid balls in a vast room, and a magnificent supper at which no less than 400 persons were seated, served with the greatest luxury, without using one single article from abroad ... They saw the streets rendered impassable by the multitude of sumptuous carriages. Every foreigner who observed such a reunion of riches could not fail to be convinced that the capital and the Kingdom were in the highest state of prosperity and opulence.'[2]

The doctors advised José to take the baths at Estoril, 12 miles west of Lisbon, so Pombal offered the use of his mansion house in Oeiras (midway between Lisbon and Estoril). The family made the journey in early July and stayed in Oeiras for three months. The house was grandiose and comfortable, surrounded by extensive grounds with citrus groves and vineyards, water cascades, and a lake where Maria tried her hand at fishing.

José received some benefit from the baths but continued to suffer from 'weakness in limbs and lowness of spirits'. The ulcer in his leg flared up again in early September and he confined himself to his bedchamber. On the 20th, Walpole reported that 'the disorder in the King's leg is of serious nature. He has been in great pain, relieved by a slight operation.' Unable to move without help, he was 'very much dejected'.

The family returned from Oeiras a few days before a brutal public execution. Shortly before the inauguration of José's statue, an elementary bomb was found in the house of João Baptiste Pele (an Italian living in Lisbon), together with a fifteen-hour fuse and two wax models of the key to Pombal's coach-house. It was assumed that Pele planned to place the bomb under the seat of Pombal's carriage the night before the ceremony. Convicted of high treason, his death on 11 October was cruel – even by the standards of the Inquisition. Having already been tortured on the rack, his hands were sliced off, his abdomen was opened up and drawn, after which he was dismembered, pulled apart by four horses.

Next day, the royal family attended a Te Deum in celebration of Pombal's escape from death and José began to feel better. He ordered a new opera to be performed in the Real Barraca and went out shooting ('with some success'). His health deteriorated again in the spring of 1776 and, when Maria's two-year-old daughter died in June, he directed that there should be no court mourning 'for a princess of such tender years'.

By the end of July, he was back in bed with ulcers on his leg and a fever. In October, he returned to the baths at Alcáçarias, immersing himself in the waters for several hours a day. On 6 November, he suffered another, more devastating stroke which affected the entire left side of his body. He lost the power of speech. He tried to speak but could only make inarticulate sounds. Pombal attended the palace every day, his tall frame bending over the sickbed, but the ranks of courtiers closed around the king as soon as he left the room and foreign diplomats wrote home to their governments that a change in politics was imminent.

On 22 November, after 'copious bleedings and blisters', José asked to be given the last rites. While prayers were read in the churches, he became fearful for his immortal soul. On the 29th, he banned Pombal from entering his rooms and appointed his 'very much beloved and esteemed wife' to act as regent on his behalf.

While her mother took charge of affairs of state, Maria prepared herself for absolute power. Up to this moment, she had been allowed no control over her life, no influence over the pattern of her days. Soon she would have total control, not only of her own life but the lives of all her subjects, an awesome responsibility for a woman of her temperament and limited education. She was 43 years old and the burden was harder to bear because she was once more about to give birth. Her last child was born on 22 December, after which she was 'very much indisposed'. She was declared out of danger by the end of the year but the infant was too weak to survive. The king continued to deteriorate and Walpole, writing discreetly about the shifting sands of power, 'was not idle in observing the motions of the different persons about the Court'.

On 23 January, nine days after Maria's new-born baby died, Pombal exerted his authority for the last time. There had been a disturbance in the fishing village of Trafaria, on the southern shore of the Tagus, and some fishermen had roughed up an official. On the excuse that the village was a hotbed of deserters and vagrants, Pombal gave orders that it should be set on fire. That night, the glow of burning houses stained the sky, the flames visible from the Real Barraca where José's family were gathered at his bedside.

The king was now 'taken out of bed for a few days' but the ulcers on his leg began to weep and fester, and like his father before him, he became bloated with oedema. During his last days of life, he made two decisions. The first, written on a piece of paper which he gave to his wife on 20 February, expressed his 'great desire' that his elder grandson, Prince José, should be married without delay to his youngest daughter Benedita.

According to Walpole, this marriage between aunt and nephew 'had long been determined upon … and it cannot be doubted that the Marquis de Pombal was privy to it'. Papal dispensation had been obtained as early as October 1775, when the royal family was staying in Pombal's house in Oeiras, but the ceremony was delayed, partly because the bridegroom had not reached puberty, partly because the king wanted the marriage to be a state occasion. Now, at the very end of his life, he decided to go ahead with a marriage which he hoped would ensure the succession of the Bragança monarchy.

The ceremony took place in the palace chapel during the afternoon of 21 February. Only the immediate family was present and, when it was over, they made their way to the king's bedroom, knelt to kiss his hand, 'and retired very much affected'. The newly married prince was 15 years old, his body still changing from boy to man. His bride was 30, full-bosomed and stout. It is unlikely that there was much sexual attraction between them but that night, according to custom, Maria helped to undress her sister and prepare her for the marriage bed.

José's second decision was communicated to Maria in a personal letter. It began with the usual platitudes, that she should rule the country well, look after her mother and sisters, pay his debts, and be kind to his servants. Finally, in the last words of a dying man, he asked her:

> 'to pardon the legal punishment of those state criminals whom she shall judge worthy of forgiveness. As to the crimes and offences which they have committed against my Person or against the State, I have already pardoned them all, that God may pardon me my sins.'[3]

Maria and her mother wasted no time. On 23 February, they revoked the imprisonments which had most distressed them. The Bishop of Coimbra was released from the fort at the mouth of the Tagus and received that afternoon in the Real Barraca; Maria's half-uncles were ordered to return from Busaco, 'restored to the establishments they previously enjoyed'; and a letter was sent to Angola to recall José de Seabra to Lisbon.

The king died shortly after midnight on 24 February 1777, his life ending 'with such ease that it required the application of a mirror to determine his death with certainty'. Maria had retired from her father's room to rest but, when told the news, 'she prepared to receive the ministers of state and admitted them into her presence to kiss her hand as Sovereign'.

On the 25th, Pombal returned to the palace to be greeted by one of his former allies with the words: 'Your Excellency has nothing more to do here.' Barred from royal circles, he returned home and hid behind the shuttered windows of his house while the people of Lisbon took to the streets, rejoicing. The tyrant had fallen. The rule of the Marquis de Pombal was over.

Part Two

Maria I

12

Absolute Power

... A dawn of brightest ray
Has boldly promised the returning day ...
Beneath the smiles of a benignant Queen
Boast the fair opening of a reign serene,
Of omen high ...

William Julius Mickle
Almada Hill: An Epistle from Lisbon, 1779

On 26 February ('with the usual pomp and ceremony'), the king's body was taken to the church of São Vicente de Fora for interment in the royal mausoleum. The following day, when Maria gave orders that the prisons be opened, more than 800 people were released from incarceration, some after an imprisonment of twenty years. Crowds of sympathisers gathered at the gates as the nobles, priests, and magistrates, men and women, emerged from the dungeons. Pale and emaciated, their clothes in tatters, their eyes screwed up against the light, it was, wrote the Austrian envoy, 'an image of the rising from the dead'.

Among those released were forty-five Jesuits, including Timoteo de Oliveira, 'her Majesty's former confessor whom she has always greatly missed'. Five of the nobles (Marquis de Alorna, Count de São Lourenço, and three brothers of the old Marquis de Távora) refused to accept their liberty until their innocence was confirmed by a tribunal, so Maria agreed to a temporary – and more comfortable – exile 60 miles from court.

Her most urgent problem was Pombal. Seventy-eight years old, he stooped slightly but his great height was still impressive and age had not impaired his vigour or his intellectual power. A few months earlier, the French envoy had written that he was 'sound in body and mind, thinking himself immortal, talking of vast projects that not even his sons could hope to see realised'.[1] Before José's death, he had written a letter of resignation to Mariana – 'on account of advanced age' – a letter which she chose to ignore. He wrote again on 1 March, this time to the new queen, asking permission to retire to the small town of Pombal 80 miles north of Lisbon, the town from which he had taken his title.

Maria asked her mother for advice. 'I suppose he must be dismissed,' she is reported as saying, 'since everyone thinks he should be.' Mariana knew that Pombal, with his powerful personality, might still persuade Maria that no one else was capable of running the country, that there should at least be a hand-over to a new administration. 'In that case,' she told her daughter, 'avoid seeing him, even once, upon business.'

On 4 March, Maria signed a decree allowing him to retire to the town of Pombal and ordering him to remain there. This was taken to his house in Rua do Século and read aloud to him at two o'clock that afternoon, at which point (according to Robert Walpole) he 'lost all his fortitude'. He set out immediately for his house in Oeiras; that evening, the people of Lisbon burned him in effigy and marched singing through the streets. The following day, he wrote to his eldest son who had been allowed to remain at court. He was, he wrote:

> 'heavy-hearted and lonely, for I have not yet the consolation of your mother's company and the escort which is to accompany us on our journey is not yet arrived. You can imagine what my night has been like, when to the strain of the last weeks has been added a separation from my children … God, who has witnessed my afflictions … will lend me strength to support them. I give you my blessing. That is all I can give you now.'[2]

On 6 March, he was joined by his wife and, the following morning, they started their journey north. They made slow progress. The roads were a quagmire from the winter rains and, to avoid encounters with angry villagers, they had to make several detours which prolonged the journey. Pombal was too down-hearted to leave the carriage but sometimes, to lighten the load, his wife had to walk. The party stumbled along, manoeuvring the carriage over the rough tracks; at night they kept moving by the light of torches.

They arrived at their destination after a journey of eight days. Pombal owned estates in the area but had neglected to maintain his property in the town, so the only accommodation available was a small rented building, an old single-storey house in the market square. The walls were damp and there was little furniture, but he and his wife settled in as best they could and unpacked the few possessions they had been able to bring with them.

…

Maria came to the throne on a wave of public enthusiasm. The people believed her accession to be a gift from God, while the church and aristocracy had high hopes of regaining their influence. 'The clergy seem to be in great expectation of a return to their power,' wrote Walpole on 26 February, 'and the nobility flatter themselves that they shall be restored to their former consideration and consequence.' It was difficult for a woman with so little experience to handle these expectations, to set up a new government, to choose men to serve as her secretaries of state, so Maria relied heavily on her mother's fortitude and strength of character.

It was important to have some continuity in state affairs so, on 4 March, they appointed two ministers who had served under Pombal: Aires de Sá e Melo and Martinho de Melo e Castro retained their portfolios of foreign affairs and marine and the colonies. Ten days later, they appointed Marquis de Angeja as president of the treasury (and first minister) and Viscount de Ponte de Lima as secretary of state for home affairs. These men were new to government and both had reason to dislike the previous regime. Angeja's brother (Count de São Lourenço) and Ponte de Lima's father (Viscount de Vila Nova da Cerveira) had both been imprisoned by Pombal – and Vila Nova had died in the dungeons.

Nine days later, Maria fell ill with measles. Her symptoms began on 23 March and it was not until 27 April that she felt well enough to meet with her ministers. At the meeting, it was agreed that her acclamation would take place on 13 May and that her husband would have the status of king-consort (as Pedro III). He would be subordinate to his wife; he would walk on her left side, he would sign his name below hers, and he was not entitled to the crown.

The morning of 13 May dawned bright and sunny. A gallery, 300 feet long by 30 feet wide, had been erected in the Praça do Comércio, 'magnificently furnished with tapestry and damask and adorned with gold fringes and gold lace'. Crowds had gathered during the night, singing and dancing through the early hours of the morning, and the square was packed with people, the river crowded with boats filled with spectators. People were crammed onto every balcony and rooftop, with a few brave souls perched at perilous height on José's equestrian statue.

At four o'clock, the procession formed and began to move into the gallery. First came the heralds and knights-at-arms, followed by the nobility, the religious establishment, and the secretaries of state. Then came Maria's two sons, Crown Prince José (now known as the Prince of Brazil) and Prince João, followed by her husband and his entourage. Pedro wore a cloak of flame-coloured stripes, a hat adorned with white feathers, and he carried a sword of solid gold.

Finally, Maria appeared, followed by the ladies of her household. She looked magnificent. She wore a robe of silk taffeta woven with silver thread and covered with diamonds, the bodice encrusted with precious stones set in a floral design. Her train was made from cloth of gold and she wore the mantle of state, a crimson cloak embroidered with gold and silver thread.

The royal musicians played as the procession entered the gallery and the family took their seats under a silk canopy. After a number of declarations had been read aloud in ringing tones, Maria knelt on a crimson cushion and, in a quiet voice, promised to govern her country well, administer justice and guard the customs, privileges and liberties of her people. Her husband and sons paid her homage, her courtiers swore allegiance, and the royal standard-bearer acclaimed her as queen. Trumpets and bugles sounded, the crowds shouted 'Viva Rainha', bells pealed, guns thundered salutes, and rockets banged into the sky.

According to the Duke du Châtelet, who was among the throng in the Praça do Comércio, 'the Queen alone seemed to take no share in the general joy; she was painfully affected'.[3] Tired from recent events, still weak from the measles, she had been warned of a plot to inflame the crowd into demanding the head of Pombal. Troops on horseback were ready to move at the first sign of unrest, but she was still unnerved by the occasional shout of 'Death to Pombal' which rang out from the mass of people in the square.

When the ceremony was over, as she was leaving the gallery with the sceptre in her hand, the crowd broke through the barriers. People knelt at her feet to kiss the hem of her dress and train. There was such a throng around her that she was prevented from reaching the carriage waiting to take her home to the Real Barraca. Touched by this demonstration of affection, she told her guards not to intervene and she stood there for several minutes, surrounded by her subjects, 'affected even to tears'.

...

Four days after her acclamation, Maria confirmed the innocence of the five nobles who had refused to accept their liberty. On 6 June, she took part in a new festival dedicated to the Heart of Jesus. The following day, she and her family moved to Queluz. It was the hottest summer for almost thirty years and she took refuge in the formal gardens, shaded by trees imported from northern Europe, cooled by fountains and running water.

The family stayed in Queluz for four months, enjoying excursions into the countryside and spending time in the Moorish palace at Sintra. The only shadow on this summer idyll was Pedro's health. On the morning of 16 August, he suffered a minor stroke, 'taken ill … while at Mass with a giddiness in his head and lay speechless some time'. He remained unwell for several weeks but, ten days after the family returned to Lisbon in October, he was fit enough to accompany Maria and her mother on the three-day journey to Vila Viçosa.

One of the most pressing matters of state when Maria came to the throne was the situation in South America, where Portugal and Spain had been embroiled in territorial disputes for several years. Pombal had taken a particularly hard line on the matter and, by July 1776, there was a risk of hostilities. Maria came to the throne declaring her 'intention of resigning the government ... rather than enter into a war', but her mother advised her to speak with more caution. According to Walpole:

> 'The Queen Mother, who has a spirit of more fortitude than the reigning Queen, is not less solicitous of seconding her daughter's pacific views, but says that this must be done with decency to the Crown of Portugal.'

It was Mariana who made the first move, exchanging letters of peace with her brother, Charles III of Spain. Formal negotiations began in May 1777. By August, she and her brother were 'writing to each other every fortnight' and a treaty was signed in October, 'setting the limits of territory in South America'. This put an end to the territorial squabbles and formed the basis of a second treaty (of 'friendship and protection') which was signed five months later.

Mariana undertook most of these negotiations personally and it was soon agreed that she should visit her brother in Spain. Her family travelled with her to the border. They left Lisbon on 21 October; seven days later, Maria accompanied her mother to the river Caya, which formed the frontier between the border towns of Elvas and Badajoz. Here mother and daughter took leave of each other 'with much tenderness on both sides'.

In Spain, Mariana continued to negotiate the treaty of 'friendship and protection' which was signed in March 1778. This was good timing, for Britain's war with its American colonies soon became a wider conflict. France entered the war in early 1778, followed by Spain a year later, so the treaty allowed Maria – despite pressure from Britain to honour her obligations under the Anglo-Portuguese alliance – to maintain a policy of 'the most strict neutrality'.

Mariana stayed in Spain for a year. To strengthen the links between the two countries, she discussed the betrothals of two of her grandchildren to members of her brother's family. In June 1778, she was again 'seized with the rheumatism' and retired to bed in the palace at Aranjuez. In July, she took the waters for several days and, by mid-August, was well enough to be 'pushed about the gardens in an old-fashioned cariole or three-wheeled chair'.[4]

When she returned to Portugal in November, Maria and Pedro travelled to Vila Viçosa to meet her. As her carriage descended into the valley from Badajoz, crowds of people lined the roads on both sides of the frontier to watch the royal reunion on the banks of the river Caya. Next day, a hunt was scheduled at Vila Viçosa. Mariana could no longer ride on horseback but nothing could deter her from the chase. Following the hunt in a sedan chair, she shot three stags and thirteen deer.

...

While her mother negotiated treaties with Spain and laid the foundations for two dynastic marriages, Maria set about restoring the power of the church. She dismissed Cenáculo Vilas Boas, her son's liberal-minded preceptor. She wrote a public letter to Miguel da Anunciação, reinstating him as Bishop of Coimbra and assuring him of 'the great confidence and esteem which I have for you'. She had no power to revive the Society of Jesus but she did her best to make amends for Pombal's persecution of the order. She gave pensions to Jesuits released from prison, sent money to the pope to cover the cost of supporting priests in exile, and restored the names of Jesuit saints to the calendar of religious festivals.

She re-established the jurisdiction of the papal nuncio's court and admonished members of the clergy who had embraced Pombal's secular policies. She rewarded people of other faiths who converted to Catholicism and stood godmother at their baptisms. And she fulfilled the vow she made on her wedding night, to build a church and convent dedicated to the Heart of Jesus if she was blessed with the birth of a son. She selected a site close to the Protestant cemetery in Estrela and appointed an architect to design an immense building in late baroque and neo-classical styles.

Meanwhile, her ministers had inherited a chaotic situation. The state papers of the previous reign were stored in great disorder in Pombal's house in Lisbon, so two officials were appointed to organise a filing system. The treasury was so depleted that Marquis de Angeja had to instigate an economy campaign. He suspended the reconstruction of the city, cut expenditure on the royal opera, reorganised the system of palace servants, and reduced the number of horses and mules in the royal stables.

The ministers were dutiful and pious men, but only two of them had any experience of world affairs. Restricted by the formality of the court, they were unable to make decisions on the queen's behalf. As Walpole explained, 'the Queen is the law and above the law, and no minister would advise her Majesty to tie her hand and circumscribe her authority'.

This was an impossible position for anyone of such limited education and experience, even more so for a woman who had been excluded from all contact with government and who had such reverence for the church. In Walpole's words: 'The Queen is timid … very devout … of unlimited obedience to the See of Rome … and easily influenced by the clergy with whom she has very much conversed.' And Pedro was no help in state affairs. He was, according to Walpole:

> 'of a confined understanding. He hears three or four Masses in the morning in the utmost ecstasy and attends evening prayers as devoutly … He has

no knowledge of mankind or of business [so] is easily governed, right or wrong, by those immediately about him, especially if they belong to the Church.'

Maria did her best to rise to the occasion. She tried to understand matters of government and discuss them with her ministers. She relied on her mother's advice in political matters and also turned to Inácio de São Caetano, a jovial man of humble birth who had served as her confessor since 1759 and did not hesitate to involve himself in affairs of state.

At the same time, she took 'every means to announce a reign of clemency'. She gave pensions and court appointments to men released from prison or returning from exile. She restored the freedom of the press which had been abolished by Pombal. She inaugurated a Royal Academy of Sciences and encouraged expeditions to record the flora and fauna of the colonies. And remembering the brutality of the Távora and Pele executions, she announced that she would not sanction the death penalty, 'even for the greatest criminals'.

13

A Time of Uncertainty

In the different excursions which I took in Portugal, I made a point of visiting such places
as contained any manufactures. In many of these places ... I observed that they were
established ... by foreigners, who were every moment in fear of losing their situation.
Pierre Cormatin, Duke du Châtelet, 1777

In Marinha Grande, William had followed the news at court with apprehension. Aware that Pombal would fall from power when José died, he was still surprised by the speed at which his friend was banished from court. It was a dangerous time for one of Pombal's most successful protégés and William had the courage to behave with honour as well as self-interest, one of the few who were brave enough to do so. He set out to ingratiate himself with the new regime; at the same time, he remained loyal to Pombal and began to correspond with him as soon as he had settled in his place of exile, 20 miles north-east of the glassworks.

He sent newspapers from England (translating the important items into Portuguese). He delivered baskets of asparagus, herbs and seeds, for Pombal shared his interest in horticulture and was planting a vegetable garden. He visited him whenever he could spare the time. Philadelphia accompanied him on these visits and soon forged a friendship with the Austrian-born marquesa who was finding it difficult to adjust to life in exile. The Duke du Châtelet described her plight when he visited Pombal in July 1777:

> 'She still retains a portion of her charms and dresses with great art and taste. She certainly is not deficient in understanding, but she has neither her husband's fortitude, nor strength of mind to endure her situation. During the prosperity of the Marquis, his wife had grandees and the people at her feet and her house was a sort of court. Men, when they called to see her, knelt to kiss her hand, according to the practice of the country. Her vanity, flattered with so many marks of respect, cannot familiarise itself to the exclusion to which her husband's disgrace has doomed her, forsaken by all and buried in the solitude of an obscure village ... These sentiments she strove to conceal from me, but they were too powerful to be repressed. After conversing about ten minutes, her eyes overflowed with tears.'

As Pombal watched his wife's face crumple with misery, he turned to his visitor. 'This is but natural in her sex,' he told him. 'To comfort her is one of my occupations.'[1]

In September, William fell ill with malaria and Pombal wrote several times to enquire about his health. 'Yesterday's fit of ague was small,' William replied on the 12th, 'and I have started to take quinine; the effects will only be known after a few days. I thank your Excellency for your concern.' Five days later, he wrote again, thanking Pombal:

> 'for your affectionate letter yesterday ... having suffered only one fit of ague since I started taking quinine, I believe that it has effected a complete eradication of my ills. As a precaution, I am drinking the extract of laxative plants, repeating the quinine at every change of moon and at each quarter. The illness, the blood-letting or the medicines have weakened my eyesight, but I am not too concerned about this because every day I am feeling better. I hope in a few days to be well enough to have the pleasure of kissing your Excellency's hand to thank you for the distinguished and much appreciated honour with which you treat me.'

The visit to Pombal was delayed because William's use of laxatives confined him to the house. 'I have had no repetition of my ailment,' he wrote on 25 September (when informing him of the 'great progress' of the British war in North America), 'but shall continue with the precautionary medicines which means that I find it embarrassing to go out.' He hoped to call on his friend 'as soon as possible'; meanwhile Philadelphia sent her 'greatest respect' to the marquesa.[2]

In February 1778, Pombal received a pamphlet of letters, written in English and published anonymously in London, which eulogised the minister and his achievements. Despite his four years as Portuguese minister in London, he was 'never able to acquire a language so difficult for a Portuguese'. Seeing his name quoted many times in the pamphlet, he spent a frustrating few days before a letter arrived from William who had ordered a copy for himself and knew that it was complimentary to his friend:

> 'In this dilemma, I received a letter from my excellent friend, William Stephens ... who informed me that he was in daily expectation of receiving some letters from London, which he would forward to me as soon as they arrived. The Marquesa, judging they were the same as those we had already received, begged me to send them to William Stephens, with a request that he would have them translated by someone who might be paid for his trouble.'[3]

Pombal took his wife's advice and William replied promptly. He was pleased to have the pamphlet for the ship carrying his copy had missed the mouth of the Tagus and sailed on to Portimão, a fishing port in the Algarve. His office was short-staffed and no clerk was available to do the translation, but 'because the letters are in praise of your Excellency, my sister has offered to translate them and will do so with much pleasure, especially as the Marquesa also wishes to read them'.[4] And so, as Pombal noted, 'Philadelphia Stephens, who had contracted a friendship with the Marquesa, they being neighbours, took the translations upon herself, and forwarded them to us as fast as they were ready'.

…

In his letters to Pombal, William made no mention of his precarious situation at the glassworks. Many of the minister's collaborators were being dismissed from their posts, subsidies to the new industries were being reduced, and he had to act quickly to protect his privileges. His annual report for 1776 was incomplete when Pombal fell from power, so he took the opportunity of sending it to Maria personally, with a covering letter stating his case for continued royal protection.

In May 1778, after he had been repaying his loan in kind for almost three years, he received a letter from the Junta do Comércio informing him that it could no longer guarantee the quantities of lime and window glass required because, 'by order of her Majesty, the greater part of the reconstruction works are suspended. It is therefore necessary that you make repayments of the loan in money, to be paid over the contracted period.'

William appealed against this decision, reasoning that some rebuilding was likely to continue, but in July he heard again from the Junta: 'The payment of the debt in the form of lime and glass is no longer viable because of the continuing suspension of public works in the city.' The buildings that remained under construction were of 'little consideration', and because treasury funds were depleted, prompt repayment was required of all outstanding debts.

There were difficulties in Alcântara too, where his brother John James was engaged in a feud with the consul. The Culm Act of 1758 had exempted the limekilns from export duties for fifteen years; a second Act in 1773 had extended the exemption for a further twenty years. Everything ran smoothly until October 1777 when the consul, Sir John Hort, became pedantic over the custom-house certificates required to prove that cargoes of culm had been landed in Lisbon. As soon as the certificates had been countersigned by the consul, they were sent to England to cancel the bond (for three times the value of the cargo) that John James's representative had signed at the port of embarkation.

Perhaps emboldened by the fall of Pombal, Hort decided that the wording of the culm certificate, which merely stated that the cargo had been unloaded, was inadequate. It was possible, he reasoned, for ships to have off-loaded some of their cargo in other countries and taken different goods on board. He wrote to John James on 31 October:

> 'You are to take notice for the future that in all custom house certificates under the Culm Act, it is necessary that it be declared ... that the ship brought nothing else except culm ...and must also certify expressly that it was all unloaded for the manufactory of lime.'

John James replied on 7 November:

> 'As I am a great admirer of regularity in office, I must acquaint you that the Culm Act only requires a certificate testifying simply "that such culm has been landed in Lisbon" ... As to the culm being "all unloaded for the manufactory of lime", it is a thing of course, culm being useless for any other purpose in this country.'

Matters came to a head on 9 November when the ship *Four Brothers and Sisters* arrived at the Alcântara quay with a cargo of culm. The customs official completed the certificate which John James sent to the consul for countersigning. It was returned unsigned, so John James sent it back with the comment that 'such scruples and trifling minutiae, Sir John, are the bane of trade and I lament meeting with them in a Consul General to the greatest commercial nation'.

The unsigned certificate went back and forth three times until John James made a formal complaint to the secretary of state in London, who duly sent a reprimand to the consul:

> 'The form that had been used for near twenty years does not seem to have wanted amendment, and all innovations in these matters, unless essentially necessary, are inconvenient to trade. I trust you will immediately re-establish the old form or state to me sufficient reasons for the alteration you have required.'

This despatch arrived in Lisbon on 27 February 1778. John James received a letter from his agent by the same packet boat and immediately wrote again to the consul, 'to resume my former request for a certificate ... for the culm per the *Four Brothers and Sisters*'. Hort, smarting from the secretary of state's rebuke, replied the same day:

> 'As you have found means to write me a few lines this morning unmixed with ill manners, I think it proper to acquaint you that I wrote by last post to your brother ... to explain to him in what manner his business continues to be impeded.'

Hort's letter reached Marinha Grande on 5 March 1778 and, as William read through the pages, he became increasingly annoyed. The consul complained of John James's arrogance and bad manners. He set out his reasons for refusing to sign the certificate, explained how easily William and John James could abuse the Culm Act, and referred to John James's 'improper letters, such as are not usually apt to forward any business within my knowledge'.

William put pen to paper the following day, one of only three letters he wrote in English to survive the centuries:

> 'I am sorry to see the dispute between you and my worthy brother with respect to a culm certificate is not yet settled. I have maturely considered all the arguments that you have offered … which suppositions, having no example, don't authorise you to stop our business. Besides which, they are … so highly improbable … that they need no serious refutation. These suspicions carried a little further would suppose more than you intend to say, but as yet I will not take the argument up in that light …
>
> 'However, as you do me the honour to place some confidence in my decision, we will set aside all altercation and I will give you my thought freely and candidly. I am of opinion that … you have not the smallest foundation to refuse the certificate we have required, and I am further of opinion that you are under the highest obligations to my brother for proceeding so prudently in his complaint and through so proper a channel. The Culm Act, you know, was made in favour of this Kingdom. My brother might have made this dispute a Court affair, but he very prudently avoided giving the Court of Portugal any notice of your stopping the trade …
>
> 'To prevent any further trouble … on this insignificant affair … permit me to say there is not the least shadow of reason on your side, the more so that, happily for us in the present dispute, not one of our culm ships ever since the first Act was made in 1758 ever put into any other port even in distress.'

William was confined to the office when he wrote this letter because of the absence of his administrator. He was making up the accounts, paying wages and invoices, ordering supplies of raw materials, and organising transport. As he wrote to Pombal on 7 April, 'I am in this factory, not only as the owner but also as a substitute, always ready to work in positions which are vacant, so much so that I have been held captive in the office for the past three months.'[5]

Freed from these duties by the autumn, he was able to spend several weeks with his family in Lisbon. Much of the city remained in ruins but the grid of new streets behind the Praça do Comércio was almost complete. Further west, reached by following the river or by climbing and descending one of Lisbon's many hills, was the corner of Rua de São Paulo and Rua das Flores. Here lay the Largo do Stephens, a large four-storey house built on a steep incline which included a warehouse for finished glass as well as a home for his brothers. Lewis and Jedediah had set up their own merchant houses in the city and John James had moved from Alcântara as soon as the house was ready for occupation.

During these weeks in Lisbon, William asked Robert Walpole to present him at court where he hoped to remind Maria that her father had placed the glassworks 'under his immediate and royal protection'. He dined at Oeiras with Pombal's eldest son and came to a decision about the limekilns. The dispute about culm certificates had been resolved in April but, with the cancellation of the building works, there seemed little point in keeping the factory open. As he explained to Pombal on 17 September, 'unless new measures are taken, which I do not expect, the lime factory will be closed down'.[6] After twenty-two years, it was the end of William's first industrial enterprise.

14

The Trial of Pombal

What was the Portuguese forty years ago and what is he now? Have I not rendered
him independent of his neighbours? Have I not everywhere founded arts, trades, and
manufactures ... Have I not revived industry and diffused wealth among the artisans?

I am particularly accused of cruelty; but I was compelled to be severe. When
I announced the commands of the King, and people disdained to attend to them, it
was then necessary to have recourse to force; prisons and dungeons were the only
means that I could discover to tame this blind and ignorant people.

Marquis de Pombal to Duke du Châtelet, July 1777

While William continued his friendship with Pombal, Maria was finding it difficult to make a decision on his fate. Members of the nobility, particularly those who had languished in dungeons, were calling for stronger punishment than exile to a small country town. Maria believed in the innocence of the Távora conspirators, but she was also aware that a posthumous pardon would damage the honour of her father whose memory she held dear. These conflicting emotions caused her great anguish and, although she might have preferred to banish Pombal to the back of her mind, she was given little opportunity to forget him.

His plaque was torn off the pedestal of José's statue ('I am happy to hear it,' said Pombal, 'it was a very poor likeness') and, in early 1779, a returning exile laid a claim for damages against him. He accused Pombal of 'having ... abused a despotic and absolute power in order to raise himself to the summit of honours and riches, at the expense of the liberties of many innocent persons'.

Pombal responded with enthusiasm, drafting a closely argued defence of his actions. It was the king, he wrote, who had signed every order against the nobles and the Jesuits. He, the loyal servant, had merely been a passive instrument in his master's service. Maria was unhappy to see her father held responsible for such tyranny and Pombal was delighted when she asked to read his defence. 'I am not displeased that my contradiction should have been sent to the palace,' he wrote to his son. 'The documents will serve to weigh the consciences of those who read them, who will see that I ought not to be treated with such barbarity.'[1]

His hopes were misplaced. On 3 September, after discussing the matter with her mother, Maria declared Pombal's defence to be libellous and an insult to her father's memory. She had spent long hours in prayer before consenting to the demands of her courtiers, but now she agreed that plans should be put in hand for his prosecution on charges of abuse of power, corruption and fraud.

On 9 October, two judges arrived at Pombal's house where they set up a temporary courtroom. Their interrogations began on 11 October and lasted for more than three months. The old man's strength was fading. Sometimes he fainted, sometimes he was carried into the courtroom on a stretcher, sometimes he was too ill to be questioned. But throughout the trial, he continued to assert that every cruel deed, every act of terror, had been instigated by the king who had signed all the relevant papers.

...

In November, William travelled to Lisbon to attend the marriage of his brother Lewis to the daughter of an American merchant. The ceremony took place on the 29th in the British envoy's house, followed by a ball in the Largo do Stephens. One of the guests was the Scottish poet, William Julius Mickle, who had recently arrived in the city and been introduced to the Stephens family by Robert Walpole. During the evening, William told Mickle about his glass factory and his friendship with the Marquis de Pombal. Mickle was curious about all things Portuguese and it was soon agreed that he would accompany William when he returned to Marinha Grande after Christmas.

The two men left Lisbon on 4 January 1780, the poet anxious about the dangers of the journey. 'Here are frequently wolves,' he wrote in his diary after passing through an area north of Vila Franca:

> 'This being the chief road to the northern provinces, and no houses, naturally is a fit place for robbery and murder. The several crosses denote the spots where murders have been committed and are erected for the prayers of good Christians for the souls of the murdered.'[2]

Having made the journey many times, William reassured him and they arrived safely in Marinha Grande. Mickle was hoping to meet Pombal so, a few days later, they set out for the minister's place of exile. The interrogations were nearly at an end, but Pombal had been so weakened by the trial that he was unable to see anyone, not even his friend from the glass factory. As Mickle explained in his diary:

> 'We waited first on two judges who were there on enquiries by order of the Court with respect to the Marquis's administration in the last reign

... which seems to be carried on with a degree of rigour against the great Minister which indicates a desire of retaliation. This extraordinary man is now in his 81 year, and retains all the spirit and memory of his youth, both of which were remarkably lively and strong ...

'After near an hour's conversation with the judges who behaved with the greatest politeness, promising to return the visit to Mr Stephens at Marinha, we went ... with the Corregidor [magistrate] to the house of the Marquis, who had some weeks been much indisposed and thought in such danger that his recovery had lately been despaired of ... His lady ... received our visit with the greatest affability and politeness, in which no person can be more accomplished than the Marquesa. After three quarters of an hour's visit, we retired with the Corregidor with whom we supped and returned to Marinha early next morning.'[3]

Towards the end of January, the judges travelled to Salvaterra to report their findings to Maria. They had learnt nothing of significance. Pombal's enemies still clamoured for his punishment but he had been able to prove that every one of his decrees had been signed by her father. At first, she hoped he would die – but although his physical sufferings were acute, the life force in the old man showed no signs of weakening. In March, she sent a doctor to report on his condition and was dismayed at the findings. Pombal, wrote the doctor (no doubt with some exaggeration), displayed 'the vivacity of spirit, the lucidity and firmness of intellect, the fresh and exact memory of a man not yet 30 years old'.[4]

In May, Marquis de Alorna called for the verdicts of January 1759 to be revoked. He and surviving members of the Távora family had been declared innocent, it was known that Duke de Aveiro had retracted his confession (obtained on the rack), and there were other irregularities at the time of the trial. It took courage for Maria to sign an edict which declared the verdicts to be 'null and unjust', and to appoint a tribunal of magistrates to review the evidence.

The edict was dated 9 October 1780 and, as soon as Maria signed her name, she threw her pen on the floor and had a fit of hysterics. Screaming that she was damned, condemned to hell for all eternity, she had to be lifted bodily out of her chair and carried from the room.

This was Maria's first major breakdown, a torrent of conflicting emotions exacerbated by the ill-health of both her husband and her mother. Pedro had suffered a second stroke in July 1779, taken ill during a performance in the theatre at Queluz. It affected one of his legs and he lost the power of speech. A few days later, after 'frequent bleedings and other remedies, his speech and mouth are somewhat restored to their former state', but there was no improvement to the leg.

The doctors recommended that he take the baths at Alcaçarias, treatment which he 'omitted taking upon various pretences, being himself much averse to it, and the distance from Queluz too great to undertake that remedy with safety'. It was therefore decided to convert the Senate House in the Praça do Comércio into royal apartments. Builders worked with 'the greatest dispatch by day and night' to prepare the building and the family moved into their new accommodation at the end of August.

Meanwhile, Maria's mother was suffering from her old complaint ('much afflicted with the rheumatism'), as well as from pains in her chest. In September 1780, she travelled to Caldas da Rainha to take the waters and, as the year drew to a close, she was 'attacked with a violent oppression at her breast which has given the greatest alarm'. Mariana died on 15 January 1781. The following day, Maria wrote to Charles III in Spain to inform him of his sister's death. For herself, she told him, the loss of Mariana was 'such a painful blow for she was a precious companion in every way'.[5]

Maria had relied on her mother's advice and support for almost four years but on 23 May, when the tribunal of magistrates reported its findings, she had to deal with the situation alone. In a lengthy report which deplored the use of torture and discredited some of the evidence, the tribunal confirmed the innocence of the Távora family (but upheld the verdict on Duke de Aveiro). This established the guilt of Pombal – but it also served as a reproach to her father who had signed the death warrants.

Three weeks later, Maria's new convent in Estrela was ready for occupation. She took a personal interest in the opening ceremonies and on 16 June, 'with the greatest pomp', the abbess and sixteen nuns arrived at the convent in a train of royal carriages. Mass was celebrated in the presence of the royal family, after which the nuns ate their first meal in the refectory, a meal prepared in the palace kitchens and served – to the nuns' amazement – by the queen's own hands.

In August, she finally made a decision on the fate of Pombal. Her decree, signed on the 16th, was remarkably charitable:

> 'The Marquis de Pombal was a criminal worthy of exemplary punishment. Nevertheless, out of regard for the advanced age of the offender, and of his heavy infirmities, consulting my clemency rather than my justice, I have been softened by the prayers of the said Marquis ... and have remitted all bodily punishments, enjoining him simply to absent himself from the Court at a distance of at least 20 leagues ... My royal intention being only to pardon him the personal chastisement which justice and the laws require.'[6]

This went some way towards meeting the demands of her courtiers but the decree made little difference to Pombal, whose place of exile was 28 leagues from court and whose iron constitution was crumbling at last. His skin was ulcerated, his blood was poisoned, and he suffered from dysentery and fever.

The doctors prescribed asses' milk and viper-broth (local people brought snakes to his door in baskets) and he was dosed with quinine. Maria had allowed his two sons to retain their positions and, as his health deteriorated, she gave them permission to leave the court. 'Be good sons,' she told them. 'Go and look after your father.'

Pombal died on 8 May 1782, a little more than five years after his fall from power. As his body lay in an open coffin, crowds of people filed through the house in the market square, crossing themselves at the sight of the recumbent figure with its long, emaciated face. The clergy came to sing masses for his soul and William arrived from Marinha Grande, to pay his last respects to the man who had befriended and enriched him. Philadelphia came too, to comfort the marquesa.

The sons buried their father on 12 May with the pomp associated with royalty. Bells tolled as the body was taken to church in a hearse drawn by six horses and escorted by eight boys carrying lighted tapers. Two bishops attended the service and a monk eulogised the minister's achievements, acts of courage for which they were duly reprimanded when the news reached Lisbon.

…

By the time of Pombal's death, William's future was secure. As an Englishman, a Protestant, and a protégé of Pombal, he had found it difficult to make a favourable impression on the new regime. But he persevered, addressing his reports and petitions to Maria personally and attending court during his visits to Lisbon. He set out to charm the queen; he made compliments in his understated English manner; he praised the wisdom of her father; and he placed his services and his factory at her disposal.

His careful handling of the situation finally bore fruit in December 1780, when Maria signed a decree endorsing all the conditions agreed by her father eleven years earlier. Congratulating William on the 'zeal he has manifested for the great utility of my Kingdom', she confirmed that the glassworks would continue to operate under royal protection. She extended the exemption from sales taxes until 1794 and widened the definition to include export tax. The high duties on imported glass would remain in force and she conferred a new privilege (one which even Pombal failed to grant): the factory would be exempt from import duties on utensils and raw materials for a period of five years.

Finally, she stipulated that the glassworks should never be divided on the deaths of William and his partner John James (or their successors), nor were they allowed to admit other partners into the business. This, she explained, was to 'conserve the integrity of this useful and beautiful factory for the benefit of this Kingdom for ever'.

It was a time for celebration and his family made a special occasion of William's fiftieth birthday in May 1781, travelling to Marinha Grande to join the festivities. A banquet was served in the mansion house while musicians played in the minstrel's gallery and the workers assembled in the courtyard. In the afternoon, they entered the house two-by-two. William embraced them all and, as the last pair left the room, he followed them out of the house to find them reassembled in the courtyard. The administrator removed a sheet of paper from his pocket, cleared his throat, and read a poem which the workers had written in his honour:

Duly grateful and contented,
We desire to render unto you
Such services, praise and considerations,
As are worthy of our reverent hearts.

And also to erect outstanding statues,
Pyramids, obelisks and epigraphs,
The burnt offerings and tributes
Produced by a grateful people.

It's no easy task to do as we proclaim;
Our only gift is the highest loyalty
Of the tender heart we've already given you.

This heart, Sire, wishes most sincerely
That the course of your years be long
In righteous peace and with much prosperity.

William was deeply touched. 'I shall remember this demonstration of affection,' he told his workers, 'to the very end of my days.'[7]

15

The Double Marriage

Expect neither a fair wind nor a good marriage from Spain.
Portuguese proverb

Pombal's death lifted the shadow which had darkened Maria's life for more than a quarter of a century. The next four years were the most relaxed and happy of her reign, although life at court remained stiff with formality. Nothing had changed since the days of her grandfather, João V, who had been a stickler for protocol. With the unique exception of Maria's confessor, no person was allowed to sit in her presence. Everyone else had to stand, including the secretaries of state who attended the queen on matters of government.

Courtiers would kneel from time to time to rest their feet; others would retire from the state rooms to lie down on the floors of antechambers. Gentlemen-in-waiting were permitted to drop to one knee when talking or playing cards; the ladies were sometimes allowed to sit cross-legged on the floor. Maria's favourite courtier, Marquis de Marialva, admitted to William Beckford (a wealthy Englishman who had become his friend) that attending the royal family was a tedious and tiring servitude.

In December 1782, Maria's second son, Prince João, fell ill with smallpox while the family was making plans for the journey to Salvaterra. He complained of fever and pains in his head. Red spots appeared on his skin; the spots turned into pimples and then into blisters containing a pale yellow liquid. Smallpox – a common disease – had a mortality rate of around one in five. A mild or benign attack, which involved only a few blisters, provided immunity for life; when the blisters joined up over the body, it was known as a confluent attack and was often fatal.

Initially, the doctors feared the worst, João's blisters having 'the appearance of being the confluent sort'. By mid-January, they had changed their minds. The attack was benign, they said, so Maria left for Salvaterra, leaving her son to convalesce in the Real Barraca. 'He gave me quite a fright as his load of pox blisters was very heavy,' she wrote to a cousin in Spain, 'but he has already left his bed and all he has to do now is to convalesce.' When João joined his mother in Salvaterra on 15 February, she was delighted to find him 'fully recovered and not much changed in his appearance'.[1]

Meanwhile, Pedro was afflicted by an ulcer on one of his legs. This prevented him from hunting and continued to trouble him on his return to the Real Barraca. As Maria wrote on 6 April, 'the ailment, although it causes no alarm, mortifies him so we cannot enjoy the good weather'. The ulcer had improved by July when they moved to Queluz; Pedro still had 'the remains of a sore' but was well enough to join his family on excursions into the countryside.

On 10 August 1783, they set out on a more unusual outing, a visit to Pombal's mansion house in Oeiras, now occupied by his elder son. According to Pedro, they made the journey to see the formal gardens and the water cascades, but Maria may also have intended the visit as a kindness to Pombal's family. Arriving in the mid-afternoon, they strolled through the alleys of citrus trees, visited the waterfalls, and stopped at the lake where – once again – Maria tried her hand at fishing. In the evening, refreshments were served in the house and, by the time the family climbed into their chaises for the return journey to Queluz, wax tapers had been placed in every window to illuminate the darkness.

A few days later, the family moved to the convent-palace in Mafra where, on 2 September, Pedro suffered his third stroke. 'Being on a walk in the open air,' wrote Sir John Hort (the consul standing in for Walpole who was on leave in England), he was 'seized with a slight paralytic affliction in his mouth from which he recovered sufficiently to resume his exercise.' Three days later, the ulcer in his leg flared up again, keeping him in bed for more than a week. In October, he made several public appearances, 'yet the reports, even from within the palace … are not uniformly favourable'. Pedro was 66 years old, older than his father and his brother had been when they died from the same condition. The strokes should have been taken as a warning but, on 24 November, Maria felt able to write that her husband's health was 'entirely better'.

He remained well through the winter and spring, taking part in the celebrations for Prince João's seventeenth birthday in May 1784. A few days later, the family set out for the annual festival of Nossa Senhora do Cabo. They boarded ship at Belém and sailed down the coast to the Setúbal peninsula where campaign tents had been set up for their accommodation. For three days, they enjoyed processions, bullfights, and displays of horsemanship; at night, there were concerts and fireworks.

The marriage negotiations with Spain had been finalised a few months earlier, so this was the last time Maria's three children would celebrate a spring festival together. Her daughter, Mariana, was pledged to Gabriel de Bourbon, fourth and favourite son of Charles III, and her second son, João, to the 8-year-old Carlota Joaquina, daughter of Charles's eldest son. Final arrangements were made during the next ten months and, as the date of the nuptials approached, special couriers travelled between Lisbon and Madrid with last-minute adjustments of detail. It was customary in royal marriages for the ambassador of the groom's country to make a formal demand for the bride. The Spanish and Portuguese ambassadors were due to make their demands in Lisbon and Madrid on 27 March 1785, the marriages to be celebrated by proxy the following day, but Prince João fell ill with measles so the proceedings in Lisbon were delayed.

On 2 April, news arrived that the proxy marriage between João and Carlota in Spain had taken place on schedule. The bridegroom was now feeling better and the demand for his sister took place during the afternoon of 11 April. The Spanish ambassador drove to the Praça do Comércio in a procession of seventy-five coaches accompanied by more than 100 men on horseback. He was received by Maria and Pedro in the Senate House and, on behalf of Gabriel de Bourbon, made the formal demand for their daughter. The marriage by proxy took place the following afternoon, a wedding ceremony 'conducted with all due pomp and magnificence' in the chapel in the Real Barraca. Maria gave her daughter away, Pedro stood proxy for Gabriel, and when the formalities were over, the Spanish ambassador made his way to Mariana's apartment and gave her a portrait of her husband, the first time she had seen his face.

Walpole was amazed at the cost of the proceedings. As he wrote to London on 23 April:

> 'When I consider the very great quantity of ready-made clothes and laces and everything belonging to the toilet of the finest and of the greatest magnificence ... as well as several new carriages, and also the presents that are to be made to the same extent and in as great a number as are to be given by the King of Spain, I am entirely lost in the excess of expense that will accompany the completion of these marriages. Her Majesty has already given the Spanish ambassador her picture very richly set with diamonds of a value very much beyond that of the usual present to an ambassador and a ring of a single diamond of very high value.'

This was indeed a different approach from Maria's marriage twenty-five years earlier, when her father had ensured that 'the nobility and gentry are put to no expense ... not so much as the additional expense of a suit of clothes'.

On 22 April, Maria and her family set out on the journey to Vila Viçosa for the exchange of the two princesses. They crossed the Tagus on royal barges, then travelled overland in 'five four-wheeled carriages accompanied by a numerous and splendid train of courtiers'. They spent the first night of the journey in Vendas Novas, the palace built by João V to house the court when it travelled to the frontier for the double marriage in 1729, the second night in the bishop's palace at Évora.

The Spanish princess, Carlota Joaquina, left Aranjuez on 27 April and reached Badajoz on 7 May. The following morning, her cortège descended into the valley, crossed the river Caya, and travelled on to Vila Viçosa. As her carriage arrived in the palace square, the guns of the castle and the regiments drawn up on parade gave her three 21-gun salutes. Prince João helped her down from the carriage; José and Benedita welcomed her to Portugal.

Maria and Pedro were waiting inside the palace and, as Carlota made her entrance, they were taken aback by what they saw. She was not only a child, she was extremely small for her age and unattractive in appearance, with frizzy hair and ungainly features. That evening, Maria wrote a disingenuous letter to her uncle in Spain, informing him 'of the safe arrival of our beloved Carlota, who is so pretty and lively and grown-up for her age'.[2]

Carlota's retinue stayed in Vila Viçosa for four days, after which it accompanied Maria's daughter Mariana across the border to Badajoz and on to Aranjuez to meet her husband. In the meantime, the court was in gala as Portuguese and Spanish nobility mixed for the first time in fifty-six years. Maria and her family dined together in public to the sound of trumpets and kettle drums. Musicians played in the evenings, the princesses sang arias, and fireworks exploded into the sky.

During the night of 11 May, the queen and her daughter said their farewells in private; it was unlikely they would meet again. The following morning, Maria heard the 21-gun salute; she heard Mariana's carriage rumble across the palace square. She knew the road the carriage would take. Eight years earlier, she had accompanied her mother to Elvas and down to the river Caya, but it would have been too distressing to make the same journey with her daughter, to perform their final embrace in public.

A few hours later, her sons mounted their horses, but João was as miserable as his mother and galloping after deer in the hunting park did little to take his mind off his loss. 'As soon as we reached the first thicket,' he wrote to his sister that night, 'there was a great storm which crowned this sad and bitter day, a day when I passed not a single moment without tears in my eyes.'

Mariana arrived in Aranjuez on 23 May. The following morning, she wrote to her mother, a letter which described her husband and gave details of their first night together. Maria showed the letter to João and he wrote again to his sister:

> 'It is good what you said about your husband, that he likes you very much, that you feel the same way towards him, that you are having very little sleep. I should like to take possession of my wife also. She is very small but the time will come when I can do the same things to her as your husband does to you.'[3]

The family returned to Lisbon on 8 June. The following afternoon, João and Carlota were married in person in the chapel of the Real Barraca and during the ceremony – as a portent of things to come – the bride turned her head and bit her husband on the ear.

It was no longer believed that Benedita (now aged 37) would have children, so the marriage of Maria's second son was of paramount importance to the future of the Bragança monarchy. The marriage was followed by the usual three-day celebrations but the people of Lisbon showed no joy at the occasion. They were unimpressed by Carlota and made the comment that, in the exchange of princesses, they had given away a grown fish in exchange for a sardine.

João was ambivalent about his child bride and heartbroken at the loss of his sister, from whom he had been inseparable since childhood. He wrote to Mariana every week, letters which described his grief at her absence. 'I miss you so much,' he wrote on 17 June after the family moved to Queluz. 'I cry every time I pass your bedroom door because it reminds me of our great conversations.'

Mariana also wrote regularly and a letter which arrived towards the end of June gave Maria cause for concern. The shock of being torn from her family, finding herself alone in a foreign court, and going to bed with a man who was still a stranger, was affecting her body which responded by almost continual bleeding. 'I should like to know when you are expecting,' wrote João rather obliquely, 'because today I heard my mother mutter through clenched teeth that you had that thing again – you know what I mean.'[4]

Meanwhile, Carlota was proving to be vivacious, energetic and badly behaved. She refused to get up in the morning; she refused to get dressed, complaining about corsets and uncomfortable shoes; she ate with her hands and threw food at her husband; she remained mute during lessons. João tried to act as an older brother; at first, he was even a little impressed. 'She is very clever and has lots of common sense for one who is still so small,' he wrote to his sister, but then added that she was also 'very uninhibited, without any shame whatsoever'.

Maria took on a motherly role and became the only person capable of keeping the unruly child in check. It was she who disciplined Carlota, threatening to withdraw her favourite activities, riding on donkey back and driving through the grounds of Queluz in a pony cart. She taught her Portuguese phrases, they went out riding together and visited convents, but the strain of coping with her disruptive daughter-in-law soon led to an attack of conjunctivitis which confined her to the palace 'for some weeks'.

She was still suffering from her eyes in mid-November when a special courier arrived from Spain. Her daughter was now two months pregnant. Maria was delighted by the news, but João felt unsettled. Nineteen years old, too shy to

1. Church of St Sidwell, Laneast, Cornwall. William was baptised here on 20 May 1731: 'William, ye son of Jane Smith of Landulph, father unknown.' *Photograph by Jenifer Roberts*

2. Hornafast on the banks of the River Tamar, Pentillie estate, Cornwall. The cottages are Victorian but they almost certainly stand on the site of the house where William lived until the age of twelve. *Photograph by Hazel McHaffie*

3. Pentillie Castle, where William's mother was employed as a domestic servant. Engraving by Thomas Allom, 1832. *Private collection*

Two engravings by R. White of the Cathedral Church of St Peter in Exeter, 1744.
North Devon Athenaeum

4. 'The North Prospect', viewed from Cathedral Close where William lived with his parents for three years (1743–6).

5. 'The West Prospect', viewed from Cathedral Yard. The tower of St Mary Major, where William's parents were married on 11 May 1743, can be seen on the right.

6. Terreiro do Paço and Ribeira Palace before the earthquake (arrival of a new papal nuncio, 1693). *Coleção de Jorge de Brito*

7. Maria de Bragança at the age of four. Painting by Francisco Pavona, 1738/9. *Palácio Nacional de Queluz*

8. William Stephens aged 21. Miniature painting set in gold brooch, Lisbon, 1752. *Private collection*

9. Maria, crown princess of Portugal. Painting attributed to Francisco Vieira de Matos (Vieira Lusitano), c.1753. *Palácio Nacional de Queluz*

10. Maria's mother, Mariana Vitória de Bourbon, painted in early middle age. *Palácio Nacional de Queluz*

11. Maria's father, José I. Painting by Francisco José Aparício. *Museu Nacional dos Coches*

12. The Lisbon earthquake, 1 November 1755. Engraving by Christoph Henrich Bohn after drawing by Reinier Vinkeles, late eighteenth century. *Rijksmuseum, Amsterdam*

13–14. Details from a panorama of Lisbon. Pen and wash by Bernardo de Caula, 1763. *Biblioteca Nacional de Portugal*

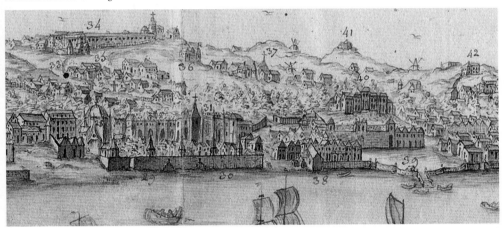

13. Belém and Ajuda, showing the Real Barraca (no. 34), the town of Belém (no. 38), and the royal palace at Belém (no. 39).

14. Alcântara. The lime kilns (closed at the time this drawing was made) are somewhere behind the jumble of houses on the waterfront.

15. The ruins of the Casa da Ópera in Lisbon, completed just a few months before the earthquake. Aquatint by Jacques Philippe Le Bas after drawing by Miguel Tibério Pedegache, 1757. *Biblioteca Nacional de Portugal*

16. Garden façade of the palace of Queluz, constructed by Pedro 1747–52. *Direção-Geral do Património Cultural*

17. Sebastião de Carvalho e Melo, Marquis de Pombal. Painting attributed to Joana do Salitre, c.1769. *Museum of Lisbon*

18. The royal glass factory, Marinha Grande. Engraving by Alberto from drawing by Nogueira da Silva, 1868. *Câmara Municipal da Marinha Grande*

19. Interior view of the workshop for crystalline glass. Engraving by D. Netto from drawing by Ribeiro Christino, 1890. *Câmara Municipal da Marinha Grande*

20. Exterior view of the glass factory. Engraving by Oliveira from drawing by Ribeiro Christino, 1890. *Câmara Municipal da Marinha Grande*

21–24. Glassware made in Marinha Grande, second half of eighteenth century.
Museu Nacional de Arte Antiga

21. Tumbler engraved with a portrait of José I and the words 'Vivat Rex Josephus I', c.1772.

23. Tankard.

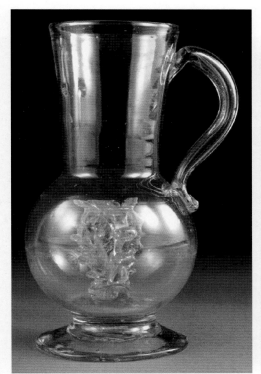

22. Flower vase with four apertures.

24. Vase with handles.

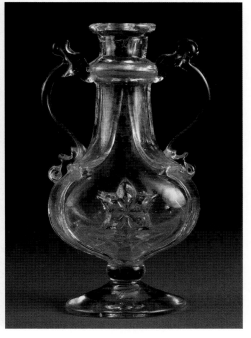

25. Maria I and her consort Pedro III, painted after her acclamation in 1777. Maria's hand is placed on the crown, signifying her role as monarch; Pedro's hand is hovering above it, signifying his more humble role as king-consort. *Museu Nacional dos Coches*

26. The queen mother, Mariana Vitória, painted after Maria's accession to the throne. Maria relied on her mother's fortitude and strength of character during the early years of her reign. *Museu Francisco Tavares Proença Júnior*

27. Benedita, Maria's youngest sister and wife of Prince José. Painting attributed to Jean Baptiste Debret, c.1785. *Museu Nacional dos Coches*

28. Prince José aged 15, painted after his mother's acclamation in 1777. *Museu Nacional dos Coches*

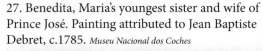

29. The palace at Vila Viçosa. The marriages of Maria's younger children, João and Mariana, were celebrated here in May 1785. *Photograph by EDARF*

30. Maria I. Engraving by Marie Anne Bourlier from original miniature portrait, probably by Daniel Valentine Rivière. *Private collection*

31. Carlota Joaquina, painted in celebration of her marriage to Prince João, 1785. *Palácio Nacional de Queluz*

32. Prince João. Engraving from original miniature portrait by D. Pelegrim, 1808. *Fundação Biblioteca Nacional, Brazil*

33. Maria I. Painting by Guiseppe Troni, 1783.
Palácio Nacional de Queluz

34. William Stephens aged 67. Engraving by A. Smith from drawing by Bouck, published in London, 1799. *Private collection*

35. William's mansion house in Marinha Grande, described by a Portuguese aristocrat as 'a pretty little palace with an exterior both grandiose and simple'. Maria stayed here for two nights in the summer of 1788 and 'liked her Situation so well that she regretted leaving it'.
Photograph by Edwin Green

36. The factory courtyard in Marinha Grande, showing the mansion house and the workshop for crystalline glass. During Maria's visit, the courtyard was lit by 2000 lights strung diagonally on wooden frames attached to the buildings. *Private collection*

37. The Basilica da Estrela, completed in 1789. The buildings of Maria's convent can be seen on both sides of the church. Lithograph by Salema, c.1870. *Biblioteca Nacional de Portugal*

39. Dr Francis Willis, painted after his 'cure' of George III in 1789. Pastel by John Russell. *National Portrait Gallery*

38. Maria I, holding a miniature portrait of her husband, c.1786–91. The strain which led to the breakdown in her mental health is etched on her face. *Palácio Nacional de Mafra*

40. The Dona Maria Pavilion at Queluz. Maria lived in seclusion here for almost twelve years until the royal family fled to Brazil in November 1807. *Direção-Geral do Património Cultural*

41. Largo do Paço, Rio de Janeiro, as it was when Maria arrived here in March 1808. The royal palace (the viceroy's residence) is on the left. At right angles to the palace is the convent where Maria spent the last eight years of her life. Engraving from original painting by J. Stainmann. *Private collection*

43. Monument over William and John James's grave in the Protestant cemetery in Estrela. *Photograph by Jenifer Roberts*

42. Maria's tomb in the Basilica da Estrela. *Photograph by José Luiz*

44. The Treasurer's House in Christ's Hospital (London). Philadelphia spent the last seven years of her life here.
London and Middlesex Archaeological Society

45. The glass factory in Marinha Grande, early twentieth century.
Deolinda Bonita

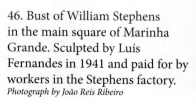

46. Bust of William Stephens in the main square of Marinha Grande. Sculpted by Luís Fernandes in 1941 and paid for by workers in the Stephens factory.
Photograph by João Reis Ribeiro

seek an outlet elsewhere, he longed to get his hands on his little wife. As he wrote to his sister:

> 'It will be many years before I can go to her, and this is mortifying for me. There can be no pleasure for now because she is so young and her body so small, but the time will come when I shall play with her. How happy I shall be then!'[5]

16

English Comfort

*The Queen is a woman truly worthy of esteem and respect, but she has not
the qualities which constitute a great sovereign. No one can be more humane,
more charitable, more tender than she is, but these qualities are spoiled by an
excessive ... devotion.*

Pierre Cormatin, Duke du Châtelet, 1777

Maria delayed her return to the Real Barraca in the autumn of 1785
because of an outbreak of smallpox in Belém. Prince José had never
shown signs of the disease, so it was thought wise for the family to
remain in Queluz until 'the contagion had diminished' in December. Three
months later, in early March 1786, Carlota suffered an infestation of head lice.
'You wouldn't believe the amount of lice she had,' João wrote to his sister, 'they
are like a plague.'

Her scalp was wet with weeping sores so they shaved off her thick unruly hair,
leaving only a forelock to grace the front of a cap. Confined to her apartments
until her scalp dried out, she was visited twice a day by her husband who,
'playing donkey for her amusement', circled around the room on his hands and
knees while his child-wife rode jockey-style on his back.[1]

Carlota's hair had grown to a halo of brown frizz when the family made plans
to travel to Caldas da Rainha in early May, but Pedro felt unwell and the journey
was postponed. Less than three weeks later, he suffered the same fate as his
father and brother. 'I am very sorry for the cruel blow you are about to receive,'
João wrote to his sister in Spain, before giving her a detailed description of their
father's last twelve days.

At first, Pedro had suffered from 'a great tightness in his voice'. The doctors
applied leeches and Maria suggested that he remain in bed during the official
audience to celebrate João's birthday on 13 May. The following afternoon, he
insisted on leaving the palace:

> 'He was walking very slowly and when he came back, he took twenty-five
> minutes to reach his room. He sat down on his chair and stared at us in a
> daze and would not speak unless we spoke to him. My mother asked if he
> wanted to write to you. He said Yes and then he wrote nonsense and we

were all quite dismayed. When he relieved himself, he did it in his chair. He could no longer stand.'

It was another stroke, so Pedro was taken to bed where he slept fitfully through the night. Next morning:

> 'His legs were useless which frightened us very much. He went to his chair and held himself up by his arms, still dazed and staring at us. All he would say was Yes or No. He was purged in the afternoon. It worked well but, after the last motion, we found him even weaker, so he was put to bed again.'

On the morning of the 16th, the doctors applied blistering ointments and Maria ordered that the statue of Senhor dos Passos be brought to the palace. Four days later, Pedro 'began sweating and was soon soaked', after which more blistering ointment was applied, this time to his forehead. The priests administered the last rites, 'and gradually he stopped taking anything other than little sips of breast milk'. On the 24th, João went to see his father shortly before midnight:

> 'He looked the same as he had on previous nights. He did not look as if he was dying. He was very florid and the veins all over his face were engorged. Then it struck twelve and, within a quarter of an hour, he started agonising until half past two in the morning when he died.'

Pedro had remained in the same comatose condition for four days; with no warning of a sudden change, Maria had retired to bed in an adjacent room and was sleeping through the night. Her two sons waited until she woke in the morning and, when they entered the room 'to give her our condolences, she became very agitated at the news'.[2]

Later that day, she issued a statement: according to custom and 'in demonstration of her grief, the Queen has determined to retire for eight days, beginning this day, and goes into mourning for a year, six months strict and six months slight'. On the evening of the 27th, she kissed her husband's hand for the last time before his coffin was carried out of the palace and taken ('with the accustomed pomp and ceremony') to the royal mausoleum in São Vicente de Fora.

During her days of confinement in the palace, Maria banned all public entertainments and ordered her courtiers to attend a series of requiem masses to pray for his soul. Her first outing after his death was to the convent in Estrela. She had been a regular visitor since the nuns took up residence in 1781 and had forged a friendship with the abbess, a woman on whom she became increasingly reliant for spiritual guidance.

She also relied on her confessor, Inácio de São Caetano, who had been given the title of Archbishop of Thessalonica and, alone among her subjects, had the privilege of being allowed to sit in her presence. A large, red-faced man who tucked into enormous meals, he was, according to Robert Walpole, 'of a plain, good understanding, without any extensive knowledge beyond his profession, and has certainly great influence over her Majesty in matters of conscience'.

São Caetano was always smiling. 'I never saw a sturdier fellow,' wrote William Beckford. 'He seems to anoint himself with the oil of gladness, to laugh and grow fat.'[3] When Maria confessed that her father's complicity in Pombal's acts of terror lay heavily on her conscience, São Caetano reassured her. 'Be easy concerning your soul,' he told her. 'I shall take that upon myself.'

...

On 21 June, a special courier arrived from Aranjuez with news of the birth of Maria's first grandchild, a boy named Pedro Carlos after his two grandfathers. The news did little to raise her spirits, so the doctors advised her to take the baths at Alcaçarias. The baths seemed to calm her so, in the early autumn, she and her family set out for Caldas da Rainha where the hot spa waters were thought to be especially beneficial.

There was no palace in the town – her grandfather visited Caldas only when his health was in decline; her parents were more interested in hunting than in taking the waters – so the house of the *provedor* (the most important man in town) was prepared for their accommodation. This was by no means a palace. When the French ambassador stayed here the following year, he was shocked by the meanness of the apartments. The house was a '*bicoque*', he wrote in his diary, 'a hovel, by no means suitable for the dignity of the throne of Portugal'.[4]

Maria arrived in Caldas on 9 September to spend her days in the 'large and handsome bathing house' which covered the spa waters in the centre of town. Five weeks later, William Stephens came to the provedor's house to offer his condolences and present a petition about his tax exemptions.

His loan had been fully repaid earlier in the year. Profits from his monopoly were now unencumbered by debt repayments but he was disappointed that, in her decree of 1780, Maria had not extended his tax exemptions for longer periods. The exemption from sales taxes would remain in force until 1794, but the exemption from import duties had expired the previous December. His petition requested an extension of both these privileges, not only to protect the profitability of the factory, but also 'to preserve the good faith of our workers who, at present, are not inclined to educate their sons in this art for fear that the exemptions will soon expire, rendering their work useless and obliging them, in their old age, to seek alternative employment'.

Maria granted him an audience on 12 October, at which she agreed to extend both exemptions for a further ten years – and as she thanked him for his condolences, he raised the courage to suggest a visit to the factory. Marinha Grande lay 30 miles north of Caldas, but only 15 miles from the convent of Alcobaça where 'a suite of spacious rooms' was kept for the sole use of the royal family.

The queen was aware that William had achieved great things at the glassworks. Stories were told at court, not only about the volume and quality of his glass, but also about the welfare state he had created in the village and the theatre where his workers performed in plays with music and dance. She was still in strict mourning for Pedro, but she was curious to see the factory and – perhaps to William's surprise – she informed him that she would visit Marinha Grande five days later.

As Maria and her family travelled to Alcobaça on the 14th, visited the monastery of Batalha on the 15th, and rested in Alcobaça on the 16th, the workshops and open spaces in the glassworks were cleaned and tidied, creating an excitement among the workers reminiscent of Pombal's visit fourteen years earlier. Shortly before noon on 17 October, the royal carriages clattered through the factory gates to be greeted by William and Philadelphia on the steps of the mansion house. Maria was the first to alight, followed by her sisters, her two sons and little Carlota who scampered out of the carriage, her short locks hidden beneath a cap. Refreshments were served on the first floor of the house, after which the queen and her family made a brief tour of the workshops and Maria praised the 'good taste, perfection and regularity of this most useful factory'.

Later that afternoon, the family drank tea in William's garden while the carriages were prepared for the return journey to Alcobaça. Maria had enjoyed her few hours in Marinha Grande and told William that she hoped to come again the following year. And according to the *Gazeta de Lisboa*, the day was 'all to her Majesty's satisfaction'.[5]

A few days after she returned to Lisbon, a new French ambassador arrived in the Real Barraca for his first official audience. The Marquis de Bombelles kept a private diary and, during the next few months, he recorded the improvement in Maria's spirits. In November, she lifted the ban on public entertainments. In December, she engaged in cheerful conversations with her courtiers. 'Little by little,' he wrote, 'the Queen emerges from the profound sadness into which she was plunged by the death of her husband.' By the turn of the year, she was coaching Bombelles in the use of Portuguese phrases.[6]

Despite this easing of her grief, Maria was in another low mood when she returned to Caldas in May 1787. She stayed in the town for seven weeks but failed to make a second visit to the glassworks. Several matters were preying on her mind. She was concerned about her daughter in Spain, distressed by her elder son's attitude to the church, and unnerved by the need to reorganise her cabinet.

Mariana had inherited her mother's timid nature. She was lonely in the court of Spain and missed the company of her own people. In a letter to London on 16 June, Walpole speculated on the appointment of a new ambassador to Madrid:

> 'It would be agreeable to the Portuguese Infanta married to Don Gabriel to have an ambassador of this country there, to be frequently in her company to relieve her from the embarrassment to which her natural timidity and taciturnity frequently expose her.'

Prince José also had a 'reserved disposition'. He was lacking in grace and charm, frustrated at having so little to occupy his time, and his secular approach to state affairs was encouraged by his courtiers who were spreading rumours that Maria might abdicate, that she was thinking of entering a convent.

Meanwhile, the men in her cabinet were ailing. Aires de Sá (secretary of state for foreign affairs) had died the previous year, reducing the number of her ministers to three, two of whom were over 70 and in poor health. Marquis de Angeja was semi-retired, while Martinho de Melo was subject to 'frequent violent attacks of illness [which] may be attended with the most serious consequences at his advanced age'. After Sá's death, Melo had taken on foreign affairs in addition to his own portfolio and was now handling a 'multiplicity of business ... which he said was too much for him in his advanced years'. The third minister, Viscount de Ponte de Lima, was inexperienced in government; he was also unwell from time to time, 'having been afflicted with a fever in his head'.

These matters were preying on Maria's mind when she returned to Lisbon on 26 June, travelling by road to Vila Nova da Rainha and thence by river to the city. The *Real Bergantim*, the royal barge built in 1785 to celebrate the double marriage, was a magnificent longboat and Maria reclined on red velvet cushions in the gilded cabin, 'fanned by refreshing breezes'. She had recently abolished the tax on sales of *bacalhao* (dried and salted fish) and, as the barge approached Lisbon in the late afternoon, the people of the city gave her a special welcome.

Hundreds of boats 'transformed into arbours of flowers and garlands' had sailed upriver to meet her, some with musicians on board who serenaded the queen during the last stage of the journey. The Praça do Comércio was crowded with 'a great concourse of people' who had gathered to greet their sovereign. A carriage was waiting at the quayside but Maria, 'affected by these testimonies of the satisfaction of the people', chose to walk across the square to the Senate

House, 'without guards amidst a multitude worked up to the highest pitch of grateful enthusiasm. Such genuine rejoicings are seldom seen in Portugal, and the Queen was affected by them almost to tears.'

Cheered by this reception, Maria came up with a solution to the crisis in cabinet. Her elder son needed employment and a role in state affairs; her confessor, Inácio de São Caetano, had advised her on matters of government for several years. Now she decided to appoint both her son and her confessor to her council of state. The inclusion of the prince was greeted with satisfaction ('it ought to have been done some years ago') but São Caetano's elevation was met with less enthusiasm. Ponte de Lima tendered his resignation, which Maria refused to accept, and Melo complained that São Caetano was 'so exceedingly ignorant that when he could not be made to comprehend any business beyond his capacity, it became an object of conscience for the Queen not to adopt it'.

Maria was distressed by the reaction of her ministers, particularly since they (and Prince José) were treating her confessor with disrespect. She retired to the palace in Sintra where, in mid-October, she had a frank conversation with Marquis de Marialva – and Marialva was indiscreet enough to tell William Beckford. 'He told me in the strictest confidence,' Beckford wrote in his diary, 'that the Queen had thoughts of retiring from government, that she was worn out with the intrigues of the Court and sick of her existence.'[7]

On 8 November, nine days after Maria returned to Lisbon, a special courier arrived from Spain with news that Mariana had given birth to her second child, a daughter named Maria after her grandmother. The birth was announced with the usual pealing of bells and cannon-fire, and the Te Deum was sung in the churches. As dark fell that evening, Beckford set out to see the illuminations in the city. He watched rockets in the Praça do Comércio rising to a 'vast height', bursting into 'innumerable clear blue stars', and returned to his house to find 'every apartment … filled with the thick vapour of wax torches' which his servant 'had set most loyally a-blazing'.[8]

Three days later, another courier arrived from Spain. Maria's infant granddaughter had died on 7 November, one day before the whole of Lisbon celebrated her birth.

…

In March 1788, the death of Maria's first minister, Marquis de Angeja, reduced the number of her secretaries of state to two. It was vital that she appoint new ministers but, with her usual indecision, she merely asked Ponte de Lima to assume Angeja's role on an interim basis. And for the next nine months, he and the elderly Martinho de Melo conducted all business of state between them.

In early April, a courier arrived from Spain with news that Maria's daughter had conceived for a third time. On the 25th, there was an official audience to celebrate Carlota's thirteenth birthday. All foreign diplomats attended, all trying to think of a suitable compliment, all lying through their teeth when they congratulated the tiny princess on how much she had grown. 'Such great flattery,' wrote the Marquis de Bombelles, 'was embarrassing to sustain.'

The family returned to Caldas on 3 May. A few days later, William Stephens arrived at the provedor's house with another petition. His monopoly of supply had come under threat from foreign glass merchants, who were trying to avoid import duties by building their own factories in Portugal. Maria granted him an audience, at which he asked for confirmation that foreign factories would not be permitted on Portuguese soil. As she gave him the assurance he needed, she told him that she was ready to make another visit to Marinha Grande. She was curious to know more about his achievements in the village and she would arrive at the factory on 30 June, not for a few hours as she had done two years before, but for a stay of almost three days.

This was an unprecedented honour and William rode home to Marinha Grande aware that he and Philadelphia had just six weeks to prepare for such a momentous occasion. During his birthday celebrations on 16 May, he stood on the steps of his mansion house to address the assembled workers. He congratulated them:

> 'on the industry and enthusiasm which have enabled this factory to reach the summit of its achievement. It is the admiration of your compatriots and fills the hearts of importers with envy and malice. But their efforts to build new factories will come to nothing because our factory makes sufficient glass to supply the entire kingdom and its colonies. Her Majesty will not permit factories to operate with foreign craftsmen; she knows that this would prejudice her subjects, the workers in this factory who have applied themselves so well to the art of glassmaking that they can compete with the most skilled glassmakers in Europe.'

Then he told them of the impending royal visit:

> 'When I went to Caldas, I was given the clearest demonstrations of kindness and encouragement from her Majesty. The care and contentment we show in our work have led to such high esteem at Court that she has deigned to honour the factory for a second time with her royal presence.'[9]

Maria was an absolute monarch, ruling by divine right, yet she was about to spend three days in an industrial complex and sleep for two nights in the house of an Englishman, a man who was not only low-born but also a Protestant, a heretic in the eyes of the Portuguese. She rarely slept outside the precincts of royal palaces, the convent at Alcobaça or the provedor's house in Caldas. There must have been something in William's demeanour to give her comfort; his English reticence in a court of flamboyant flattery, his understated dress, his big square reassuring face. The man who was worshipped by his workers and the lowliest villagers in Marinha Grande also had the power to woo a queen.

17

The Great Occasion

*My Brother has achieved what nobody else in the Kingdom can boast of, which
is the honour of entertaining the Royal Family and all the Court for two days
and given universal satisfaction to everybody from the Queen down to the
Scullions and Stable Boys.*
Philadelphia Stephens, 25 July 1788

*I have gone thro this affair with great Eclat. It was an honour they have never
done any of their own subjects. I was therefore without a precedent to go by. I
requested nothing from the Palace but their Cooks and the kitchen Utensils.*
William Stephens, in conversation with Robert Southey, March 1801

William's brothers, Lewis and Jedediah, made the journey to Marinha
Grande a few days before the visit was due to begin. Only John James
remained in Lisbon, perhaps because he was needed to handle the
sale of finished glass in the city, perhaps because he disliked the journey to the
glassworks, the rough roads, the nights spent in country inns.

On the morning of 30 June, the factory complex was a hive of activity as final
preparations were made, and William and Philadelphia ensured that everything
was clean, tidy and well-rehearsed. During the morning, large numbers of
people ('an assembly of many thousands') arrived in the village to witness the
occasion, 'a vast concourse from all the Country round this Neighbourhood
which Curiosity had brought together to see their Sovereign'.

At four o'clock in the afternoon, a messenger brought news that the
royal carriages were approaching. Everyone took up their allotted positions
in the factory courtyard. 'Our Praça on this Occasion made a very Brilliant
Appearance,' wrote Philadelphia in her account of the visit:

> 'On each side of the House, the Soldiers were drawn up in form belonging
> to the Guard and opposite, before the Door of the Fabrick, all the Artificers
> belonging to the Manufactory in their Working Dress which does not
> admit of either Coat or Waistcoat. Their Hair was dressed and powdered,
> their Shirts clean and ironed with the Sleeves tied round the Middle of the
> Arm with Red Ribbons, Black breeches and clean white Stockings which
> altogether gave them a very neat Uniform Appearance.'

As the carriages drove into the courtyard, the workmen – almost 200 men – shouted '*Viva Rainha! Viva toda a Família Real!*' three times. Most of these men had never travelled more than a few miles from Marinha Grande. They had never seen Lisbon, or Caldas da Rainha, yet here was the queen arriving at their place of work, not for a passing visit but for a stay of three days.

William and his family were waiting outside the front door of the mansion house ('which on this occasion was called the Paço or Palace'), together with Inácio de São Caetano and Viscount de Ponte de Lima. As the queen alighted from her carriage, Philadelphia 'had the Honour of kissing her Majesty's Hand … and received a Gracious Smile in return'. She found Maria 'greatly improved in her looks since she was here in the year 1786, being now fatter, of a better colour and more cheerful countenance'.

The greeting ceremony was repeated with the other members of the family: Prince José, a fairly tall young man 'with a pale and delicate face'; Prince João, who had a pronounced underbite and a habit of keeping his mouth 'somewhat open' as his grandfather used to do; Benedita, who had lost weight since the previous visit 'but still retains a pleasant agreeable aspect'; her sister Mariana, who was 'fatter and, although not handsome, has something agreeable … in her appearance'; and Carlota, who was 'just the same as when she was here last, lively but very short, nor does her countenance indicate that she will ever grow much taller. I have seen children as Lusty at nine years of age; she is now in her fourteenth.'

The ladies-in-waiting arrived next and, after São Caetano introduced them to Philadelphia ('and recommended them to my particular care'), the royal party entered the house and ascended the staircase. The first floor had been transformed into royal apartments. Beds had been brought from Caldas and heavy curtains ('of Crimson Damask trimmed with Gold Lace and Valance of Crimson Velvet with a Deep Gold Fringe') hung over the doors and windows. Maria inspected the apartments, then 'went up to the Attic Storey to see the Accommodations of her Female Attendants with which she expressed great satisfaction'. After viewing the house:

> 'She intimated a desire of seeing the Fabrick. Accordingly a Procession of the Royal Family and Attendants walked across the Praça from the House to the Fabrick amidst a vast concourse of people. On their entrance into the Fabrick, they were again saluted by the Manufacturers with *Viva Rainha, Viva toda a Família Real* repeated three times.'

A pavilion covered with green baize and red taffeta had been installed in the main workshop, so the family could sit in comfort while they watched the glass-masters wield their blowing rods while assistants and apprentices hurried around them with pincers, scissors and tongs. Maria stayed here for half an hour, but her sister Benedita:

> 'afraid of being so near the Glass Furnace on account of the Heat so soon after finishing her Baths at the Caldas, immediately on entering the Fabrick called me to her and desired I would shew her the way up Stairs to the Packing Warehouse. Accordingly I ordered a Chair to be placed for her by the Window where she amused herself in admiring the Prospect and talking to me … in a very agreeable familiar style.'

After 'satisfying her Curiosity of seeing the People at work and applauding them all very much', Maria followed her sister upstairs and 'examined everything very attentively'. In the room where the glass was engraved and painted, 'they sat some time admiring the work, the Queen and Princess both asking me a number of questions'.

…

William had spent over £20,000 in today's values on furnishings, decorations and provisions for the visit. He had bought 50 yards of velvet, 100 yards of green and white baize to line the dinner tables, and four plumes of feathers to decorate the queen's chair. He borrowed houses in the village to accommodate members of the court and acquired 'some hundreds' of beds, 'which we got from Leiria and its Neighbourhood, it being impossible to collect so great a number in this place'. He built a marquee of wood and sailcloth 'at the upper end of our great Walk in the Garden', hung with tapestry and large enough to seat sixty men at table. He provided stabling for the horses and mules, and cleared the wood sheds to accommodate the servants:

> 'You may guess a little more or less of the number of People belonging to her Majesty's Suite when I tell you that we had Stables provided with Straw and Barley for six hundred Beasts exclusive of the Troops … The Livery Servants, Coachmen and Soldiers with their Beasts were all well accommodated under the Wood Sheds, where they had their Kitchen and Dining Rooms according to their several degrees, with a plentiful supply of the best Beef, Rice and Bread that could be got in this Country and as much Aljubarrota wine as they chose to drink.
>
> 'Notwithstanding this, for their honour, I must not omit saying that there was not one got Drunk, nor the least disturbance happened during the whole time they were here, and as a remarkable proof of their Honesty, I can assure you that on this, and the former Occasion of their being here, we lost nothing but two dessert spoons which I suppose to be mislaid or

thrown out with the dirt of the Kitchen, it being not an object to be stolen where there was an opportunity of stealing things of much greater value ...

'The Livery Servants and Soldiers were delighted to find they had got decent beds to sleep in. It was a Luxury they enjoyed for the first time since leaving Lisbon on the 3rd of May. During the whole time of their being at the Caldas, they were obliged to sleep on loose straw in the Stables, on the Ground, or wheresoever they could find a place to lay themselves down, such is the Hardship these poor fellows endure when Travelling with the Court and is probably the reason of their committing many Outrages, but I must again repeat that their good behaviour here entitled them to every Indulgence.'

A few days before the visit, the director of the royal household had arrived in Marinha Grande with his chief assistant. They brought with them 'five Beds for the Royal Family and Curtains for the Doors and Windows of the Principal Rooms'. The assistant hung the drapes and assembled the beds, a ritual which took place every time the family travelled from one place to another. This gave Philadelphia a rare opportunity to see details of the royal sleeping arrangements.

José and Benedita shared a 'very large and elegant' bed; Maria's bed was smaller but equally sumptuous; João and Carlota still slept in separate rooms. Each of the five beds had three mattresses. The first was a linen case 'which they brought empty and filled here with Rye straw'; the next two were 'of very fine Irish Linen stuffed with Wool'. These were covered with a fine linen sheet, 'which four men pulled with all their strength and tucked in under the Straw Mattress'. The two larger beds were dressed with headboards and valances of deep red damask, covered with 'a most Beautiful fine Muslin worked with small spots of silver, the edges trimmed with an elegant Silver Blond Lace plaited on pretty thick'. These beds were normally assembled with testers and curtains:

'but her Majesty, most graciously recollecting that our Rooms, being elegantly furnished with Stucco, the Testers could not be fastened without driving Hooks into the Ceiling ... gave positive orders for the Beds to be made without Curtains as she would not consent by any means for the most trifling thing to be done to injure the House which she often admired for its neatness.'

William had bought vast quantities of food for such an immense gathering, not only top quality ingredients for the royal family and the court, but also good quality provisions for the servants and soldiers of the guard. The accounts book shows purchases of fat oxen and calves and 400 gallons of wine. The queen's chief cook and twenty-three assistant cooks had arrived in Marinha Grande on the morning of the 30th:

'Everything was provided for them so that, on their arrival, they had nothing to do but begin their Work. We required nothing from her Majesty's Household but the Damask Hangings for the Doors and Windows and the large Coppers for the use of the Kitchen. China, Damask, Table and Plate we have sufficient for the service of all the different Tables. Having had some reason to expect this visit last year, we got a large supply of silver-hafted knives and forks and spoons from England, of the best quality and newest fashion …

'A little Anecdote happened which is scarcely worth mention only as a proof of Her Majesty's determined resolution to be pleased with everything she met with. The Queen and Princess have each a particular Teapot and Cup and Saucer which they always make use of. The Princess brought hers. The Female Servant who packed it up enquired of the Queen if she would have hers packed up also, to which her Majesty said *No*, that she knew very well that Stephens had provided everything required, and she was determined to make use of nothing but what belonged to his House.'

After their tour of the workshops, the family relaxed in William's garden 'where Chairs were placed in different situations for them to rest themselves'. At six o'clock, 'they retired to the House and drank Tea' before William led the way across the courtyard to the factory theatre.

The workmen were well-rehearsed, the scenery and costumes newly made, and the interior lit by large numbers of wax tapers. The royal gallery had been 'elegantly prepared … with Crimson Damask Curtains trimmed with Gold Lace and hung in Festoons, the Rails covered with Crimson Velvet ornamented with a Deep Gold Fringe'. This was flanked by side galleries for Maria's confessor and her ladies-in-waiting, 'behind which was sufficient room for all the rest of the Female Attendants to see the play'. The pit was 'allotted for such People belonging to the Suite as were not … in immediate waiting, as also for the Gentlemen of this Neighbourhood and the Ministers of the City of Leiria'. Under the royal gallery was 'a Private Box … for the Principal Ladies of Leiria who were here to see the entertainments'.

A painting over the front of the stage depicted 'two female figures representing Tragedy and Comedy … supporting a target with the following label – Come and Rest from your Labours – alluding to the motives for which the theatre was built'. The curtain was painted with a pastoral scene illustrating William's philosophy at Marinha Grande:

'It represents a Lady sitting upon a large Tree with the Arms of Portugal by her side and a Youth in a light Gardener's Dress emptying a Cornucopia in her Lap as the Emblem of Plenty and Industry. The expulsion of Indolence is represented by a Beggar who is a healthy, stout, hearty looking Fellow covered with Rags, his Pockets stuffed with Bread and a Staff in his hand pointed with Iron serves as an offensive or defensive Weapon as best suits his purpose. He is going off with a look of contempt on Industry. The explanation at the bottom is in the following words – Portugal receives Abundance from Industry and Indigence is exiled.'

The performance on the first night of the visit – 'by particular desire of her Majesty' – was the queen's favourite play, the tragedy of *Sésostris*. Set in ancient Egypt, this three-act play was often staged in Lisbon and, although the workers at Marinha Grande 'had not a fortnight to study it, they performed their parts exceedingly well'. Between the acts, 'there were different Dances and Pantomimes, during which the Royal Family were served with Ice of different sorts and other Refreshments', and the evening ended with a farce received with much laughter.

The factory orchestra consisted of four violins, two French horns and four cellos, and the quality of the music and acting came as a surprise to the audience:

'The Performers acquitted themselves with Honour and received universal Applause, not only from the Royal Family but from all the Audience who thought it impossible that a rude Country Place like this could have produced such good Actors. Their Surprise was greatly increased on finding that the greatest part of them had never been more than two or three leagues from this Parish, and that they all worked in the Fabrick. They perform only for their Amusement, which you must allow is very different from the Public Theatres where the Actors have no other Employment than studying their parts and their whole subsistence depends upon the favourable Opinion of the Public.'

After the curtain came down for the last time that night, William and Philadelphia escorted the royal family across a courtyard lit by 2,000 candles strung diagonally across the façades of the buildings and with 'an Obelisk in the middle of the Praça crowned with a Sphere at the top'. The royal dining table had been set up on the first floor of the mansion house. Fifteen feet long by 8 feet wide, it was covered with a pink silk tablecloth and decorated with 'a very elegant Glass ornament made here, representing a Temple'. This had been designed by the Marquis de Marialva's confectioner, who also provided the ice creams and sorbets, 'of which there was a great variety and exceeding good'.

Except for rare occasions (such as the double marriage in Vila Viçosa), the royal family never dined in public – 'their usual custom at Lisbon and the Caldas is to sup and dine each in their different Apartments' – so Philadelphia, standing in the doorway, watched a protocol that few people had the opportunity to witness.

The royal women sat at one side of the table, the two princes on the other, and 'they seemed to be very happy in each other's company'. All the courses were placed on the table at the same time ('Meat, Fruit, Sweetmeats etc.') and each member of the family was served separately by their *camarista* (lord of the bedchamber) and *reposteiros* (footmen). The ritual began as soon as they entered the room:

> 'On the Queen's entering the Dining Room, she is presented by her Camarista on his knee with Water and a Towel to wash her hands, which being done she takes her Seat and the Camarista stands behind her Chair. The same Ceremony is observed with all the rest of the Royal Family. The Camarista then carves such dishes as they choose to eat of, and when anything is required from the Side Boards, the Reposteiros reach it to the Camarista who puts it on the Table. When water or wine is required, the Reposteiro draws the Cork and brings the Bottle and Glass on a Salver to the Camarista who, on his knee, pours out the liquor and presents it to the Queen, remaining in the same attitude to receive the Glass when she has done drinking. When Dinner is over, they again wash their hands and retire to drink Coffee.'

Even the provision of water had its own ceremonial:

> 'They are very particular with respect to the water they drink which is all brought in flasks from Lisbon, some from the Chafariz da Praia and some from the Ajuda. One of the Reposteiros who was Provedor das Aguas I observed had nothing else to do but to keep the Key of the Water Chests and take care that there was always a Bottle full of water ready on the Side Board and on a Table in each of the Apartments. Her Majesty's Bottle was distinguished by having a bit of narrow White Ribbon tied round the Neck. Claret is the wine chiefly made use of, and that only a very small quantity.'

During the meal, 'two Triumphal Cars with Musick were drawn round the Square and played under the Windows ... and as soon as the Royal Family got up from Table, some pretty fireworks were displayed off, which amused them about a quarter of an hour, when they all retired to their Apartments'.

Now it was the turn of the court and local dignitaries. Philadelphia and the ladies-in-waiting took their places at the royal table on the first floor, Ponte de Lima and the gentlemen-in-waiting on the ground floor at a 'Table of State' covered with a blue silk tablecloth adorned with 'a Pyramid of Glass Salvers ... decorated with Sweetmeats'. The 'Gentlemen of the Neighbourhood' and ministers of Leiria dined with William and his brothers in the marquee in the garden.

When everyone had eaten, the 'great concourse of people' slipped away to bed. São Caetano slept in a house to the right of the main gates, Ponte de Lima and the gentlemen-in-waiting in the best house in the village ('where we had very excellent Beds made for them'). Other members of the court were distributed around the village. And now, wrote Philadelphia, 'a total Silence commenced for the night'.

...

The first to rise next morning was Prince João, who left his bed at four o'clock to ride out to his estates in Monte Real and inspect the works at Foz de Vieira where engineers were clearing the mouth of the river. By the time he returned to Marinha Grande four hours later:

> 'The Queen and all the Royal Family were up and dressed. They breakfasted in their different Apartments on Tea and Toast à Inglesa. Breakfast being over, their Travelling Altar was erected in the Queen's Dressing Room, where Mass [was] celebrated by one of her Majesty's Chaplains in the presence of the Royal Family and a few of their Attendants. This being over, they amused themselves in walking about the House and conversing very affable with any persons who came in their way.'

Philadelphia watched the royal women as they moved through her house and garden. Two years earlier, they had been dressed in black in mourning for Pedro. Now they wore 'Silk Riding Habits, every day a different one', with 'Broad Black Velvet Girdles round the waist, fastened before with two monstrous large Medallions set and ornamented with steel, which I believe were English'.

Maria wore her hair 'twined up before in a plain tight Toupet, behind in a Bag like the Gentlemen or in a Queue'. She carried 'a little old-fashioned Cocked Hat ... in her hand or under her arm. It is seldom she puts it on her Head but when she rides on Horseback'. Benedita's hair was 'frizzed before and tied in a Club behind' and she wore 'a large Hat in the English fashion, round the Crown of which was a Ribbon with a Knot on one side ornamented with Steel bows'.

Dinner was served at one o'clock, after which Maria told Philadelphia that 'she had eaten very hearty, everything being exceeding good'. Coffee was served while the royal carriages were prepared for an outing to Leiria. The family visited the cathedral and the bishop's palace and, later in the afternoon, the princes rode into the pine forest to inspect the sawmill, while the queen and her sisters visited a convent in the city. They 'examined every corner of it with satisfaction [and] left the poor Nuns highly impressed with Gratitude, not only for the Honour of the Visit, but also for her Majesty's Gracious Bounty of twenty Moydores which she left for their support'.

Tea was served after they returned to the factory, followed by another evening in the theatre. There was a comedy ('a laughable piece ... acted with great Humour'), a farce, more dances and pantomimes, and 'a Solo ... played on the Violoncello by a Young Man of Leiria who is studying Physic at Coimbra'. After the performance, 'the Royal Family returned to the house where Supper, Illuminations, Triumphal Cars and Fireworks concluded the diversions in the same manner as on the preceding night'.

Next morning, the family rose early and, while they dressed, ate breakfast and celebrated mass, the servants made preparations for departure. Horses and mules were brought from the stables and the royal carriages driven into the factory courtyard. The first to leave were José and Benedita, who were travelling direct to Caldas:

> 'On taking leave of her Royal Highness, I kissed her hand and thanked her for the Honour she had done us in this Visit and wished her a good Journey. In return she gave me an Abraço, thanked me for the Hospitable Entertainments she had received, and wished me Health and Happiness. My Brother took leave of the Prince in the same manner and attended him to the Door of the Carriage.'

The rest of the family, who were making a detour to the fishing village of Nazaré, departed an hour later. As she left her rooms on the first floor, Maria thanked Philadelphia:

> 'for the Entertainment we had given her, with a Countenance that indicated she was pleased with everything she had seen. [She] applauded very much the Industry of our People, the good order and management of the Fabrick, and the Harmony which subsisted between the People belonging to the Manufactory.'

As William accompanied the queen to her carriage:

> 'she again repeated her thanks for his Hospitality and drove away amidst the Acclamations of a great number of people who remained penetrated with love and respect for their Sovereign and all the Royal Family for their pleasing and affable deportment during their stay in this place.'

The carriages rumbled across the courtyard and passed through the factory gates. When the sound of the wheels had faded into the distance:

'Our House was open for every person who chose to see it. We had a large Company from Leiria and the Neighbourhood who dined with us at the Royal Table and, at night, the same Illuminations were repeated. The Tragedy of Sésostris, with the same new Dresses, Dances and Pantomimes as on the first night, were performed with universal applause to a numerous Audience, free admittance being granted (as is our usual custom to every person of all Ranks and Denominations). After the Play, our Company supped with us at the Royal Table, drank her Majesty's health, and concluded our three days Festival with no small satisfaction to ourselves and all our Neighbours, it being altogether such a sight as they had never seen before.'

Three weeks later, Philadelphia finished her long letter to Thomas Cogan in London. 'The first time of her Majesty's coming here,' she explained:

'was not so surprising, as curiosity to see the Glass Fabrick was supposed to be the motive, but that she should come a second time and sleep two Nights in the house of a private person, an Englishman and a Protestant, is a thing that never entered the Idea of the Portuguese and has struck all ... People with amazement. Her Majesty liked her Situation so well that she regretted leaving it and would have stayed longer had it not been for the unavoidable necessity of returning so soon to Lisbon. The Orders were already passed for the change of Beasts on the Road and everything to be got ready for their reception at the Praça de Comércio, and it was now too late to recede.'

During the visit, Maria had 'very politely taken every opportunity of praising everything'. She also hinted that she might come again the following year, 'as the royal family have some thoughts of going to Coimbra'.

18

A String of Tragedies

When sorrows come, they come not single spies,
But in battalions.
William Shakespeare, *Hamlet*

Maria and her family travelled through the dappled shade of the pine forest towards the fishing village of Nazaré. They stopped to pray at the chapel of Nossa Senhora de Nazaré (built to commemorate a foggy day in the twelfth century when a man was saved from riding his horse over a cliff by the miraculous appearance of the Virgin), before driving into the village to watch teams of oxen hauling boats up the beach and women laying the fish out to dry.

Meanwhile, José and Benedita travelled direct to Caldas, 'being afraid to stop … at Nazaré on account of the Smallpox which raged there, it being doubtful whether the Prince [has] had this disorder or not'.[1] Maria and Prince João were immune to the disease but José had never been diagnosed with smallpox, so it was thought wise for him to avoid the area.

Eight weeks after the family returned to Lisbon, José began to feel unwell. He complained of headache and fever and red spots began to appear on his skin. At first the doctors were optimistic. 'His Royal Highness is ill with the smallpox,' wrote Walpole on 6 September. 'This is the fifth day of its eruption and all the circumstances at present are favourable. He is said to have a considerable quantity, but of a good sort.'

Maria was confident in the diagnosis. Assuming that José would recover as quickly as João had done five years earlier, she continued to go out riding in the afternoons. On 8 September, the doctors changed their minds. The pox blisters had joined up over José's body; they had become 'the confluent sort'. For three days, Maria stayed in the palace, talking with the doctors, praying with her confessor. Her son's condition became critical in the early hours of 11 September. He was given the last rites as dawn broke over the Tagus and he died in the afternoon, 'at about three quarters after four'.

Church bells tolled, the air reverberated with discharges of artillery, and José's body was taken to the royal mausoleum in São Vicente de Fora. During her eight days of confinement in the palace, Maria's grief was exacerbated by guilt. Several royal houses had used inoculation against smallpox to protect their children but she had refused to consider it, partly because of the risks involved (a mortality rate of about 1 per cent), but mostly because of religious scruples. The procedure was, she said, against the will of God.

On 20 September, the foreign diplomats arrived in the palace to present their condolences. 'Her Majesty ... bears very strong expressions of affliction in her countenance,' wrote Robert Walpole, 'I think more than upon any former occasion.' The following day, she fled to Queluz.

José's death had several implications. The first was his widow, Benedita, who had lost the prospect of becoming queen-consort ('being so unfortunately and so suddenly deprived of the most brilliant prospect') and now had to give precedence to a tiny 13-year-old child. There was an 'affecting scene' one morning in chapel, 'a contest ... accompanied by tears and expressions of grief on both sides', as Carlota went through the motions of insisting that her sister-in-law retain her precedence. Maria grieved for Benedita, but she had to enforce the rules of etiquette. A few days later, when she settled 100,000 cruzados a year on her widowed sister, she was 'so much affected as hardly to be able to go through this afflicting ceremony'.

A second problem was the conflict between José's secular opinions and the queen's religiosity. In an emotional meeting between Walpole and Martinho do Melo a few days after the prince's death:

'A comparison was [made] between the pompous, vain, and expensive establishment of the Patriarchal Church and its attendants, and the more sober and beneficial public relations of King José, whose principles of government the late Prince of Brazil was disposed to adopt ... and I must do Monsieur de Melo the justice to say that everything he offered upon this subject appeared to come from the bottom of his heart, and with great emotion and sensibility he added that the reflecting upon what has happened was enough to make him mad, at the same time exclaiming upon the absurd prejudices received here against the practice of inoculation.'

Meanwhile, rumours were circulating that José had been 'allowed to die' by an establishment troubled by his liberal education. As Walpole explained:

'The nobility ... are very cautious and prudent upon the present occasion and silently lament the late melancholy event. But the imprudent of a lower class have not refrained ... from reflecting even upon the highest personages, as well as upon the ignorance and unskilfulness of the principal physician which, having reached her Majesty's ears, may have contributed to her resolution of retiring ... to Queluz.'

A third concern was the future of the monarchy. Benedita had no children and there was a 'great uncertainty of heirs by the Spanish Infanta ... who is as yet of a very diminutive stature'. The Marquis de Bombelles (who called Carlota 'an embryo' in the private pages of his diary) wrote that her restricted growth was an abnormality in an already defective family, 'more bad blood poured into narrow veins'.

The issue was more serious than the matter of children alone, for Bombelles also made the comment that João was 'angry at having resigned himself to marrying this stunted princess, this little spider monkey'. Walpole tried to put it more delicately:

> 'I avoid troubling your Lordship with the private speculations of some, or the greater freedom in language of others, with regard to what may be, or ought to be in contemplation upon the future fate of the Spanish Infanta ... as this is a subject of too delicate a nature, even for the most sincere well-wisher to the prosperity of this country.'

He not only referred to the 'great improbability of her having children', he also mentioned the 'dislike which the Prince may be disposed to have towards her'. He hinted that Portugal might ask for an annulment, so that Carlota could be sent back to Spain.

There was a precedent for this. Maria's mother was betrothed to Louis XV of France when she was 3 years old. She was taken into the French court and remained there for three years until it was thought expedient for Louis (aged 15 and in frail health) to beget an heir as soon as possible. Mariana was therefore returned to Madrid, a rejection which caused a political rift between the two countries. Walpole was concerned that an annulment might have the same result, a breach with Spain which Maria would find distressing. It was she who had nurtured good relations with her uncle Charles III, she who had arranged details of the double marriage in Vila Viçosa. Her ministers may have discussed the idea among themselves; it is unlikely that they were brave enough to bring it to her attention.

...

Maria remained in seclusion at Queluz for almost three months. On 4 November, she was heartened by the arrival of a special courier from Madrid with news that her daughter had given birth to a second son on 31 October. But Mariana was running a fever when she gave birth – and soon the familiar red spots appeared on her skin. For the next two days, as the spots turned into pimples and the pimples into blisters, special couriers left Madrid with the latest news. On 6 November, a letter arrived from Charles III: 'What I feared so much has become a reality, the loss of our Mariana. It grieves me to send you this terrible news.'

This second tragedy in less than two months 'occasioned a considerable degree of affliction to her Majesty', an affliction which deepened four days later when another letter arrived from her uncle in Spain:

> 'In all my life, I have never felt so sad. The day before yesterday, the doctors found smallpox in our new-born grandson, a disease he brought with him from his unfortunate mother's womb. It seems the pox is benign but God knows whether such a tender child will overcome this dreadful malady.'[2]

The infant died a few hours after this letter was written. Three weeks later, Maria received news that his father Gabriel had died from the same disease.

On 28 November, Inácio de São Caetano – the confessor on whom she placed her entire trust and confidence – suffered a massive stroke in the palace of Queluz. He was 70 years old and, as he lay dying, he asked Maria to pardon him 'for any harm he may have caused her, for any discredit he may have brought upon her'.

In the space of eleven weeks, Maria had lost two of her three surviving children, as well as her main pillar of strength and support. Alone amongst her advisers, São Caetano had the ability to soothe her troubled mind. His death was, as Walpole put it:

> 'a serious loss to the Queen as she had been accustomed to put her confidence in this person for a considerable number of years and had permitted her conscience to be guided by him since her accession to the throne, in matters very much out of his sphere, or education or intelligence.'

In December, another letter arrived from Spain. Charles III had died on the 14th, three weeks after his favourite son. 'Gabriel is dead,' he had written in November. 'I shall follow him soon.'

...

On 16 December, Maria raised the courage to appoint two additional secretaries of state. This had become a matter of urgency since Marquis de Angeja died in March, leaving the cabinet in the hands of Martinho de Melo and Ponte de Lima, both of whom were 'overloaded with business'. Now some fresh blood entered the cabinet. Luís Pinto de Sousa Coutinho (who had recently served as Portuguese minister in London) was given the portfolio of foreign affairs, and José de Seabra e Silva (whom Pombal had exiled to Angola) was appointed secretary of state for home affairs. Ponte de Lima would continue to run the treasury and act as Maria's first minister.

The delay in making these appointments was partly due to the queen's indecision and partly the result of a disagreement between São Caetano and Prince José. São Caetano had been lobbying for the inclusion of Seabra but José held a grudge against him ('the Prince is not favourably disposed towards that gentleman'), perhaps resenting his intervention in 1774 which (probably) cost him the throne. Now, with both José and São Caetano in their graves, the abbess in Estrela had taken up the matter. As Walpole explained:

> 'The sudden resolution in favour of these two gentlemen has been a complete defeat to the nobility, who had planned for themselves the different departments of government ... This measure is said to be another of the requests of the late Confessor ... and has been accomplished by means of the Abbess.'

The following day, during an official audience to celebrate her fifty-fourth birthday, Maria and Robert Walpole discussed her new secretaries of state, particularly Luís Pinto who had impressed the British government during his years in London. They also spoke of the mental health of George III who was suffering his first attack of madness (a mania now believed to have been a form of bipolar disorder). The illness had first appeared in November and the king was in the care of Francis Willis, a doctor who specialised in treatment of the insane. During the conversation, Maria 'expressed her concern for his Majesty and her sincere wishes of a speedy re-establishment of his Majesty's health'.

These were poignant words, for Maria herself was on the cusp of insanity. Her grandfather, Philip V of Spain, and her uncle, Ferdinand VI, both suffered from mental illness and both had lost all reason by the end of their lives. There are many parallels between their symptoms and Maria's condition which began to appear at about this time.

Philip believed that fire was consuming him from the inside as divine punishment for his sins. His moods swung between extreme lethargy and outbursts of violent frenzy. He screamed and howled for hours at a time, he sang aloud and bit himself. He refused to have his beard shaved or his hair and toenails cut. He believed himself unable to walk because his feet were of different sizes.

Ferdinand inherited his father's illness. He lived in fear of sudden death, convinced that his body was being destroyed internally, that he would die if he lay down. He refused to be washed, shaved or dressed. He refused food, taking liquid refreshment only. He banged his head against the wall and attacked his servants. In a manic phase, he would spend ten days or more without sleep. At other times, he would become completely inert.

This was the illness which lay in wait for Maria – and the abbess of the convent in Estrela did her no favours when she recommended her nephew, José Maria de Melo, the 30-year-old Bishop of Algarve, as her new confessor. Appointed to the post on 5 December, he was described by Walpole as 'very devout', and by William Beckford as a 'very young looking' man, 'whose small, black, sleek, schoolboyish head and sallow countenance was overshadowed by an enormous pair of green spectacles'.[3]

Inácio de São Caetano had made light of the horrors of hell; by taking 'her soul upon himself', he had kept Maria on a reasonably even keel. Her new confessor was the worst possible choice. Related to the nobility, he put pressure on Maria to rehabilitate families implicated in the Távora conspiracy. At the same time, he enjoyed preaching about the terrors of hell and he gave his queen no comfort, preferring to heighten her dread of hellfire which, he told her, was waiting for her just around the corner.

For more than thirty years, Maria had agonised over her father's complicity in the persecution of so many of his subjects. Now she became convinced that his soul would suffer eternal damnation. There was nothing she could do to repair the damage, so she believed that she too was damned and would burn forever in the infernal flames.

19

A Fragile Mind

Her Majesty was firmly persuaded she was in hell, saying that a skilful
physician may sometimes cure madness, but never reverse the decrees of fate.
Dr Francis Willis on Maria I of Portugal[1]

aria's mental state was growing increasingly fragile but, despite
anxieties and night panics, she retained a grip on reality for most of
the next three years. She was sometimes 'indisposed', unable to meet
with her ministers, but she managed to deal with most of her public appearances.
In early 1789, she spent several weeks in Salvaterra. In April, she 'testified her joy'
at the recovery of George III, attended a Te Deum in a convent of English nuns,
and 'visited a Portuguese ship of war in Lisbon harbour'. In June, she watched
the army on manoeuvres near Queluz. In early July, the outbreak of the French
Revolution gave rise – as Walpole put it – to 'a great deal of seriousness at Court'.

A few weeks later, Prince João suffered an attack of mumps, an illness which
led to 'a good deal of uneasiness, chiefly on account of the particular situation
of this Royal Family'. Partly because of the mumps, but mostly because of
Carlota's doubtful fertility, the secretaries of state hatched a plan to bring
Maria's only grandchild, Pedro Carlos, to Lisbon. 'There seemed to be nothing
left for the security and tranquillity of this country,' Luís Pinto told Walpole,
'than bringing the Prince into Portugal.'

Pedro Carlos was a Bourbon but, if the fundamental law against foreign
princes was repealed and the boy was brought up in the Portuguese court, the
people might, if João and Carlota failed to have children, accept him as their
sovereign. Charles IV of Spain agreed and it was soon arranged that the boy
would leave for Portugal in the autumn with the extended name of Pedro Carlos
de Bourbon e Bragança.

By the end of August, João was feeling better and Maria ordered celebrations
to mark his recovery. In October, the 3-year-old Pedro Carlos arrived in
Portugal, received at the border by Marquis de Marialva who accompanied
him to Lisbon. The first time the child appeared in public, Maria ordered that
all members of the court should kiss his hand in submission. 'It may not be
improper to observe,' commented Walpole, 'that this intimation has not been
received without having been silently criticised.'

Maria's new church, the Basilica da Estrela, was now almost complete. Constructed of white limestone, the interior lined with 'a great variety of fine marble', it had been built 'at enormous expense which is supposed will amount to not much less than a million sterling'. The building was consecrated – in a service of 'great solemnity' – on 15 November in the presence of the royal family and the court. The proceedings, which lasted all day, must have been painful for Maria who had commissioned the church in thanksgiving for the birth of her elder son who now lay in the mausoleum at São Vicente de Fora.

Her distress at this time was increased by events in France which the *Gazeta de Lisboa* was reporting in colourful detail. Terrified that the people of Portugal would rise against her, she banned the editor from publishing any further bulletins from Paris (which 'had produced some shrewd observations from the lower class of persons here'). She asked Luís Pinto to arrange for confidential dispatches to be sent from France and, as the news worsened, every report of mob violence, every example of disrespect to the French royal family, filled her with dread.

...

In March 1790, Carlota experienced her first period, a loss of blood which led to much rejoicing. 'It is a matter of great joy and satisfaction to this Court,' wrote Walpole on the 24th, 'that the state of nubility of the Infanta Dona Carlota … is no longer doubtful and it is decided therefore that she is to cohabit with the Prince of Brazil about the 25th of next month, her birthday.'

João was unwilling to wait for four more weeks, so Maria brought the date forward. 'Our beloved Carlota has reached full womanhood without the slightest trouble,' she wrote to Carlota's mother (Maria Luísa) in Spain:

> 'Even before this, I was intending to let them get together, however briefly, as she was so well-informed about everything and João was so keen for conjugal relations. Now we are beyond doubt, it will happen over Easter and I feel great happiness.'[2]

During the evening of 5 April, Maria helped to undress Carlota and place her in the marriage bed. She waited until João arrived, prayed with them for the success of their union, then left the room. It was a night for which João had been waiting for almost five years. He and Carlota had grown to dislike each other intensely, but he still wanted to 'play with' his little wife. Next morning, Maria wrote another letter to Maria Luísa: 'Our beloved Carlota joined herself with her husband yesterday. They spent the night together well and are very happy.'

In May, Maria and her son 'amused themselves with reviewing the infantry'. In October, she was 'somewhat indisposed'. In December, she reduced the number of her official audiences. She also signed an edict lifting the mark of infamy from Duke de Aveiro's son, an occasion which triggered another attack of hysteria. In January 1791, she left for Salvaterra and Walpole assured the British government that she was 'in perfect good health'.

In June, news arrived from France that Louis XVI had been captured while trying to flee the country and was now imprisoned in the Tuileries. 'Considerably affected' by the news, Maria sent two million cruzados 'to the service of the French King's cause'. In August, she spent two weeks at Mafra where she laid the foundation stone of a new convent. Despite sharing a bed with João for sixteen months, Carlota showed no signs of pregnancy and the stone was inscribed with a dedication to St Anthony: 'in hopes of the continuance of the progeny of the Royal Family.'

On 28 September, Maria attended the launch of a frigate. A few days later, she 'began to sink into a great melancholy, with night-time distress, interrupted sleep and a sinking of the spirits'. In November, she failed to appear at official audiences. At the end of the month, with masterly understatement, Walpole reported that 'her Majesty, although not afflicted with any very serious disorder, does not think herself perfectly well and complains of pains in her stomach and want of sleep'.

She remained 'very low spirited' throughout December and doctors were called to 'consult upon the causes of her uneasiness and apprehensions'. On 4 January, she was 'blooded', a procedure she found distressing ('she was very averse to the bleeding... She does not allow that she was in the least relieved by it'). João made plans to take her to Salvaterra, to remove her from the influence of the abbess to whom she was making 'frequent and long visits' and returning to the palace full of gloom and 'melancholy reflections'.

The winter rains had arrived and the departure for Salvaterra was postponed several times before the family finally embarked on 14 January. Two weeks later, Walpole reported that 'her Majesty's health has not received any advantage from her removal to Salvaterra where the rains, which have continued since her arrival there, must have rendered that residence very unhealthy as well as inconvenient'.

Towards the end of the month, Maria's new confessor produced a paper for her to sign. It was connected to the rehabilitation of families implicated in the Távora conspiracy and it 'made a deep impression' on her mind. She became 'very much indisposed' towards her confessor and he, 'suspecting he had gone too far ... fell sick and was blooded in consequence of it'.

This reminder of her father's complicity in Pombal's reign of terror was too much for Maria to bear. She became hysterical. Doctors were called from Lisbon and, by the end of the month, it was decided that 'her Majesty should return to Lisbon to take the baths of Alcaçarias'. On the evening of 2 February, she was considered calm enough to attend an opera in the theatre – but she broke down completely during the performance, throwing a fit far worse than any she had suffered in recent days. She had to be lifted up and carried into her bedroom where she screamed and howled through the night.

The morning of 3 February dawned overcast and grey as the servants prepared to take the queen home to Lisbon. On the river, the *Real Bergantim* was cleaned and polished, the gold dragon on the prow shining bright through the morning drizzle. Eighty oarsmen dressed themselves in resplendent livery of red and gold. Servants in the kitchen prepared refreshments which were carried on board: plates of exquisitely prepared food, flagons of spring water, lemonade and wine.

When everything was ready, Maria was led to the river bank and settled on the velvet cushions in the cabin. During the next few hours, the creaking of timbers, the rhythm of the oars, the sound of rain falling on water, all helped to calm her distress. She was 'in a tranquil state' when the barge arrived at the Praça do Comércio. The great square was filled with people who had heard rumours of her 'indisposition' and come to see their queen. The oars were raised to the vertical, the barge came to a halt at the quayside, and Maria was hustled into a carriage for the short journey across the square to the Senate House. A short time later, her pale face appeared at a first-floor window, greeted by cheers from the crowds below.

Since October, the doctors had given out that Maria had no 'serious or alarming disorder'. By the evening of 4 February, 'the government could no longer conceal … the real state of her Majesty's health'. Public entertainments were cancelled, prayers were intoned in churches and convents, sacred images were carried in procession to the Senate House, and Luís Pinto wrote a long letter to the Portuguese minister in London:

'It is with great sadness that I inform you that her Majesty is suffering from a melancholic affliction which has descended into insanity, into what is feared to be a total frenzy. In view of this unfortunate situation, I believe it would be helpful for Dr Willis, the principal doctor who assisted his British Majesty in similar circumstances, to come to this Court as soon as possible. You will provide him with all the money he might request, with no limitations. You will agree to all he proposes, should you enter into a contract with him, and will leave the remuneration to the generous discretion of this Court …

'The Queen has always been of a gloomy temperament and subject to nervous afflictions. Her disposition is one of great meekness and a certain shyness, her imagination vivid, her habits inclined towards spirituality. For years she has suffered from stomach ailments and spasms of the abdomen, which are worsened by the aversion she has to purgative medicines, especially enemas to which she would never consent.'[3]

During the next few weeks, Maria's behaviour swung between extreme lassitude and violent excitement, sometimes remaining awake at night 'with very little repose'. She was bled again on 11 February. She was taken to the baths at Alcaçarias and struggled violently as she was placed in the water, with a force 'greater than could naturally have been expected'. She refused to eat ('though in the course of the day, she eats as it were by stealth what is placed in different parts of the apartment'). She refused to take medicine. She dismissed the royal musicians who were playing in an adjacent room, alleging that it was 'improper' to listen to music 'while prayers and processions are observed for the recovery of her health'.

Religion – and the fear of damnation – caused her the greatest anguish. Sometimes she was quieter, with 'intervals of reminiscence and reasonable talk', but she became agitated if she was taken to chapel or saw a religious procession from the windows of the palace. When she did speak coherently, 'she returns to the first idea that afflicted her, that she is condemned, that there is no help for her salvation'.

The abbess in Estrela wrote to the pope, asking for dispensation to leave the convent and visit the queen, an offer which Prince João had the sense to refuse. Maria's ministers begged him to take charge of affairs of state, but he found it impossible to conquer what Walpole referred to as 'his respect and condescension to the Queen'. Although he agreed to sign documents in his mother's name on 10 February, he was unwilling to pick up the reins of government and state business came to a standstill for several months.

...

Meanwhile, the Portuguese minister in London was negotiating with Dr Francis Willis who ran a private lunatic asylum in Lincolnshire. He had been called to treat George III in December 1788 and his reputation was greatly enhanced when the king recovered his senses a few months later. Now he was summoned to Lisbon and paid £20,000 (almost £3 million in today's values) to treat the queen of Portugal.

Willis had some psychological insight, but treatment of the mentally ill was brutal at the time and he favoured straitjackets, coercion, blistering, and water baths, as well as complete physical and mental domination over his patients. He arrived in Lisbon on 15 March 1792 and soon discovered that Maria's condition (which appears to have been a particularly severe form of bi-polar disorder) was not susceptible to his 'scientific' treatments.

His first suggestion was that the family should move to Queluz; it was more peaceful in the countryside and Maria could be taken into the gardens away from public scrutiny. He also hoped to remove her from the courtiers and ministers who were encouraging her to attend mass and say prayers. 'Whether the doctor will succeed in this part of his recommendation is very doubtful,' explained Walpole, 'considering the difficulty of changing the customs of etiquette of this Court.' Protocol demanded that courtiers pay their respects to the queen every day and Prince João was too timid and immature to direct otherwise.

Another visitor to the queen's apartments was Maria's confessor who was, according to Walpole, 'exceedingly distressed in regard to the scruples of his office'. When his behaviour at Salvaterra became public knowledge, he found himself blamed for the queen's 'alienation of mind'. He was insulted in the streets and treated at court 'with very little respect'. Denied access to the queen, he lurked about the antechambers and engaged her ladies-in-waiting in earnest conversations.

Maria's condition continued to deteriorate at Queluz. Sometimes she was violent and distressed ('returned to her state of despair upon the subject of her salvation'). At other times she was more cheerful ('in a humour of singing which I doubt very much is a favourable symptom'). Now Willis began to use his more brutal treatments. She was constrained in a straitjacket, she had blistering ointments applied to her legs, she was immersed in ice-cold baths ('not without a considerable amount of resistance … followed by an aguish fever'). To rid her body of evil humours, she was given enemas and emetics, and because she refused to eat, an instrument was made 'for the conveying of nourishment down her throat'.

His treatments may have been cruel but Dr Willis understood, in a way that no member of the court was willing to accept, that Maria's condition was exacerbated by religious imagery. In June, he asked her a few probing questions:

> 'Dr Willis endeavoured by his conversations with her Majesty to discover whether her malady is not occasioned by political as well as religious motives. Her Majesty answered that that was a matter of the greatest secrecy. He then asked her whether any paper which related to the noblemen of a passed period had been produced for her to sign. She answered in the negative. He then asked her why she had forbidden the confessor to appear in her presence, to which she remained silent. After reflecting on this conversation, she appeared to be uneasy at having gone too far and said too much.'

Meanwhile, he was unable to prevent 'the bustle and preparations' for the Corpus Christi procession at Queluz and soon realised that his only hope was to remove the queen from the source of her terror. The journey downriver from Salvaterra had calmed her and when (after 'some opposition') she allowed João to take her sailing on the river, she behaved 'pretty quietly' on board the royal yacht. So Dr Willis recommended a sea voyage.

This led to a misunderstanding. The doctor's intention was to remove Maria from the people who surrounded her, but João simply assumed that the government and the court would embark with her. He ordered several ships to be fitted out for the purpose. When Willis explained that this was not what he had in mind, ministers, nobles and priests were all asked for their opinion. Most of them raised objections, and some of them talked to Maria about the 'dangers of going to sea', giving her 'an aversion and opposition' to the idea. On the night of 8 July, her 'apprehensions were so much increased that a very severe fever ensued'. Next morning, the plan was abandoned and Dr Willis resigned.

Maria was distressed that the doctor was leaving. He had gained her confidence and she was 'persuaded that she shall grow worse when he shall have left the country'. In August, 'upon a pretext that she had desired to hear Mass ... she was carried to chapel ... but behaved in a very extravagant manner and has since been so very much disturbed that her attendants have been obliged to use constraint'. By September, she was declining 'towards a state of childishness'.

João appointed a new doctor from Coimbra, a man with no experience of mental illness, and Maria sank further into her private world of despair. 'Her Majesty is in a most melancholy state,' wrote Walpole on 31 March 1793. 'Her memory seems to have left her and she has but a confused idea of persons and things.'

Four weeks later, concerns about the future of the Bragança monarchy came to an end with the birth of Carlota's first child on 29 April. João ordered the usual celebrations in Lisbon, as well as great festivities at Queluz: bullfights, displays of shifting lights, and an illuminated hot-air balloon that, released from the gardens, rose into the night sky until it disappeared from sight.

...

As the months passed, there was little change in Maria's condition. By the summer of 1794, she was still 'in the same unfortunate state of mind ... frequently very fretful, very much disposed to a perfect indifference to everything, and dreading every incitement to exertion'. Soon her sister Mariana began to show signs of the same disease – 'afflicted with the same melancholy disorder' – the third of José's four daughters to fall prey to this distressing inheritance.

On 8 November, after spending the summer and autumn in Queluz, the family returned to the Real Barraca accompanied by a long train of carriages and carts piled high with the royal furniture and furnishings. Two days later, a fire broke out in a servant's room. The alarm was raised at eight o'clock in the evening and 'the flames began to spread so rapidly that the whole family was obliged to make their escape in the greatest haste'. Maria, who remained remarkably calm, was taken 'to a place of safety at a little distance'. Benedita walked to a nearby house 'on the arm of one of the helpers in the kitchen'. Only Mariana showed signs of distress, becoming 'exceedingly violent in an increased paroxysm of the disorder'.

By ten o'clock, 'the whole edifice was in a blaze' and João and Carlota stood in the gardens, watching the flames devour the wooden building which had served as the royal palace for almost forty years. According to the British consul, 'the jewels, most of the plate, the papers and part of the library, some wearing apparel and a very small portion of the furniture are the only things saved'. Later that night, the royal carriages returned to Queluz. The servants made the family as comfortable as they could but, because all their furniture and furnishings had been consumed in the fire, 'the royal personages suffered considerable inconvenience'.

After the loss of the Real Barraca, João and his family took up official residence at Queluz. A pavilion had been completed in the grounds in 1789, originally intended to house the apartments of José and Benedita. Now it became Maria's place of confinement where she lived in seclusion with her servants and attendants. Every day, she was taken into the gardens for fresh air and exercise, and travellers on the road to Sintra – who could look down into the palace grounds from a nearby hill – sometimes saw her there, her long white hair hanging loose around her shoulders.

Part Three

Prince João

20

The Hat-Trick

Persist in this brave patriotism.
And should this brutish world
Overlook your heroism,
Never fear that it will be forgotten
Amongst right-thinking men,
The good you have done to so many people.

Leonor de Almeida Lorena (Marquesa de Alorna),
Ode to William Stephens, c.1795[1]

The death of Prince José so soon after his visit to Marinha Grande came as a shock to William and Philadelphia, particularly since he had avoided the detour to Nazaré because of the smallpox there. They grieved for Maria, the gracious and dignified woman who had enjoyed a few days of simple pleasure at the glassworks, time to relax in congenial surroundings away from the formality and intrigues of the court.

On the few occasions that William attended court during the next three years, he found the queen much changed. She no longer responded to his compliments with a warm smile or engaged him in conversation about music and the theatre. There was no royal journey to Coimbra, no more visits to the factory. Maria's withdrawal from public life was distressing from a business perspective too. Five years after he had forged a friendship with the Marquis de Pombal, the minister fell from power and he had to make the effort again, wooing the new queen with his personality and charm. He had succeeded – possibly beyond his wildest dreams – but her mental breakdown led to another transfer of power. So, making the effort for the third time, he set out to charm Prince João. And he was sharp enough to turn the problems at court to his advantage.

In the spring of 1789, he had come under renewed attack from the glaziers of Lisbon, who complained that their exclusive right to cut sheets of window glass had been contravened by the decree of 1773 which gave permission for window glass to be cut at Marinha Grande. Their petition was considered by the Junta do Comércio and, on the grounds that 'cutting and preparing glass for use in window panes is an essential part of the glaziers' specialist trade', William lost the right to sell pre-cut window panes in Lisbon, the largest market, but retained permission to do so elsewhere in the country.

This represented a considerable loss of added-value. It also meant that William had to compete like-for-like with window glass from Bohemia, which was of better quality and (by defrauding the customs) still entering Portugal in significant quantities. Because of these illicit imports, William's sales had failed to keep pace with production for several years. His stocks were accumulating and, in 1792, he geared himself up for another fight with the merchants.

He produced a set of accounts showing the annual value of glass produced between 1769 and 1791 (with estimated figures for 1792), together with the value of sales in Lisbon and Oporto. He then wrote a petition to the government. He explained that capital was tied up in more than 1,000 boxes of unsold window glass, valued at more than 38 contos of reis, sufficient to meet consumption in Portugal and its colonies for at least two years. To maintain employment, the workshop was continuing to operate at normal capacity and he asked that all imports of window glass be prohibited, 'for the benefit of the national industry and the numerous families who work in this factory'.

Although the petition was well-written and appeared plausible, the value for unsold window glass was heavily inflated. Stocks had accumulated to less than 19 contos of reis by 1791, but the total value was boosted by estimated figures for 1792 which showed production increasing by more than 50 per cent over the previous year. Too intelligent to have increased production at a time when his stocks were accumulating, William had exaggerated the figures to give greater force to his petition.

This was a time of turmoil and uncertainty at court; Maria was losing her senses and Prince João was reluctant to assume responsibility for affairs of state. Taking advantage of this hiatus in government, William timed his petition well. No questions were asked about his estimated figures and, in January 1793, his monopoly was enhanced when the prince signed a decree prohibiting all foreign window glass from entering the country.

This infuriated the merchants, prompting one of them to publish an official complaint against him. If William had been 'less preoccupied with ambition, he would have been content with the privileges and exemptions already conferred on him and would not have prevented her Majesty from receiving taxes on imported glass while he pays no tax at all'. Glass from Marinha Grande was 'of poor quality [and] should not be protected with such diligence, as if it was the most important item in the kingdom, as if the happiness of the monarchy depended on it'.

William's glass had always been of lower quality than that produced elsewhere in Europe. With a monopoly of supply, he had little incentive to improve standards and he was certainly aware of the value of repeat sales, particularly at the lower end of the market. One evening, when he was staying in a tavern in Rio Maior, he dropped his wine glass on the floor. Surprised that it remained intact, he borrowed a hammer but the glass was so thick and strong that it took several blows to shatter it. On his return to Marinha Grande, he ordered the administrator to alter the composition of tavern glasses. 'It is against the interests of the factory,' he told him, 'to make tableware that is difficult to break.'

With his tax exemptions due to expire in 1794 and concerned that the merchant's complaint might damage his standing at court, William turned his attention to Prince João, a placid man with a good heart who had enjoyed his three days at the glassworks. But João was slow-thinking and indecisive, and it was not until May 1794 that he confirmed his royal protection of the factory. He extended the exemption from sales taxes for a further ten years (but made no mention of import duties on utensils and raw materials).

William had achieved the hat-trick, the patronage of three people who wielded supreme power in Portugal. They each enriched the glassworks for a decade – Marquis de Pombal in the 1770s, Queen Maria in the 1780s, Prince João in the 1790s – and by the turn of the century, he had built up one of the largest industrial fortunes in history, a fortune estimated at more than £100 million in today's values.

...

William was not the only foreigner to run a successful factory in Portugal. The Frenchman, Jacome Ratton, had set up several industries in the country, also with help from the government. He and William were of similar age. They were on friendly terms and, in his memoirs, Ratton described William as 'a man of genius and sound judgement who, although an Englishman, has always showed the greatest interest in the advancement and prosperity of the Portuguese nation'.[2]

One of Ratton's many projects was the preservation of the port of São Martinho, 25 miles from Marinha Grande and used to dispatch consignments of glass by sea to Lisbon and Oporto. The shallow circular harbour, protected from the Atlantic by two projecting arms of rock, was slowly silting up. On the assumption that sand causing the damage was carried by two rivers which discharged into the basin, Ratton asked William to investigate the matter. William surveyed the area and recommended that the rivers be diverted along a canal cut through the hill to the south of the harbour. He drew a map detailing the course of the new waterway and – not a man to be unnerved by a large undertaking – hired a team of workmen and started digging through the rock.

The project was cancelled for lack of funds, but the port remained in use and glass from Marinha Grande continued to be dispatched in small ships from the harbour. When William built a second house behind the Largo do Stephens in 1789, he used the port to transport wooden beams from the pine forest. The sale of timber for building purposes was prohibited at the time (all trunks were reserved for use in the royal dockyard), so he could only take 'the refuse beams that have lain here a considerable time unsaleable, the interior part of them greatly decayed'. At the same time, he reopened one of the kilns in Alcântara to provide lime for the new building.

Two years later, he was granted free use of the sturdier trunks in the forest to build an eight-mile road linking Marinha Grande with the new public highway from Lisbon to Coimbra. Still known today as the *Estrada do Guilherme* (William's Road), it was completed in 1793 and allowed him to transport a greater proportion of his glass overland. He had taken advice about load-bearing and drainage from engineers in England, and his road was built using techniques which were new to Portugal. When Prince João renewed his privileges the following year, he congratulated him on 'a gift to the country, an undertaking which has earned the benefit of my royal protection'.

The Estrada do Guilherme made the journey to Marinha Grande much easier, particularly after 1798 when stagecoaches began to travel the highway to Coimbra. William was well-known for offering hospitality to English travellers; he entertained poets and writers, statesmen and diplomats, and men of science and the arts, many of whom made the journey north from Lisbon to visit the great monasteries of Batalha and Alcobaça. 'Batalha will be more conveniently visited from Marinha,' explained *The Lisbon Guide*, 'where the noble glass factory of Mr Stephens presents a picture of English liberality and industry, highly gratifying to the vanity of his countrymen.'[3]

William Withering, the doctor who discovered the benefits of digitalis in the treatment of heart disease, stayed at the glassworks in the winter of 1792 when he was conducting a study into the benefits of the spa waters at Caldas da Rainha (which he found to be 'truly efficacious'). He arrived in Marinha Grande before the new roads were completed and made the comment that 'what would have been considered in England as only a journey of a day, was in Portugal a formidable undertaking, from the miserable accommodation on the road, and the difficulty in making progress'.

Withering was a member of the Lunar Society of Birmingham, a group of men who met monthly – near the time of the full moon – to discuss new developments in science and technology, a society which included such luminaries as Erasmus Darwin, Josiah Wedgwood and James Watt. He and William talked long into the night, their discussions ranging through scientific discoveries, industrial progress, advances in horticulture, and political developments in Europe (Withering had been an advocate of the French Revolution and his house had been targeted during the Birmingham riots of 1791).

They also discussed the financial operation of the glassworks. William explained that, in full production, 'three furnaces are lighted, each of which produces £50 value of glass per day'. He employed 300 men, including carters working in the pine forest, and his 'weekly wages amount to about £200'. The factory buildings had cost £22,000, although 'the same buildings in England would have cost perhaps more than one fourth less ... the carriage to this place of the materials for them having been very considerable'. This investment in buildings, together with 'about the value of 30,000 moydores in glass always on hand', provided a total capital of 'more than £100,000', from which William was making '10 to 12 per cent profit'.

A friend of Josiah Wedgwood, Withering would certainly have visited Etruria, the factory in Stoke-on-Trent which Wedgwood opened in 1769 (the same year that William reopened the factory in Marinha Grande). His high opinion of the glassworks is the more remarkable considering the lack of industrial technology in Portugal and the relative shortage of skill among Portuguese workers:

'The buildings of this manufactory ... are remarkably complete, and the utmost regularity prevails in each department. The genius of this worthy man has changed the face of the country, and the character of its inhabitants. The workmen are clean and industrious; men, women and children appear to be excited by a laudable emulation; and a general spirit of exertion pervades the whole district ... their habits are civil, obliging and orderly [and] labour and amusement are happily combined.'[4]

As well as establishing a profitable and well-run factory, creating a welfare state which was revolutionary for its time, reorganising the agriculture and horticulture of the region, and building roads and surveying harbours, William wrote treatises on bee-keeping and the cultivation of alfalfa, burnt seaweed to provide alkali for industrial use, and experimented with the production of tempered glass.

During his visit to Marinha Grande, Dr Withering asked him to send samples of his tempered glass to England. Almost five years later, he forwarded them to James Watt and Sir Joseph Banks, president of the Royal Society. As he explained to Banks on 31 October 1797:

'When I was in Portugal, I had the pleasure of forming an acquaintance with Mr Stephens, the proprietor of the great glass manufactory in that country. Acting immediately under the patronage of the Government and unrestrained by the laws of excise, he has made many experiments to improve the properties of glass and to ascertain the best and cheapest modes of its composition. In one of these experiments, he made a kind which he calls "tough glass" and which he describes as having the property of bearing the vicissitudes of heat and cold much better than the common flint glass.'

William had proved the 'toughness' of his glass to Withering, first by placing a tumbler on a marble slab and filling it with boiling water, then by heating the glass in a lamp before dropping it into a tub of cold water. In both cases, the glass had remained intact:

> 'These experiments convinced me that a glass with such properties must be highly acceptable to the chemical philosophers, and I requested Mr Stephens to make me a few chemical vessels which he was so good to do, and though I have hitherto made but little use of them, I am satisfied of their utility … Mr Watt has made some further trials on this kind of glass which I shall leave him to relate. I shall not forget your request to Mr Stephens to send a piece of a proper thickness for optical purposes; but from what I recollect of its composition, I doubt whether it will have sufficient density.'[5]

James Watt subjected William's 'tough glass' to a series of experiments which he detailed in a long letter to Sir Joseph Banks on 5 November. 'From all that I have seen,' he concluded, 'the glass in question bears the alternatives of heat and cold much better than any other I have had occasion to try.'[6]

Banks was less fortunate and had to wait for another consignment from Marinha Grande. 'I fear it was my inexperience in manipulation which broke Mr Stephens's glass,' he explained to Withering on 23 December. 'I shall heartily rejoice to have it in my power to do it more justice if you favour me with any part of the cargo you expect.' Five months later:

> 'Mr Stephens's glasses are not yet in my hands but I expect them tomorrow as I gave the bill of lading to my broker some days ago. I wish much to put their beneficial qualities to a fair trial before I write to Mr Stephens and I mean to put them into the hands of my chemical friends the moment I get them. If they prove useful in the chemical, the optical or any other line, I shall know how to thank Mr Stephens for having confided the receipt to me.'[7]

The samples were delivered to Banks on 19 May 1798, after which he began to correspond with William in Marinha Grande. By December, as the merchant Antony Gibbs explained:

> 'He is now in correspondence with Sir Joseph Banks … who has lately suggested to him a still further improvement, and will probably have ordered experiments of the same kind to be made in England.'

…

Antony Gibbs was a friend of the Stephens family who stayed in the Largo do Stephens whenever he was on business in Lisbon. He spent a week in Marinha Grande in December 1798 and was deeply impressed with William's achievements in the village. 'In the delightful retreat of the Glass Fabrick at Marinha,' he wrote to his brother:

'I shall endeavour to amuse you by talking a little of this charming establishment. I really never saw or heard of so excellent an establishment of the kind in all its points. Whether you look to it as calculated for the promotion of useful industry, going hand in hand with the pecuniary interest of its master, or take it simply as an establishment for the promotion of happiness among the people employed in it, a careful observer must ... allow that the end proposed seems to be most effectually obtained ...

'The fruits of industry are so often squandered at an alehouse instead of going to the families of industrious men. One may see clearly here that this consideration has all along been uppermost in the mind of Mr Stephens; he saw that innocent amusement for the leisure hours of his people was what was wanted in order to make them happy and their families comfortable in consequence of their working hard through the week ... I will confess to you that, without having seen it, I should not have thought it possible that a life of constant occupation at proper hours ... could be so nicely blended as we see it here with hours of great and varied entertainment ...

'On seeing those things ... one is apt to conclude that they must be acquired at the expense of neglecting some other of the more necessary callings in life, but I declare I never saw any fabrick where such strict discipline was established and observed with respect to the hours of attendance, or where more diligence appeared through the work of the day. Mr Stephens tells me that no drink but water is ever allowed in the fabrick at working hours and, generally speaking, the people here live to a great age ...

'Mr Stephens has some great advantages, and if he were a necessitous man, might make, I believe, a vast deal more money by the fabrick than he does. But he is already one of the richest men in Portugal, and there is not, I suppose, a better man in any country ... His will is a law with the whole fabrick. No monarch had ever more absolute power, he reigns in the hearts of all the people here, they only want to know what he likes in order to do it. I was always proud of his friendship, but never so much so as now ... There is hardly what may be called a poor family in the place.'[8]

21

The Gathering Storm

*No result of invasion ... would be more hateful than banishment ... across
the Atlantic to those whose excursions had hitherto been confined to a journey
between their town and country residence at home.*
Henry Brougham, secretary to Lord St Vincent's mission to Lisbon, 1806

The French Revolution, which caused such dread in Maria's mind, led to the outbreak of war in April 1792, less than three months after Prince João began signing documents in his mother's name. Following her example, he declared a state of 'most perfect neutrality' but, after Britain entered the war in February 1793, he agreed to provide 'mutual aid' during the hostilities. The most important aid that Portugal could offer its ancient ally was a safe harbour in the Tagus, so the closure of Portuguese ports to British shipping became an important objective in French military strategy.

Maria had done little to improve the country's defences; João did little to prepare for the coming hostilities. Apart from a few ships and some military manoeuvres, he made no preparations for war, no contingency plans for invasion. His lack of education, limited intelligence and indecisive personality left him paralysed in an increasingly dangerous situation. 'No one doubts the natural good qualities of the Prince of Brazil,' wrote a visitor to Portugal, 'but his talents are questionable and ... he has no striking passions or inclinations except, perhaps, that for the chase.'[1]

In August 1796, Spain entered the war in alliance with France. Four months later, a British squadron arrived in the Tagus (under the command of Admiral Sir John Jervis) with orders to report on Portugal's naval defences. Jervis was unimpressed. As he wrote to the Admiralty on 28 December:

> 'It becomes me to apprise you that no reliance whatever can be placed on the Portuguese marine for the defence of the country. The arsenal is unprovided, owing to ... the bad state of the finances of the country, and the supineness of the Government which appears to me at a lower ebb than I ever remember it.'[2]

The squadron remained in the Tagus for a week before leaving for an encounter with a Spanish squadron almost twice its size. The ships were intercepted off

Cape St Vincent and the battle was a great success for the admiral – and for one of his subordinates, Commodore Horatio Nelson, who succeeded in boarding two of the enemy vessels. Lisbon was illuminated in honour of the victory and, when the squadron returned to the city, the officers were entertained in the homes of English merchants.

These early years of war passed without much danger in Lisbon. Merchant vessels and packet boats sailed in armed convoys, but life for the English community carried on much as usual and William continued to worry about his tax exemptions. In 1794, Prince João had renewed the exemption from sales taxes for a further ten years, but the exemption from import duties expired two years later and had not been reinstated. The prince had been signing documents in his mother's name since February 1792, but it was not until July 1799 that he gave up all hope of her recovery and agreed to the formal appointment of regent.

With the government on a more sensible footing, William tried again to have the exemption reinstated and, on 7 October 1799, João signed a decree explaining that William 'deserves praise, not only for re-establishing the glass factory at Marinha Grande, but also for operating it with the utmost care and expense'. In order that 'the progress of the factory can be carried to its ultimate and complete perfection', he reinstated the exemption from import duties for ten years and also extended the exemption from sales taxes for a similar period·

...

William was now feeling the infirmities of age. As Antony Gibbs wrote from Marinha Grande in December 1798, 'several of the people have been lamenting with me that time should have gone her usual course with him and brought on old age so soon'. To reduce his workload, he had employed a new manager at Marinha Grande, an efficient administrator who moved into the mansion house, assumed responsibility for all aspects of management, and with the aid of the music master, continued to stage the weekly concerts and plays. This allowed him to spend more time with his family in Lisbon.

His eldest brother Lewis (born while William was a schoolboy in Exeter) had died in 1795 and was buried near his uncle John in south-east corner of the Protestant cemetery. Four years later, William made a hurried journey from Marinha Grande to visit his brother Jedediah who was suffering from a gastric ulcer and had 'brought up many pounds of blood from his stomach'. He arrived in the Largo do Stephens towards the end of March 1799 and, despite having travelled in relative comfort by chaise and stagecoach, he was so tired from the journey that he remained in Lisbon for the next eighteen months.

From the flat sandy landscape of Marinha Grande, the peace of his garden and the affection of his workers, he was now surrounded by a busy, noisy city.

From the windows overlooking Rua São Paulo, he could see the shipping in the harbour: warships, merchant vessels, and little ferry boats with striped awnings which carried passengers up and down the river. In the hot summer months, he would sometimes make the journey to Sintra for cooler air. Stopping his chaise on the hill near Queluz, he would look down into the palace gardens, hoping to catch a glimpse of the white-haired queen flanked by her attendants, a very different figure to the elegant woman he had entertained in Marinha Grande.

He felt well enough to return to the glassworks in the autumn of 1800. Five months later, Prince João received an ultimatum from France. If Portugal wished to remain in peace, it must abandon the English alliance and close its ports to British shipping; if he failed to comply, the country would face invasion from Spain. As Robert Southey (on a visit to his uncle who was chaplain to the English Factory) wrote on 22 February:

> 'The state of Portugal is become uncertain and dangerous. The force of the country is absolutely nothing, no preparation whatever of magazines or even ammunition … The merchants are preparing to secure their property, those who can. To the many whose trade is selling to the natives it will be utter ruin.'[3]

After a few weeks of indecision, Prince João refused the terms of the ultimatum and Spain declared war. 'We are threatened with speedy invasion,' wrote Southey on 28 March, 'and the critical hour of Portugal is probably arrived.'[4] English traders were sending their goods and money to England, and many families discussed the possibility of sailing for home. William returned to Lisbon in the spring but had no intention of leaving the country; his duty lay with the people of Marinha Grande. He gave 6 contos of reis to the exchequer as a contribution towards the cost of military defences; he obtained exemption for his workers from military service; and when the high level of recruitment among peasant farmers resulted in a shortage of grain, he imported corn from England which was ground, baked into bread and distributed to the villagers of Marinha Grande free of charge.

The invasion was brief. Franco-Spanish troops crossed the border on 20 May 1801, four days after William celebrated his seventieth birthday in the Largo do Stephens. Prince João capitulated on 6 June. He closed his ports to British naval and merchant shipping, and when the government collected a new 3 per cent tax on production (raised in March to help pay for defence), William felt aggrieved that his thirty-two-year exemption from taxes had been eroded. It was normal for a proportion of finished glass to be damaged during transport and, using these breakages as a bargaining lever, he asked for a reduction in the rate payable at Marinha Grande. João took the point and, on 3 November, he signed a decree reducing the tax by one fifth on the domestic production of glass, china and porcelain.

By this time, it seemed that the danger was over. A general armistice had been signed in late September, after which the ports were reopened to British vessels. The merchants brought back their goods and their money, the English community held banquets and balls, and Philadelphia hosted 'an elegant entertainment' in the Largo do Stephens. But Lisbon rejoiced too soon; by the spring of 1803, it was common knowledge that a renewal of hostilities was imminent. This led to renewed depression among the merchants, a depression exacerbated in the Largo do Stephens by William's deteriorating health.

He had made his last journey from Marinha Grande the previous autumn. His body, grown fat with good living, was wasting away; the big square face had become thin and drawn. His family gathered at his bedside and, a few hours after he died on 11 May, his brothers raised the presence of mind to summon the vice-consul. They knew the whereabouts of the will and, in accordance with custom, the vice-consul opened the papers and 'read the contents in an audible voice in the presence and hearing of witnesses'.

Written in March the previous year, the will appointed John James (his partner at the glassworks) as his sole heir and executor, and he recommended that his workers should 'serve my brother and successor with the same zeal, fidelity and obedience with which they have served me during my administration of the factory'. Under Maria's decree of 1780, John James was forbidden to bring in new partners, so William reminded the state that the glassworks operated under royal protection:

> 'I humbly request that the Sovereign will not delay in making a decision on any representation my successor may make, for such delays would drain the enthusiasm and energy of any good-willed person.'

Finally, he recommended that John James should, at the appropriate time:

> 'petition the Sovereign to buy the factory of glass with all its belongings. Since the Crown is the owner of the pine forest on which the factory depends, its perpetuity in private hands will need the continued protection of the Monarch, or other protector at Court, to avoid the malice and envy which I myself have experienced many times.'

Protestant burials in Lisbon were simple ceremonies, 'without any funeral pomp or attendants'. After the reading of the will, William's body was placed on a carriage shaft and pulled by mules to the cemetery in Estrela. He lay overnight in the mortuary chapel and was buried the following day, in a grave close to his brother Lewis. 'The spot of interment is so beautiful,' wrote an English visitor who strolled through the cemetery a few years after William was buried here. 'Though the trees give a somewhat melancholy shade, everything around is calm, silent and cool; verdant shrubs adorn the avenues and the fairest and sweetest flowers are placed upon the graves.'[5]

...

In the pavilion at Queluz, Maria knew nothing of the death of her favourite Englishman. She knew nothing of the war in Europe which broke out again just seven days later. When Spain re-entered hostilities in December 1804, Portugal was once again in danger, the closure of its ports to British shipping of renewed importance in French military strategy.

Pulled by Britain and France in different directions, Prince João did his best to please both sides. For a short time, he fell ill from stress; he complained of chasms opening in the ground beneath his feet and it was feared that he too might be going insane, a fear fostered by his wife who was hoping to take over the regency.

Carlota had proved her fertility by giving birth to nine children (not all of them fathered by her husband). She had also grown into a malicious, vindictive woman who hated Prince João for his lethargy and indecision. On his part, João avoided his wife's company and, by the time her last child was born in October 1806, they were living apart, he at Mafra, she at Queluz or in her country house at Sintra. And by this time, Portugal was in great political danger.

A British squadron under the command of Sir John Jervis (now Lord St Vincent) returned to Lisbon in August 1806, this time with a mission to ascertain whether Portugal had any intention or capacity to defend itself – and if not, to persuade the royal family to sail for safety in Brazil. He found the army:

> 'very much diminished in numbers since I was last in Portugal. Thirteen thousand ill-armed infantry is the utmost that can be counted upon, and the cavalry beggars all description, both as to horses and men.'[6]

The squadron stayed in Lisbon for several weeks and great parties were held on the flagship, HMS *Hibernia*. As St Vincent wrote to his brother on 10 October:

> 'We were in perpetual masquerade the whole time of our stay in the Tagus, not less than a thousand Portuguese on board the Hibernia every day; some days three or four thousand, nobles, priests, merchants, shop-keepers ... All the Ministers, both domestic and foreign, dined on board, except the Spanish and French ... The principal nobility, of all ages and of both sexes, also dined on board, some of them more than once, and we had very pretty

dances – your friend, Captain Ricketts, having the best taste for turning a Quarter-deck into a ball-room I ever saw.'[7]

St Vincent left Lisbon having concluded that Portugal was unable to defend itself and that no British force of any practicable size could prevent an invasion. A few weeks later, Napoleon issued the Berlin Decree which closed the ports of continental Europe to British vessels, an effective blockade of Britain and her colonies. As Prince João came under increasing pressure to close his ports, British officials urged him to seek safety in Brazil. Terrified at the thought of a long sea voyage, of leaving the only country he had ever known, he felt himself pulled this way and that. To appease France, he pretended that he had a mind to close his ports; to appease England, he hinted that he might sail for Brazil.

In July 1807, France issued another ultimatum: Portugal must close its ports to British shipping or face invasion. While João continued to prevaricate, an invasion force gathered in Bayonne under the command of General Junot. The British envoy did his best to persuade the prince to leave the country but, as João explained, 'every feeling of religion and duty forbade him to abandon his people until the last moment'.

On 1 October, when the French and Spanish ministers left the country, João referred to his 'well-grounded hopes that their absence will be temporary and that no hostile act will follow'. It was only when he was shown an announcement dated 13 October in the official journal of the French government – 'the House of Bragança has ceased to reign in Europe' – that he realised the full gravity of the situation. He closed his ports on 20 October, but it was too late. The French army had crossed the border into Spain two days earlier, with orders to march on Lisbon and seize the royal family.

The Portuguese fleet was anchored in the Tagus, a British squadron arrived to escort the royal family to Brazil, but João continued to wait, refusing to leave until the last possible moment. On 22 November, news arrived that the invading army had crossed into Portugal; two days later, it had reached Abrantes, less than 60 miles from the city. Only now did João make the painful decision. It was time to leave.

The next two days were filled with intense activity. The royal family, the nobility, secretaries of state, officials, their families, friends and servants, all were sailing for Brazil, leaving behind a council of regents nominated by Prince João to rule the country in his absence. The palace of Queluz was packed up in great disorder. One man described 'the mass of belongings lying exposed to the elements'; the carriages which 'rode about aimlessly, abandoning the protocol usually accorded these occasions'; the courtiers who refused to be separated

from their luggage and their servants; others who were 'eager to get going …
frightened they were running out of time'.[8]

The royal family boarded ship on the morning of 27 November. Rain had
been falling for several days, drenching the roads and creating a sea of mud at
the Sodré quay where a sullen crowd had gathered to watch the embarkation.
Prince João was the first to arrive, accompanied by his nephew Pedro Carlos
(now a young man of 21), travelling in a carriage with no sign of royal livery. As
he picked his way across planks laid over the mud, he heard shouts of 'Death to
the Prince who abandons us!' and was seen to hold back tears as he boarded the
galley which rowed him to his flagship, the *Príncipe Real*.

Carlota arrived next, with her two sons, Pedro and Miguel, followed by her
six daughters (aged between 1 and 14). Maria travelled from Queluz in a closed
carriage. 'Don't drive so fast,' she cried as the horses galloped towards Lisbon.
'They will think we are fleeing.' When the carriage reached the quayside, she
had a fit of hysterics and refused to step down onto the mud. 'I don't want to,
I don't want to,' she screamed, until a ship's officer put his arms around her,
picked her up, and dropped her into the galley.

The last carriage brought Maria's sisters, Mariana and Benedita, and after
they were safely on board, the servants brought the luggage. More than 700
vehicles transported the trunks and treasure chests to the waterside. Most of
the contents of the royal palaces were on their way to Brazil: furniture and
paintings; gold and silver; vast quantities of diamonds and precious stones; the
contents of several libraries; and all the state papers. There was great confusion
on the quays as members of the court, the government, and large numbers of
officials and priests arrived in carriages, bringing their most valuable pieces of
furniture as well as chests packed with their possessions.

By evening, the embarkation was complete. More than 10,000 people were on
board the fleet of fifteen warships and thirty merchant vessels anchored in the
Tagus, but a strong wind was blowing from the south-west, trapping the ships
in the harbour. They lay at anchor all the following day while the invasion force
was marching closer by the hour. João paced the deck in fear and frustration
until, in the early hours of 29 November, the wind shifted to the north-east.

At seven o'clock that morning, the ships moved downriver to join the British
squadron waiting outside the bar. As the flagship emerged into open waters, it
was greeted by a 21-gun salute from the English fleet, a fearful sound to Maria
who had become terrified of loud noises. The return salvo from the *Príncipe
Real* was even more terrifying as it reverberated through the hull. Storm clouds
gathered during the afternoon. The wind veered to the west, the sea took on a
heavy swell, and by the time it grew dark, the winds were at gale force. All night

and during most of the following day, the ships tacked into the wind, the waves dousing the decks with water.

The *Príncipe Real* carried at least 1,500 people, including Maria, Prince João and his two sons, with insufficient supplies of food and water. The royal passengers were comfortable enough in the staterooms, but most of the refugees slept on deck 'with no beds and no coverings'. The hull leaked, the rigging was frayed, many of the timbers were rotten, and the ship creaked and groaned as it rode the waves.

It took two months to cross the Atlantic, eight distressing weeks for Maria who was unaware of the reason for this dramatic flight across the ocean, this sudden plunge into discomfort. 'Where are you taking me?' she kept asking her son. 'What am I doing here?'

22

Exile

*The Queen was advanced to an age when changes make but slight
impressions ... Her state of mind ... prevented her from feeling the whole
extent of her misfortune.*

John Luccock, 1820

The *Príncipe Real* dropped anchor in the bay of Salvador de Bahia,
800 miles north of Rio de Janeiro, on 22 January 1808. As João and
his family disembarked the following morning, the streets were lined
with welcoming crowds who were taken aback at the tattered state of their royal
masters. The prince took his mother and his elder son to stay in the governor's
palace; the rest of his family slept on board the flagship for another five days
before they took up residence in the law court.

The fleet set sail again on 26 February and followed the coastline south to
Rio de Janeiro. The ships had been provisioned in Salvador, the weather was
calm, and this second leg of the voyage proved that Dr Willis had been right
about the calming effects of a sea voyage. Maria became quiet and pliable – but
her demons returned when the *Príncipe Real* sailed into Rio harbour during the
afternoon of 7 March to the sound of cannon-fire, 'booming salutes that could
be heard for miles around'. She heard the thunderous sounds in her stateroom
and trembled in fear.

Soon the viceroy came on board to welcome Prince João to the city. He
had known for some time that the royal family might arrive for an extended
stay. Workmen had converted his residence in the Largo do Paço into a palace,
monks of the adjacent Carmelite convent had been rehoused and the convent
linked to the palace by a covered walkway. The newly named Paço Real had been
scrubbed and painted, and the state rooms lined with silk. Churches had been
cleaned, streets swept, and preparations made for the welcoming ceremonies.

That evening, João stood on deck, watching a display of fireworks on the
waterfront. The following day, he disembarked with his family, leaving Maria
on board the flagship. To the sounds of gunfire and pealing of church bells, a
brigantine ferried them to the quayside at the Largo do Paço where they were
greeted by the viceroy, large numbers of priests and officials, and a 21-gun

salute from the artillery drawn up on parade. It was the beginning of a nine-day celebration.

It was intended that Maria should disembark on 9 March and preparations were made to receive her with the same pomp and ceremony which her family had received the previous afternoon. Once again, the quayside was lined with priests and officials, the army and militia were drawn up on parade, and Prince João sailed out to the *Príncipe Real* to escort his mother to her new home. But Maria had been agitated by the salvos fired the previous day. She threw a fit when she saw her son, so the landing was postponed until the following afternoon when the welcoming party gathered for a third time at the waterside.

At five o'clock, as João helped a trembling, black-clad figure into the brigantine, cannons were fired from the forts and from every ship in the harbour. Maria flinched in fear and, when the guns fired again as the brigantine reached the quay, she shrieked and covered her face with her hands. This demented and terrified old woman was greeted under a silk canopy, bundled into a sedan chair, and carried in procession across the square, 'surrounded by thousands of cheers from her vassals, peals of church bells and the cacophonous noise of hundreds of fireworks set off into the air from different places at the same time'.

Extracted from the sedan chair, she was hustled into the palace and led along the covered walkway to rooms on the first floor of the Carmelite convent. She was followed by her family, her ladies-in-waiting and her servants, all of whom queued up to kiss her hand in her new home.

That evening, João and his family appeared at the palace windows to an eruption of noise from a military parade drawn up in the square. 'There was a 21-gun salute from the artillery,' wrote a priest who had welcomed Prince João to the city:

> 'followed by a volley of muskets from the whole infantry, with lots of cheering and applause from the troops and the crowd. This was followed by a second salvo and volley of muskets and more cheering. Then came the third salvo, with a third volley and the same applause.'[1]

Maria cowered behind the closed windows of her bedroom. 'Make it stop! Make it stop!' she cried until one of her attendants passed a message to Prince João. Nine salvos had been scheduled, nine 21-gun salutes outside Maria's window, but João stopped the proceedings while the guns were being reloaded for the fourth salvo, 'in order not to trouble her Majesty with so much continuous noise'.

...

The new Paço Real lay on the south side of the Largo do Paço. The ground floor had been converted into guardrooms and offices, the first floor into accommodation for the royal family, the attics into bedrooms for the royal children. On the west side of the square, the two-storey convent provided a chapel as well as accommodation for Maria and her attendants. Fourteen members of the royal family, together with 300 servants and courtiers, were crammed into these two buildings and a few single-storey structures on the north side of the square.

Rio was a noisy, smelly city and it was not long before João and Carlota found alternative accommodation in the countryside. João and his two sons set up home at Boa Vista, a country estate on a wooded ridge three miles west of the city. Carlota, her daughters and Maria's sisters moved into a beach house at Botafogo, a quiet inlet inside the bay. Only Maria was left in the city.

João visited his mother several times a week, but she rarely spoke as he knelt before her and kissed her hand. Carlota and her children made duty visits from time to time. Maria never forgot her position in life ('I am always the queen of Portugal') but other memories surfaced only occasionally. 'This child will wear my crown,' she said one day as she stroked the hair of João's elder son. And she turned to Pedro Carlos, her grandson born in Spain. 'You poor boy,' she said. 'You have no mother, no father.'[2]

It was said that Maria believed she was still in Lisbon. If so, she ignored her senses. The windows of her apartment overlooked the Largo do Paço, beyond which lay the waterside, the harbour filled with shipping, the great bay edged with high granite mountains. The vegetation was tropical, the heat greater than in Lisbon. The seasons were different too. She was accustomed to the winter rains in Portugal but the rainy season in Rio, which started in September with fierce thunderstorms, was unlike anything she had experienced before. 'There is thunder like I never heard in my life,' wrote a courtier, 'and lightning strikes constantly in the mountains which surround the city.'

Every day in good weather, she was taken on outings through the streets of Rio or into the surrounding countryside. There were few horses or mules in the city, no stables attached to the palace, and her escort was a shabby sight. Accompanied by one of her attendants, she travelled in 'a small chaise … drawn by two very ordinary mules and driven by a servant in an old and discoloured, if not tattered livery'. The chaise was escorted by a guard, 'two soldiers in advance, and an officer and twelve others following, a single trumpet and a private footman'.[3] The guard prepared the way as the chaise moved through the streets and ensured that royal etiquette was obeyed. People had to dismount or alight from their carriages and kneel on the ground with bowed heads as the royal chaise passed by.

As the days spread into weeks, the weeks into months, and the months into years, Maria continued to endure her living hell. Sometimes she was in a state of lethargy and torpor, impossible to rouse. Other times she was in a frenzy, erupting into fits of hysteria and violence which kept her attendants awake for nights at a time. She slapped and punched them when she was agitated; she threw plates and screamed abuse. As a result, she had a high turnover of servants. Some of them would mimic her cries of distress ('the devil has gotten into me'); others used the pretext of illness to retire from her service.

Meanwhile, Carlota continued to behave badly, displaying 'great pride and imperiousness', unable to 'forgive the slightest disrespect'; Benedita settled into old age, becoming 'of mild and sedate habits'; and João's two sons, Pedro and Miguel, grew into reckless young men of little education. Pedro mixed with rough company; he toured the taverns in disguise and became renowned for his sexual adventures. Miguel (his mother's favourite) took up bullfighting and drove his carriage drawn by six horses at full gallop through the streets of the city.

Every year in December, the court celebrated Maria's birthday according to protocol. Troops marched past the palace windows with the usual discharges of artillery: three salvos from the cannons accompanied by soldiers firing their muskets. While Maria trembled behind the windows of her apartment, members of the court, foreign diplomats and city dignitaries came to compliment Prince João on his mother attaining another year of her age.

Discharges of artillery were not confined to birthdays. In May 1810, when Maria's grandson, Pedro Carlos, married João's eldest daughter, the festivities lasted for seven days. There were equally noisy celebrations in November the following year to mark the birth of their son, Sebastião, Maria's first great-grandchild.

There were deaths too. The first to die, just two years after his marriage, was Pedro Carlos. Several reasons were given for his demise, ranging from smallpox, through 'a violent nervous fever', to – this from the palace gossips – 'excessive conjugal activity'. The following year, it was the turn of Maria's sister Mariana, who died in May 1813 and was interred in the convent of Nossa Senhora da Ajuda.

Maria herself was next in line. Her robust physical health kept her alive until the advanced age of 81, by which time she had been insane for almost twenty-five years. Her final illness was distressing. She suffered from dysentery and fever, from oedema in her hands and feet, and she lost all feeling in her legs. 'There have been moments of relief,' wrote a court official, 'but, once over, the symptoms return stronger than ever.' Every day, she was taken around the palace in a wheelchair, an ancient figure wracked with inner demons as well as physical pain.

Confined to bed for the last two months of her life, she screamed that she wanted to see no one, that she wanted to be left alone. But a queen had to die according to protocol, surrounded by family, ladies-in-waiting, doctors and attendants. Every day, as João knelt by the bed to kiss her hand, she would tell him again, 'I don't want to see anyone. I want to die.'

She received the last rights on a warm autumn evening in May 1816, while crowds gathered in the square beneath her windows. Early next morning, João came to kiss her hand for the last time. When news of her death was announced, the bells of the city tolled all day and night, and 21-gun salutes were fired every ten minutes until midnight – but at last she was safe from the sounds which had terrified her for so many years.

Her attendants dressed her in a black gown and red velvet cloak. They laid a cloth of gold damask over her body, leaving her right arm exposed. A crucifix hung on the wall and four silver candelabras were placed around the bed. The following day, her family, the nobility, priests and city dignitaries, all came to kiss her right hand, to pray for her soul and sprinkle her body with holy water. The ritual lasted all day as large numbers of people filed through the room to pay their last respects to a queen whom most of them had known only as *Maria A Louca*, Maria the Mad.

To protect his mother's modesty, João gave orders that her body should not be embalmed. Instead, she was placed in an inner coffin lined with llama wool; this was inserted into a second coffin made of lead and, before the lids were sealed, both coffins were filled with aromatic gums, spices and dried herbs. The lead coffin was put inside a third coffin of polished wood, with a cross of gold damask on the lid. This was fastened with two locks and the keys given to Marquis de Angeja, grandson of Maria's first secretary of state.

On the evening of 22 May, the coffin was carried into the Largo do Paço where the royal coach was waiting. The streets were lined with soldiers, crowded with people who fell silent as the royal cortège passed by. The queen's arrival at the convent of Nossa Senhora da Ajuda was greeted by a 21-gun salute from the battalions drawn up by the door. A requiem mass was performed in the chapel, after which Maria was carried into the mausoleum to be interred alongside the body of her sister.

According to custom, João confined himself to the palace for eight days. On 28 March, he held an official audience to mark his return to public life. On the 29th, he visited the mausoleum in the convent. His mother had been insane since 1792 but he found it difficult to let her go. He declared court mourning for a full year and ordered that the anniversaries of her death (the week, the month, the year) should be marked by solemn ceremonies.

It was expected that his acclamation as João VI would take place a few weeks later, but João deferred the ceremony for almost two years, partly because of the marriage of his son Pedro to a Hapsburg princess in 1817, partly because of a revolutionary uprising in the province of Pernambuco, but mainly because he was concerned about his mother's immortal soul, the truth of her salvation.

He had lived for more than two decades with his mother's conviction that she was destined for hellfire. He asked the priests for confirmation that she had passed from the state of purgatory, but 'on this point the wise men differed, the priests of the Chapel Royal declaring that she had entered upon perfect bliss, while those of the Candelária warmly maintained that she was not yet purified'.[4]

...

Five thousand miles away, the Peninsular War had taken its toll on the people whom Prince João abandoned to their fate. When peace was declared in 1814, it was assumed that he would sail home to reinvigorate a country exhausted and disorganised after eight years of war. A British squadron was sent to escort the royal family to Lisbon but, happy in Rio and dreading the thought of another sea voyage, João decided to remain in Brazil.

He was only persuaded to return home after a revolution in Portugal brought a constitutional government to power in November 1820. The world Maria knew – a world of absolute monarchy, clerical dominance of affairs of state, and ancient court protocol – had been swept away by revolution and war. João had been isolated from events in Europe; he hated the very idea of a constitution but, after riots broke out in Rio in February 1821, he finally agreed to return to Portugal and accept the new political reality. He would leave his elder son Pedro to act as regent in Brazil.

On the morning of 25 April, the royal family (João, his aunt Benedita, his wife Carlota, his younger son Miguel and four of his daughters) embarked on the *Dom João VI*, the new flagship of the Portuguese fleet. The bodies of Maria and her sister Mariana were travelling with them; their coffins had been disinterred from Nossa Senhora da Ajuda and carried on board. Maria's coffin was placed in a stateroom fitted out as a chapel. She would lie here for ten weeks as the flagship took her home across the ocean.

Next morning, thirteen ships set sail for Lisbon. When they arrived in the Tagus on 3 July, the harbour was filled with boats, the river banks lined with people eager to catch a glimpse of a royal family which had been absent for fourteen years. The flagship was 'surrounded by small boats crowded with people,' wrote Marianne Baillie, an Englishwoman who watched the proceedings through a telescope:

'The river and its far distant shores resound with the roar of various royal salutes, poured from the brazen throats of every gun on board the numerous ships of all nations now in the harbour. [An] English frigate … is covered with innumerable flags of the gayest variety of colour, and the crew are attired in their gala costume; they are swarming amid the rigging … like clustering bees, and I can perceive some of the officers fearlessly stationed at the same dizzy height.'[5]

After three invasions of their country, with appalling destruction and loss of life, the king and his family appeared like relics from another age. João stood on deck wearing a plumed hat, his pronounced stomach emphasised by a uniform embroidered with gold and studded with medals and orders. Carlota was seen in animated conversation, her younger son Miguel by her side. Benedita, now 75 years old, wore a black dress embroidered with diamonds; she appeared, wrote the French ambassador, 'just like a picture that had stepped out of its frame'.

The family went ashore the following day and João was taken to parliament where, 'with a wild and distrustful expression', he swore to uphold the constitution. Having loathed each other for decades, he and Carlota set up separate establishments, João in the palace of Bemposta in Lisbon, Carlota and Miguel in Queluz. And during the next nine months, Maria's body was moved from one convent to another while a tomb was built in the Basilica da Estrela.

João had decided to break with custom. His mother would not join her husband, her elder son and three infant children in the royal mausoleum in São Vicente de Fora. Instead, she would lie in the church she had built in thanksgiving for the birth of Prince José, the church she had dedicated to the Heart of Jesus. A marble tomb was constructed in the right transept, close to that of her much-loved confessor, Inácio de São Caetano, which stands across the nave in the sacristy.

Maria was given a state funeral in March 1822. 'The ceremonies lasted for three entire days and nights,' wrote Marianne Baillie:

'during which period the great guns on sea and land, and the bells of every steeple in Lisbon, thundered and pealed without intermission. It is really a great hardship for us little people that a Queen cannot be interred without the chance of rendering many of her invalid subjects distracted. I am sure many sick persons must have been hurried out of the world by the sheer noise.'[6]

The coffin of polished wood was brought to Estrela in a torchlight procession during the night of 19 March. The cortège was headed by João and his family in state carriages, followed by the nobility on horseback, wearing black cloaks and hats with long black streamers; the religious establishment ('an army of bishops, monsignors, priests, and monks'); and the military, regiment after regiment with bands playing funeral music.

Received in the church 'with great state and formality', the coffin was placed in the main aisle where it was 'carefully watched until the next morning by a select number of ladies and gentlemen of the court, who remained standing ... in dead silence around it the whole time, without once sitting down to rest their weary limbs'. Next morning, Marquis de Angeja delivered the keys he had been given in Rio. The locks of the outer coffin were opened, the lead coffin was cut open and the lid of the inner coffin unscrewed.

João had appointed two of his daughters to preside over the ceremony of dressing the corpse in new clothes, a duty performed by their unfortunate ladies-in-waiting. The body had not been embalmed. It had spent five years in a tropical climate and, despite the herbs and spices, the smell was overpowering. According to Marianne Baillie:

> 'One of the princesses fainted twice, and was too ill to reappear; but her
> sister was obliged to remain, while the ladies raised the body and completely
> re-clothed it in a black robe, a dress cap, gloves, shoes and stockings, and
> adorned it with four splendid orders upon the breast.'[7]

A requiem mass was performed in the afternoon, with music especially composed for the occasion. Maria's body remained exposed all the following day, watched over by a guard of honour, while members of the nobility came to pay their last respects and kiss her freshly gloved hand. It was said that the corpse was still entire, the limbs still flexible, although the face had turned a deep shade of black.

23

Invasion

Junot took possession of Lisbon … without having at hand a single trooper, a
single gun or a cartridge that would burn; with nothing indeed save the 1500
grenadiers remaining from the four battalions of his advance-guard.

General Paul Thiébault, November 1807

Above Maria's tomb is a carved plaque with her portrait in profile, held on one side by an angel blowing a trumpet, on the other by a relaxed and cheerful cherub. João commissioned this image of his mother accompanied by angels, perhaps to reassure himself that her fears were unfounded, that she had earned her place in heaven, that she had indeed 'entered upon perfect bliss'.

Three hundred yards away, in the south-east corner of the Protestant cemetery, lie the bones of William Stephens, the Englishman who had entertained her so royally at the glassworks. His life came to an end in May 1803, but the story of his legacy continues for a further twenty-four years. The Peninsular War is part of this story for the French invasions of Portugal had a devastating impact on the country – and on the factory in Marinha Grande.

As Prince João came under increasing pressure from the warring powers of Britain and France, a faction sympathetic to French revolutionary ideas began to take root in Lisbon. It was time for a steady hand on the tiller, both in affairs of state and at the glassworks, but João had inherited his mother's indecision and John James Stephens lacked the qualities required to steer the factory through troubled times.

He had been orphaned at the age of 7 and, from the day he arrived in Lisbon, William had been a father to him, giving him affection, support and encouragement. For more than forty years, his brother had led and inspired him, and standing by William's graveside on that warm spring day in 1803, he realised that life without him was unimaginable. On his return to the Largo do Stephens, he called the servants together. 'My brother should not have died,' he told them as he locked the door to William's study, explaining that the room should remain exactly as his brother had left it. He included himself in this prohibition and the door would stay locked for twenty-four years while inside, gathering dust on the desk, were copies of royal orders affecting the glass factory and its privileges, as well as papers which required attention: correspondence, invoices, bills of exchange.

The death of Jedediah in September deepened the sense of gloom in the Largo do Stephens. A few weeks later, John James and Philadelphia escaped to England where they stayed for many weeks with James Palmer, the treasurer of Christ's Hospital in London, with whom they formed a firm and lasting friendship. John James was paralysed by his sense of loss and it was not until he returned to Lisbon in the spring of 1804 that he wrote a petition requesting confirmation of his ownership of the factory. At the same time, he asked that the tax exemptions be prolonged by a further twenty years.

Ownership was an easy matter to prove. Foreigners were not permitted to own land or buildings in perpetuity, but William had overcome this difficulty in August 1772 when José signed a decree allowing him to 'own, retain and convey his properties to his heirs and successors, even if foreigners, notwithstanding any law or custom to the contrary'. The tax exemptions were another matter. The factory was in good financial shape when William died and John James should have acted promptly to protect its profitability, but he was too miserable to think about procedure or to flatter Prince João as his brother had done. Meanwhile, some of João's advisers were coming under the influence of a French faction in Lisbon and were absorbing anti-British attitudes.

The Junta do Comércio considered John James's petition in July 1804. In a critical report to Prince João, it made two recommendations: first, that John James be confirmed as William's successor, his privileges for the next five years (as already granted) confirmed but not extended; second, that the prohibition on imports of window glass be revoked with immediate effect. This would, explained the Junta:

> 'benefit the Royal Exchequer and the convenience of the people, both of which have been sacrificed to the interests of the Stephens brothers. No other factory in the Kingdom makes window glass, so they have had no competition and have made incalculable profits. It must not be forgotten that this factory seems more English than Portuguese, for the owner has taken to England immense sums of money that have been made over the years at the expense of our nation.'

William had never taken money to England – but John James had done so during his recent visit to London, investing several million in today's values (including £10,600 in 'new 4 per cent annuities transferrable at the Bank of England' and £3,000 in East India Stock). He had thought it prudent to protect some of his fortune from the threat of occupying forces, but it played into the hands of those who were hostile to British interests in Portugal.

Matters deteriorated during the next three years. The factory lost its privilege of free use of firewood (ordered to pay the sum of 80 reis per cartload) and the customs in Lisbon began to impound consignments of glass from Marinha Grande for supposed non-payment of taxes. This was on the assumption that the exemption from taxes (other than the 3 per cent tax imposed in 1801) had expired in 1804. The customs administrator had asked John James many times for proof that the exemption was still in force; this had not been provided, so he refused to release the consignments until he had seen papers which confirmed that all relevant taxes had been paid on them.

John James had lost his ability to think clearly. He should have remembered the decree signed by Prince João in October 1799, which extended the factory's exemption for ten years, but the document was on William's desk, locked up in the study, and he refused to enter the room to look through the papers. Instead, he presented the decree of November 1801 (which reduced the newly imposed tax on production by one fifth to allow for breakages) as evidence that all relevant taxes had been paid, claiming that this tax included within it all other taxes.

This was not an effective strategy to use with officials familiar with domestic taxation. The administrator accused John James of subterfuge and, in the autumn of 1807, the matter was taken to the Junta do Comércio for arbitration. With the submissions of both parties based on incorrect assumptions, the decree of 1799 was also overlooked by the Junta. This was a time of great uncertainty in Portugal and the officials can perhaps be excused for the oversight. But John James should have been better informed about the privileges granted to his factory, particularly since, in July 1804, Prince João had approved the Junta's recommendation that he should 'continue to enjoy for a further five years the privileges already conceded to him'.

After considering the matter, the Junta reported that John James's reasoning was faulty and his exemptions had indeed expired in 1804. However, since 'the glass factory deserves the protection of his Royal Highness because of the great benefit it provides to the country', it recommended that the exemptions be reinstated. It also recommended that the consignments of glass be released from the custom house.

These conclusions were published on 17 November 1807, by which time Prince João had more important matters on his mind. The French invasion had begun and it was just ten days before the royal family boarded ship in the Tagus. It was also several weeks after most of the British community had fled to England.

...

The English Factory held its last meeting on 6 October, disposing of funds and paying off its agents. As one of the merchants wrote four days later:

> 'You cannot conceive the dejection that reigns here, nor how melancholy it is to see such numbers of families so long here … hastily obliged to make the best liquidation they can of their affairs, making forced sales of their furniture and effects and obliged to quit the country.'[1]

The British departed on a convoy of sixty ships which left Lisbon on 17 October. Philadelphia travelled with them but, just as William had done six years earlier, John James decided to stay in Lisbon to protect his interests in Marinha Grande. He was not the only Englishman to remain in the city; a few merchants also chose to stay, perhaps hoping that the invasion would be as short-lived as that of 1801.

The first contingent of General Junot's invasion force straggled into the city on 30 November. The soldiers had marched over 600 miles in forty-three days, traversing mountain paths and fording rivers with gun-carriages and tumbrels. Under-nourished and drenched by winter rains, large numbers had died on the journey and many of the survivors walked barefoot into the city. In the words of Junot's chief of staff, General Thiébault (who was offered hospitality by William's old friend, Jacome Ratton):

> 'The state we were in when we entered Lisbon is hardly credible. Our clothing had lost all shape and colour; I had not had a change of linen since Abrantes; my feet were coming through my boots; and in this guise I took possession of one of the handsomest suites of rooms in the capital.'[2]

On 2 December, Junot ordered the seizure of 'all possessions of any kind, personal property, jewellery and silver, as well as real estate, belonging to British subjects in Portuguese territory'. Five days later, the factory at Marinha Grande was sequestrated by the chief magistrate of Leiria, acting on behalf of the occupying forces. The administrator, José de Sousa e Oliveira, was ordered to extinguish the furnaces and dismiss the workers. The factory had ceased to operate; it no longer belonged to John James Stephens.

As soon as the news reached Lisbon, John James sent a petition to Junot, explaining that his workers would now be unable to feed themselves or support their families. The French commander took the point:

> 'Being informed that the glass factory at Marinha Grande provides employment for 500 people … and wishing to protect and encourage all useful establishments in Portugal, I order that the activity and control

established by its founders be observed in the continuation of work at the factory. All people employed prior to its sequestration are directed to return to work.'[3]

Junot delegated the matter to José Diogo Mascarenhas Neto, a lawyer and civil servant who had built the road from Lisbon to Coimbra. A French sympathiser, he was now in charge of all dealings with British subjects, including property under sequestration. He sent specific orders to the magistrate in Leiria: he was to travel to Marinha Grande and check the inventory, for which Sousa was to sign a formal receipt; he was to inspect the factory every week, examine its records of production, and send copies of his reports to Lisbon; he should ensure that lands belonging to the factory were farmed efficiently and inform him of the volumes of crops harvested; and because Sousa required money to run the factory (sales being at a standstill), he should obtain a loan from the tobacco monopoly in Leiria.

On 7 January 1808, a month after the sequestration of the glassworks, a Lisbon magistrate and his secretary arrived in the Rua São Paulo to sequestrate the Largo do Stephens. John James led the way through the buildings as the secretary listed their contents. Most British residents had been imprisoned by this time but, on condition that he behaved well and complied with regulations, Junot was willing to allow the occupier of a 'useful establishment' to remain under house arrest.

Meanwhile, no decision had been made about his tax exemptions and the crates of glass impounded by the customs. Prince João would certainly have agreed to the recommendations made by the Junta do Comércio, but when the council of regents considered the matter, they refused to take action in favour of an Englishman. On 9 January 1808, they signed their names to the Junta's report. '*Escusado*,' they wrote in the margin, 'petition rejected.' A separate document referred to John James's request for free passage of glass through the customs. '*Indeferido*,' they wrote, 'not granted.'

Annoyed by this decision, John James broke the terms of his house arrest. On 13 January, he was collected from the Largo do Stephens and taken to the British Hospital in Estrela which had been requisitioned to house English prisoners. The windows had been fitted with bars to prevent escape, and John James would spend four months and eleven days incarcerated in this building which stood within the precincts of the Protestant cemetery. When he lay awake at night, he thought of his three brothers in the south-east corner of the burial ground, their bones lying just yards from his makeshift bed.

During the next few months, the prisoners made such a nuisance of themselves that most of them were allowed to return to their homes. John James was released on 24 May, on condition that he signed a document guaranteeing good behaviour and presented himself to Mascarenhas Neto once a fortnight. He was also ordered to pay bail which, because his assets had been taken from him, a Portuguese merchant paid on his behalf. Returning to the Largo do Stephens, he found French officers billeted there, drinking his wine and giving orders to his servants. Moving back into his home of thirty-five years, he had to endure the situation as best he could, for the house was now in French ownership and the terms of his parole meant that he could cause no trouble.

Meanwhile, the news from abroad was improving. Charles IV of Spain had been forced to abdicate in March and, when Napoleon placed his own brother on the throne, the country rose in rebellion against its ally. French troops were attacked and a deputation arrived in London asking for money and arms for war. By early July, peace had been declared between Britain and Spain, and arrangements made for British troops to be sent to the peninsula.

By this time, the rebellion had spread to Portugal. Junot sent troops to suppress the uprisings and for several weeks, 4,000 French soldiers were stationed near Leiria, looting the town of Pombal, burning the fishing village of Nazaré and (according to a English intelligence officer) 'committing great excesses' in Leiria. But relief was on its way. Fourteen thousand British troops under the command of Sir Arthur Wellesley (the future Duke of Wellington) landed in Mondego bay during the first week of August. They reached Leiria a few days later, then moved south through Alcobaça to Caldas da Rainha. They defeated the French in two major battles on 17 and 21 August, after which Junot signed an armistice at the end of the month.

The hostilities were over – but it was not an easy time for the people of Lisbon. In the heat of summer, 25,000 French soldiers were camped out in the streets, many of them in the Largo de São Paulo, 'where the infection proceeding from their uncleanliness was so great as to cause many of the inhabitants of the neighbouring houses to dislodge'. People were killing the soldiers whenever they had the chance and the dead men lay as they fell, in open spaces as well as in dark corners of the city.

Much as John James might have preferred to remain indoors, the restitution of his assets was more important than the noise, smells and dangers of the streets. Closing the leather curtains of his chaise, he was driven to the headquarters of the British army where a two-man committee had been set up to organise the return of sequestered property. On 14 September, Colonel Nicholas Trant (an intelligence officer with the Portuguese militia) signed a paper ordering that:

'no obstacle is to prevent John James Stephens, from this date onwards, entering into full possession of the lands, buildings, factories, animals, cattle and stock, furniture and utensils, and all goods of whatever kind which belong to him and which were seized by the French authorities'.[4]

The following day, John James threw open his first floor windows as British soldiers marched down Rua de São Paulo. They were greeted by ecstatic crowds ringing bells, firing pistols, and throwing flowers from every window and balcony along the route. 'Long live the English!' they shouted. 'Death to the French!' The British hosted a ball to celebrate the liberation, merchants returned to the city and Philadelphia returned to the Largo do Stephens, happy to be back in the country which had been her home since she was 11 years old.

Once again, the people of Lisbon rejoiced too soon. A British army (under the command of Sir John Moore) moved into Spain in November, but Spanish resistance collapsed by the end of the year and Moore fell back to Coruña on the northern coast where his army embarked on transports for England. French forces had followed the British to Coruña and it was assumed that they would turn south for a second invasion of Portugal. 'Great alarm amongst the merchants,' wrote a visitor to Lisbon in January 1809, 'many of whom are already despatching their property on board of ships ... Many French spies are suspected to be about under the disguise of priests and friars.'[5]

In early March, Wellington persuaded the British government to concentrate its efforts on Portugal. The second invasion came less than three weeks later when a French army marched south from the northern border and occupied Oporto. During the first two weeks of April, several thousand British soldiers landed in Lisbon and, when Wellington arrived to take command, he was given a tremendous reception. According to one of the officers:

> 'No words would be adequate to convey the faintest idea of the delight exhibited by all persons. All day long, the streets were crowded with men and women, congratulating one another on the happy event; and at night, the city was illuminated even in the most obscure and meanest of its lanes and alleys.'[6]

Marching north, the troops liberated Oporto on 12 May, after which the French retreated across the border. Two months later, as Wellington's army marched into Spain, reinforcements arrived in Lisbon and embarked on boats for transport up the Tagus. 'I shall never forget my sensations on marching through the streets,' wrote an officer who left the city on 28 July:

> 'They were filled with people; the windows crowded with faces, wearing the kindest and most animated looks; loud, long and continued "Vivas" were poured forth on every side; shawls, handkerchiefs and hands were

waving from every balcony; and the women threw flowers and garlands on our heads … From the quay of the Praça do Comércio, our men sprang into our boats and our little fleet was soon sailing up the river under a favourable breeze. It must have been a beautiful sight … the polished arms, the glittering cap-plates, and the crimson dress of the British soldiers crowded into the open barks.'[7]

Another invasion defeated, another march into Spain; the people of Lisbon breathed a sigh of relief and English merchants returned to their work and their entertainments. A few weeks later, most of Wellington's troops were back in Portugal, forced to retreat from lack of supplies and the size of the French army ranged against them. It was time for a rethink – and during the autumn of 1809, Wellington spent several weeks riding over the countryside north of the city, devising a strategy which would take the whole of Europe by surprise.

A team of military engineers and thousands of local labourers set to work in October, with orders to build three lines of defence across a range of hills near the small town of Torres Vedras. The hills ran for 30 miles between the Tagus and the sea, and during the next few months, every hilltop was crowned with a fort, every valley cleared, every ditch and hollow filled. Slopes were scarped into precipices, rivers and streams dammed to flood the plains. The works were carried out in the greatest secrecy; even Wellington's staff officers had little idea of their ultimate purpose.

…

Meanwhile, none of the difficulties at Marinha Grande had been resolved. The system of using local carters to transport firewood had been disrupted by the invasion and, with insufficient fuel, the factory was operating well below capacity. The council of regents had been reinstated after the armistice, but its members were proving to be inefficient, corrupt and timid. They were referring all matters relating to royal favour for Prince João's personal consideration. As a result, long sea voyages were involved in any exchange of correspondence about the glass factory and its privileges.

Aware of the mistake he had made in 1807 (remembering that his tax exemptions did not expire until October 1809), John James wrote a petition to Brazil asking Prince João to lift the sequestration on glass impounded by the customs. It was not until May 1810 that he learnt that his request had been granted, by which time the exemptions had genuinely expired and the customs continued to demand that taxes and import duties be paid on all consignments of glass and raw materials.

John James wrote another petition to Prince João. He had hoped, he explained, that his tax exemptions would have been extended at the same time as the sequestration was lifted. He now had to face further delay, while his business was stagnating to the detriment of the people of Portugal who were in need of glass. To save time, he begged the prince to communicate directly with the administrator of the customs who should be ordered, as soon as the exemptions had been reinstated, to pass his glass and raw materials freely through the custom house.

He delivered this petition to the Junta do Comércio on 28 May 1810 – by which time Portugal was once again under threat of invasion.

24

Devastation

*From this nook of Europe proceeded that impulse by which its mightiest
kingdoms have been set free ... The arm of England was the lever that
wrenched the power of Bonaparte from its basis: Portugal was the fulcrum on
which that lever moved.*

George Canning, speech to British merchants in Lisbon, 16 April 1816

A French army (under the command of Marshal Masséna) was gathering
in Spain, close to the border with central Portugal. At the same time,
French sympathisers were planning to take control of Lisbon. On
15 August 1810, an English officer was told by his servant that 'British sick and
wounded are to be put to death this night, and the people are to take the forts
and declare in favour of the French'. But news of the plot had leaked; armed
soldiers roamed the streets and warships in the Tagus shifted their positions,
ready to fire broadsides into the city.

Masséna had led his army of 70,000 men across the border the previous day
and Wellington began to put his plan into effect. He moved his troops forward
to meet the enemy, then began to retreat, leading the French towards the trap
he had prepared at Torres Vedras. British forces were supplied from the rear
(by trains of bullock carts and river boats); French armies lived off the land,
requisitioning food from local inhabitants. Wellington's strategy was to remove
all provisions from areas through which the invasion force would pass on its
march towards Lisbon, depriving the soldiers of food once they were trapped
behind the lines at Torres Vedras. As a British officer explained:

'To give effect to this plan of defence, it was necessary, not only that the
allied army should retire to Torres Vedras, but that the whole country
between it and the frontier, which it was at all probable that the enemy
might occupy, should be abandoned by all classes of inhabitants, and that
everything which might contribute to the subsistence or facilitate the
progress of their troops should be carefully removed.

'My pen altogether fails me – I feel that no powers of description can
convey the afflicting scenes, the cheerless desolation, we daily witnessed
on our march ... to the lines. Wherever we moved, the mandate which
enjoined the wretched inhabitants to forsake their homes, and to remove

or destroy their little property, had gone before us. The villages were deserted; the churches were empty, the mountain cottages stood open and untenanted; the mills in the valley were motionless and silent.'[1]

Wellington's army marched south through towns and villages, 'sweeping before us all the resources of the country'. They were followed by the French who found a barren countryside, stripped of all food and stores. On 2 October, having passed through Coimbra and Pombal, the British army reached Leiria where Wellington set up temporary headquarters. 'This once beautiful town looked terribly devastated,' wrote a commissary. 'The place was ... entirely deserted and the houses stood open.'

The army bivouacked near Leiria until the morning of 5 October, when orders were given to resume the retreat. That evening, Wellington reached the monastery of Alcobaça and it was after this short march, when the right flank of the army passed close to Marinha Grande, that one of Wellington's officers described the plight of the villagers:

'It was altogether one of the most distressing journeys which any individual in the army was ever called upon to perform ... Crowds of men, women and children; the sick, the aged, and the infirm, as well as the robust and the young, covered the roads and fields in every direction. Mothers might be seen with infants at their breasts, hurrying towards the capital, and weeping as they went; old men, scarcely able to totter along, made way chiefly by the aid of their sons and daughters; whilst the whole wayside soon became strewed with bedding, blankets and other species of household furniture, which the weary fugitives were unable to carry further ... Those who forsook their dwellings, forsook them under the persuasion that they should never behold them again; and the agony which such an apprehension appeared to excite among the majority exceeds my attempt at description.'[2]

During the last days of the retreat, the winter rains began. The soldiers and the Portuguese struggled through the dampness and mud, the farmers driving their stocks of animals before them, cattle, sheep and pigs. On the morning of 8 October, Wellington began to shepherd his army into the area protected by the lines of Torres Vedras. Each contingent took up its appointed position. Three days later, all were in place.

On 14 October, the advance guard of the French army arrived within riding distance of the lines. As soon as Masséna was informed of the defences, he rode out to see for himself. During the British withdrawal, he had been convinced that Wellington was in retreat, that he was taking his men to a fleet of transports waiting in the Tagus. Now he returned to camp dispirited. The lines of defence were impenetrable with the number of men at his disposal.

…

Meanwhile, the people of Lisbon believed themselves to be in serious danger. They had no knowledge of the lines at Torres Vedras and, with French forces marching towards the city, another occupation seemed inevitable. English merchants formed themselves into defence corps, and marched and drilled in handsome uniforms. They also made preparations for flight. The packet boats to Falmouth (which normally accommodated up to thirty passengers) accepted bookings for four times this number – and Philadelphia fled to England for a second time.

The panic began to subside when it became known that the French had come to a standstill, although it was not until 7 November, when Wellington held a ball in the palace of Mafra (midway between Lisbon and Torres Vedras), that the city felt safe from enemy occupation. Meanwhile, large numbers of refugees were arriving in Lisbon, inhabitants of towns and villages in central Portugal who had obeyed Wellington's order to abandon their homes and travel to safety behind British lines.

In Marinha Grande, the workers and their families left the village not knowing if they would ever return. Sousa extinguished the furnaces, closed the factory, and made his way to the city where John James offered him hospitality in the Largo do Stephens. Most of the glassworkers also arrived in Lisbon, having made the journey on foot or by bullock cart. John James asked Sousa to find them and ensure that each man received his regular wages. Some of his workers had disobeyed orders and stayed in the village, but all communication north of Torres Vedras had been severed, so nothing could be done to help them.

The French army remained behind the lines for four weeks until Masséna ordered a retreat to Santarém, 25 miles to the north-east. His soldiers remained there for almost four months, drenched by winter rains and with almost nothing to eat, their suffering shared by the Portuguese who had remained in their homes. According to Jean-Jacques Pelet, Masséna's aide-de-camp:

> 'The inhabitants of the country fled and hid. They did not dare return to the villages inhabited by foreign soldiers … Most of them were roving in the woods, eating grass and wild fruit. Good God! What shelter did these unfortunates find? How many must have died during the six months we remained in this country, maintained by food that extreme necessity forced us to wrest from them.'[3]

Soldiers roamed the countryside, torturing and killing people to reveal their stocks of food. They looted the abandoned houses and set them on fire. In Pelet's words:

> 'The flames soon spread, resulting in frequent conflagrations. No one was there to put out the fires when they started, and no one came for assistance or help ... Thus the magnificent convent of Alcobaça [was] burned, and the horrors of war increased in this unfortunate country.'

At first Marinha Grande was left in peace but, when a garrison was set up in Leiria towards the end of the year, a detachment of 800 men arrived in the village in search of supplies. They killed seventy-four villagers who had remained in their homes and set fire to the factory buildings. The great workshop for crystalline glass – which contained three furnaces for melting the mixtures, three ovens for heating crucibles, and several rooms for mixing ingredients and packing glass – was reduced to a blackened shell. The soldiers broke open the crates of finished glass in the warehouse and smashed their contents. They looted William's mansion house, ripping out the doors and window frames for use as firewood. They burnt the factory theatre, as well as most of the village houses.

Thousands of Masséna's soldiers died of starvation and disease during this terrible winter. In early March 1811, he and his army marched north towards Coimbra, hoping to cross the Mondego river into a region well supplied with crops and livestock. Eight days later, harassed by British troops, with rains swelling the Mondego, and Portuguese militia defending the bridge at Coimbra, he turned east and set out for the border with Spain.

During the retreat, his soldiers cut a murderous swathe through the countryside. On their heels came Wellington's army and, although British troops could be brutal too, they were genuinely shocked by what they found:

> 'They set on fire ... almost every town and village in the line of march, while peasants hanging upon trees, priests and whole families murdered in their houses, and others lying dead by the roadside, exhibited dreadful witnesses of the savage conduct of their relentless invaders.'[4]

After passing through Leiria, eight miles from Marinha Grande, a British officer described the devastated city:

> 'It is impossible to describe the scenes of horror. The city ... had been eleven days on fire ... and burning still. Everything that could be taken away was removed, and the rest destroyed. The images in the churches

were in pieces, the graves were … opened for the sake of plunder. The nuns and friars … had fled to the mountains … and we found none but a few Portuguese perishing with hunger and ill-treatment.'[5]

On 10 April, Wellington issued a proclamation informing the people of central Portugal that they were free to return to their homes. A few days later, Sousa left Lisbon for Marinha Grande. After passing through the lines of Torres Vedras, he rode through a depopulated countryside, every village devastated, every house in ruins. Colonel Trant and his 10-year-old daughter Clarissa travelled the same route a few weeks later on their way to Oporto. Clarissa described the journey in her diary:

> 'We passed through a wild and totally uncultivated country to Leiria, and from thence to Pombal, passing many ruined villages which appeared totally deserted, and seeing and hearing much evidence of the atrocious cruelties which had been committed by the French army. Not a living being was to be seen, except here and there a little child attracted by the unusual noise of carriage wheels, with nothing but a ragged shirt to protect it from the scorching rays of the sun.'

When they reached Pombal:

> 'My father took us to the church and requested two old friars to point out to us the tomb of the celebrated Marquis de Pombal. We were shown a vacant space where the tomb had stood and on the wall the words "Respectez ce Tombeau" traced by the hand of General Loison, but such an order was not likely to be regarded by soldiers who respected neither the dead nor the living. They had broken open the leather coffin in vain hopes of finding treasure, and in revenge for their disappointment had scattered the contents in an adjoining courtyard, where they still remained.'

Clarissa helped her father collect the relics ('some fragments of bones, a pair of faded morocco slippers and a bag-wig which had once covered a very wise head') and gave them to the friars for safekeeping. 'It is singular,' she wrote, 'that the duty of seeing these relics properly disposed of should have devolved upon a British officer and a little insignificant English girl.'[6]

…

While Colonel Trant and his daughter tidied up the contents of Pombal's coffin, the people of Marinha Grande were clearing up the mess at the glassworks. The factory was, in Sousa's words, 'in a state which would have saddened and discouraged the bravest of men'. Villagers who had survived the marauding soldiers were now dying from starvation and disease. The land was deserted. Crops and grain stores had been burnt or plundered; livestock had been stolen or killed. Before 1810, the factory had supported over 2,000 people. Only half this number survived.

Sousa wrote daily to his employer in Lisbon, letters to which John James replied several times a week. There was no doubt in his mind that the factory should be rebuilt as a matter of urgency, to revive William's achievements and provide employment. Boys appeared to tidy up the factory complex, a carpenter was hired to replace the doors and windows of the mansion house, and the broken glass in the warehouse was collected and stored for reuse in the furnaces.

John James paid for 100 teams of oxen to travel to Marinha Grande from the north of the country; he sent money to help local farmers restore their land; and from London, Philadelphia sent £50 with orders that her brother should buy textiles (baize, linen and bombazine) for the women of the village to make clothes.

25

Aftermath

*Mr Stephens, an Englishman by birth … has passed his life in this country,
and is now in the enjoyment of a green old age, surrounded by friends and blest
with the smiles of fortune in a superlative degree: if general report can be
trusted, his wealth is immense.*

Marianne Baillie, November 1821

Sousa returned to the Largo do Stephens in early June 1811. During the next three months, he and John James made plans for the reconstruction of the main workshop to the exact design of William's original building. John James sent a petition to the council of regents, emphasising that the factory had been placed under royal protection and asking for as much assistance as the government could offer. On 12 July, he was granted free use of mature tree trunks in the royal pine forest, but no subsidy was made to rebuild the glassworks. The restoration would be funded entirely from John James's personal fortune.

In September, Sousa set out again for Marinha Grande and work began on the reconstruction. By March 1812, the roof of the new workshop was completed and Sousa was assembling the workforce, most of whom had fled to Lisbon during the invasion and received financial support from John James until the following spring. Despite this generosity, not all his workers remained loyal to the factory and Sousa was finding it difficult to retain a sufficient number of craftsmen.

Some of the workers had been killed by the French or were too weakened by famine and disease to return to their duties, but many of those who left the factory did so because better opportunities lay elsewhere. Some had sailed for Brazil; others were employed in a new glass factory in Lisbon where they were earning higher wages. Sousa appealed to the government. He listed the benefits the workers had received and the help John James had given them when they were refugees in Lisbon. He asked that they be sent back to Marinha Grande by royal order, a request which was granted in June.

The factory reopened in October although, because of the shortage of workmen and lack of transport from the pine forest, it would be almost two years before the workshops could operate at full capacity. But at least John James's privileges had been reinstated. In November 1810, Prince João had signed a decree re-establishing the factory's right to obtain firewood free of charge and extending the tax exemptions for a further twenty years.

…

By the time the factory re-entered production, John James had not visited Marinha Grande for at least nine years. He should have made the journey when William died but his courage had failed him. Now, when he should have been encouraging his workers after such an ordeal, supporting them in the work of reconstruction, and comforting those who had lost family and friends, his courage failed him for a second time.

Alone in the Largo do Stephens, he missed Philadelphia's company. He wrote many letters asking her to return to Lisbon – and she made many excuses. In December 1811, she was unwell and would sail for Portugal in the spring; but when spring came, she rented a new house in London. In January 1814, it was the severe winter weather. Roads were impassable, the Thames was covered in ice, and she wrote to her brother sitting close to the fire; she could barely hold her pen for cold, but she was enjoying the English winter and would not yet embark for Lisbon. In March, she agreed to return after the war but, when peace was declared in June 1815, she explained that she had recently attended the launch of a battleship and the rough water at Portsmouth had made her fearful of a sea voyage.

As John James made more urgent requests, the excuses continued: her weak health, the weather, the companionship of her friends in London. His hopes revived in November 1816 when she told him that she might embark for Lisbon in the spring, but she was tired of his entreaties and asked him to stop pleading for her return. This was the last letter she wrote in her own handwriting. A few weeks later, she suffered a major stroke, followed by another six months later.

Her physical health recovered from this second stroke – but not her faculties. Fit enough to manage a two-hour walk every day, she had (as John James explained to José de Sousa) 'lost her memory and forgets everything'. James Palmer, the treasurer of Christ's Hospital who became such good friends with John James and Philadelphia during the winter of 1803/4, brought her home to the Treasurer's House where she could be cared for by his three unmarried daughters. To make the news easier to bear, he wrote to one of John James's friends in Lisbon, asking him to go personally to the Largo do Stephens to be with him when he received news that his sister had lost her senses.

The glassworks might have returned to profitability if John James had persuaded Philadelphia to return to Lisbon. An intelligent and capable woman, she had often discussed business matters with William during the many years they lived together in Marinha Grande. Her knowledge and wisdom might have enabled John James to avoid some of his more disastrous decisions.

The high duties on imported glass had been reduced some years earlier, but the war in Europe disrupted trade and limited the amount of foreign glass entering the country. After peace was declared in 1815, imported glass began to arrive in increasing quantities and at decreasing prices. The Industrial Revolution had brought prices down in the manufacturing countries of Europe, while the costs of raw materials and transport had fallen with the ending of hostilities.

John James's prices were higher than those for imported glass; they had been set by William and approved by Pombal as long ago as 1773 when Marinha Grande had a monopoly of supply. In order to compete with imported glass, he should have reduced his prices – but this he declined to do, threatening to sack his employees if they sold glass at a discount. He also declined to cut back on production. As a result, his stocks began to accumulate. By December 1816, the warehouse in the Largo do Stephens was so full that he instructed Sousa to send no more glass to the city. During the years which followed, he was forced to build new warehouses almost every year.

He refused to accept that his problems were caused by high prices. Instead he blamed a new tax, imposed by the customs in 1815, on all goods arriving in the Tagus by sea. The public highway from Lisbon to Coimbra had deteriorated since the war, so all consignments of glass were shipped from the port of São Martinho and taxed at a rate of 3 per cent (while imports from England were taxed at the lower rate of 1.5 per cent). In 1818, when two Portuguese nobles were planning a visit to Marinha Grande, John James asked them 'to take notice of the crates of glass rotting in the warehouses because of the tax imposed by the customs.'

In failing to accept that he should lower his prices to compete with imported glass, he showed little understanding of market conditions. He even refused to depreciate the value of his older stocks as they were damaged in storage or during transport from one warehouse to another. He merely instructed his clerks to add the value of the stocks to the capital value of the factory. And as his losses increased year by year, he made up the shortfall from his own deep pocket.

His motives were to maintain the factory exactly as it was in his brother's lifetime. As well as refusing to lower his prices, he also refused to introduce new designs to keep pace with fashion or more efficient machinery as the technology of glassmaking evolved. There was a watermill at the factory, which broke down the rougher grades of sand, but the kneading of clay to make crucibles was still done by the stomping feet of a dozen men and the sand was still washed by hand in the factory courtyard. 'No one was concerned about the situation,' explained a report written in 1827, 'because the glass was simply packed and stored in warehouses, filling the accounts with imaginary value.'

There was overstaffing too. John James did his best to prevent his workers leaving the factory, perceiving those who did as 'ungrateful to the organisation which trained them and supported them during calamitous times'. Meanwhile his fortune provided full employment for the people of the village. Sons of craftsmen had a right to work in the factory, their wives and daughters employed to wash the sand and pack the glass. As a result, 'the establishment became overladen with workers, three times more than was necessary'.

...

Grateful for 'the favours and protection' he and William had received in Portugal, John James was loyal to the Bragança monarchy. In 1816, he received news of Maria's death with appropriate demonstrations of grief. In 1818, he placed lighted tapers in his windows to celebrate the acclamation of João VI. In 1820, he wrote to Sousa of his displeasure at the constitutional revolution. In July 1821, he watched João's flagship drop anchor in the Tagus. In April 1822, he found it impossible to sleep as cannons fired and bells pealed for three days and nights to mark Maria's interment in the Basilica da Estrela.

Two years later, in April 1824, he received news from Christ's Hospital. For almost seven years, James Palmer and his daughters had taken care of Philadelphia whose mind was destroyed by dementia. Palmer had retired from the post of treasurer in January, but he and his daughters stayed on in the Treasurer's House for another three months to allow Philadelphia to end her days in comfort. 'I have this instant heard of the death of my dear sister,' John James wrote to Sousa on 17 April. 'We lived together in perfect union and good friendship, and there never was, nor will be, a kinship stronger in social virtues. The next packet boat will bring me details of her funeral.'[1]

John James was the last surviving member of his family. There was no next generation. Of his four siblings, only Lewis had married but he had fathered no children. John James himself had nearly married at the late age of 53, although the arrangement involved some secrecy. 'I shall tell you something in this letter,' Antony Gibbs wrote to his wife in November 1801. 'You must not say it to anyone else but I may say it to thee, that a marriage is going on in the family of the Stephenses [but] not a word must be given to ... any other soul.'[2]

No details of this potential marriage have survived – except for a strange anecdote told by a young cousin, Francis Lyne, who visited Lisbon more than twenty years later:

'John James did once win a heart and lose his own to a very beautiful girl; and he went far up the country to get his brother's consent to the marriage. During his absence, the young lady died of a fever and, on the day of his return with his brother's approval, the poor girl was to be buried. He went to her house [where] the coffin had just before been brought; it was found to be too short so they had cut the poor girl's head off and placed it on her chest. And Mr Stephens saw it. Can anyone be surprised that a man, by nature so kind, so true, so feeling, should for the remainder of his days have lived with a sorrow in his heart.'[3]

Francis stayed in the Largo do Stephens in 1823 when John James was 77 years old. At first, he found his elderly cousin perplexing. 'I thought, and felt, that he made me welcome,' he wrote in his memoirs. 'The pressure of his hand was scarcely enough to make me feel happy; whilst the expression of his eye left a nice kind of feeling in my heart. I was young and timid and in a strange land. His words were few but kind.'

He found John James's way of living to be 'very singular and very strange'. Every afternoon, he hosted an open table for members of the English community, but the quality of housekeeping had deteriorated alarmingly since Philadelphia's departure thirteen years before:

'A public dinner daily was the order of the house and those of his acquaintance who liked it used to meet in his reception room about twenty minutes before his dinner hour ... At the proper time the butler appeared at the door, and with an extended finger, he counted heads, and then prepared the dinner table ...

'The chairs in hot climates are usually made with cane bottoms. Mr Stephens' had long been in use and, owing to the excess of his daily hospitality, some curious specimens were about the room. One day I arrived late in the reception room and, until dinner was announced, I had to balance myself on the corner of a chair as the entire bottom was, by the pressure of friends for years, entirely gone. And when I joined the dinner table and found it groaning with the weight of the good things that were upon it, I was surprised to see with what ease the servants handed to me the mustard in a broken wine-glass and ... a tablecloth darned to such a degree ...

'Men of the very highest class used to dine with Mr Stephens ... with diamond buckles to their knees and shoes ... but his own dress was drab knee-breeches, white cotton stockings, and a coat like the old-fashioned court dress, all very tidy and very clean. But I knew him more than once to 'come in to dinner' with only one string to his shoes – as if he could only afford one – and his shoes took it by turns to appear in proper order.

'When dinner was announced, Mr Stephens made his appearance through a door of another room, bow to us, say nothing, and lead the way to the dinner-table ... He spoke when politeness required, but very rarely otherwise; but his face was always beaming with kindness, as if he was happy because he saw others so ... He was well known and so were his dinners, and when he was pleased so were his friends. There was a mystic something that made every one like him and respect him – but he was strange to a degree.'[4]

...

In 1825, John James put his mind to the disposal of his assets. He was almost certainly the richest man in Lisbon, having inherited nearly all the wealth made by his brothers in Portugal. Lewis, who ran a successful merchant business, died in 1795 worth £100,000 (£14 million in today's values), half of which was divided between his brothers and sister. In 1803, William left significant legacies to his three surviving siblings. Later that year, Jedediah's estate, worth £40,000 (£4 million), was divided equally between John James and Philadelphia. In 1824, John James was the sole beneficiary of Philadelphia's wealth, valued at a massive £182,000 (£18 million). He had come a long way since that lonely day in May 1756 when he was admitted to Christ's Hospital, 'a poor child named John James Stephens whose father and mother are both dead and left him and several more unprovided for, who are assisted by friends'.[5]

His main problem was the glass factory which he had not seen for almost a quarter of a century. The workshops remained in full production, sales were at a standstill, and he was subsidising the entire running costs (estimated at more than 600 milreis a week). Meanwhile, his stocks of glass were packed in more than 12,000 crates in warehouses in Marinha Grande, São Martinho, Vila Franca and Lisbon, and valued at 'almost a million cruzados, sufficient to supply the consumption of Portugal for at least ten years'. In today's values, these numbers represent the eye-watering figures of £1 million a year for the operating costs and £11 million for the stocks of glass.

William had suggested that the factory be sold to the Portuguese nation, but crown revenues had declined since then and the state coffers were empty. Under Maria's decree of 1780, the factory had to remain in single ownership. John James was unable to pass it on to a consortium of businessmen, no entrepreneur would have been willing to accept such an unprofitable concern, and there were no family members waiting in the wings. After much thought, he decided to leave the factory to the state:

'The buildings, mansion and all other houses, farms, lands, orchards, vineyards, gardens, water courses etc. at Marinha Grande, that may be called the fixed capital of my glass concern, was agreed between

my much lamented partner and brother William Stephens and myself
should be entailed indivisible on the assigns or successors of the survivor
in benefit of this Kingdom and the people or families employed in this
undertaking ...

'In order to completely fulfil that agreement and to serve as a monument
of my esteem and gratitude for the favours and protection afforded me
in this country, I do hereby give, devise and bequeath to the Portuguese
nation all the said premises and establishment, beseeching the Government
to appoint a constituted authority to administer the same ... thus I firmly
hope and wish that prosperity, stability and permanency may afford this
useful and beautiful fabrick in benefit of Marinha Grande in particular and
the advantage of this Kingdom in general and for ever.'

Having disposed of the factory, he turned his attention to the distribution of his
fortune. First, he made three charitable bequests: £1,000 to the city of Exeter;
his £10,500 'new 4 per cent annuities transferrable at the Bank of England' to
the British consul in Lisbon to create a fund for the aid of widows and orphans;
and his £3,000 East India Stock to Christ's Hospital:

'to which I am indebted for my civil and moral education, being left an
orphan at a tender age and the prospects of my elder brother William nipt
in the bud by the fatal catastrophe of 1755, his effects and partner being
consumed in the ruins of the dreadful earthquake that befell this calamitous
city of Lisbon on the first of November in that year.'

Income on these last two bequests was to be distributed (during their lifetimes)
to individuals mentioned in the will: interest on the 4 per cent annuities 'to my
deserving friends and acquaintances hereinafter mentioned', and interest on
the East India Stock to James Palmer's three daughters who had taken such
good care of Philadelphia.

Next, he left a large number of legacies. These included totals of £24,000 to
'my paternal relations, descendants of my grandfather, Lewis Stephens, Vicar
of Menheniot'; £10,000 to 'my maternal kinsfolk, descendants from the Smiths
of Hornafast on the Tamar, whom I have frequently succoured'; £15,000
to friends and acquaintances in Portugal; and 1,000 milreis to José Diogo
Mascarenhas Neto 'for his activity in forming a public highway to Coimbra'.
He gave three months' earnings to his workers in Marinha Grande, two years'
salary to his clerks in Lisbon, and one year's wages to his servants in the Largo
do Stephens. And he left a legacy of £500 to Horatia, Lord Nelson's daughter
by Emma Hamilton, whom he described as 'the adopted daughter and legacy to
the British nation from its most renowned Naval Commander'.

Finally, on the fourteenth page of the will, he named his residuary beneficiary, the man who would inherit the remainder of his vast estate, including the 'immense fortune' made by William in Marinha Grande.

Over the years, his brothers Lewis and Jedediah had supported the families in Cornwall who had taken them in when they were orphaned in 1755. Jedediah's money enabled Benjamin Tucker's sons to achieve high positions in the navy. Lewis employed two of John Lyne's sons as apprentices and later as partners in his merchant business. The elder of these boys, Charles Lyne, arrived in Portugal in 1778 and entered into partnership with Lewis ten years later. He lived with the Stephens family and, after Lewis's death in 1795, he became a successful merchant in his own right. He returned to England in October 1803, to become senior partner of a merchant house in London, and it was expected by at least one man that he would be named as John James's heir. As Francis Lyne explained:

'Whilst I was in Lisbon, there was a certain gentleman who had a very strong fancy that "Charles Lyne would get all the old gentleman's money", and he was very anxious to stop the wheel of fortune from going that way. His mode of doing so was, with the parrot's note, saying again and again to Mr Stephens, "I believe, Sir, there is no doubt that Mr Charles Lyne is a *very* rich man". Mr Stephens learnt the parrot's note and never altered his reply, "I can't say. I never counted his money".'

The 'certain gentleman' was right. Two years after Francis's visit, John James named Charles Lyne as his residuary beneficiary:

'The Largo do Stephens, together with the furniture here and at Marinha, raw materials and glass in store, I specifically leave bequeath and devise to my much esteemed and respected cousin, Charles Lyne, whom ... I constitute and appoint my residuary legatee in order to facilitate the liquidation of my concerns and mitigate care trouble and anxiety to my survivors. That no responsibility may disturb the remainder of his days, I am sure he will with pleasure religiously comply with all my bequests.'

John James signed the will on 24 May 1825, wrapped the eighteen pages ('composed and written by myself') in a single sheet of paper addressed to Charles Lyne, and locked it in a drawer of his bedroom wardrobe, the key to which he kept in his waistcoat pocket.

During the next eleven months, he became increasingly breathless. No longer able to climb the stairs, he was confined to the first floor of the Largo do Stephens but he still attended the daily banquets in the long room overlooking

Rua de São Paulo. On 10 April 1826, he addressed a letter to one of his friends, James Bowness, marked it 'Not to be opened but in the case of the death of John James Stephens', and gave it to his butler for safekeeping:

> 'Finding myself indisposed with shortage of breath with great oppression on mounting the staircase, I apprehend a sudden cessation of it. Therefore this is to acquaint you that my will is in the small drawer towards the window of the clothes press in my bedroom, the key of which you will find in my left waistcoat pocket. Farewell. John James Stephens.'

Seven months later, on 13 November 1826, James Bowness wrote to Charles Lyne in London:

> 'It has become my painful duty to acquaint you of the demise of my much valued and respected friend, John James Stephens, which melancholy event took place yesterday, Sunday the 12th November, about a quarter past 3 o'clock in the afternoon. He was in the act of coming from his room to join his friends at dinner. When [he] arrived at the small entrance room, he was suddenly seized, and expired in the space of four to five minutes without a struggle.'

After a flurry of activity, the vice-consul (Jeremiah Meagher) was summoned to the Largo do Stephens. He extracted the key from John James's waistcoat pocket, 'with which I opened a drawer of the wardrobe in his bedroom and therein found the document purporting to be the last will and testament'. This he read aloud in the presence of James Bowness and four other friends, after which (as Bowness explained to Charles Lyne) he accompanied Meagher to the consul's office to have the will registered 'and an authenticated copy of it taken in order to be forwarded to you, which you have now enclosed'. There was much more for him to do:

> 'With the sudden and unexpected death of Mr Stephens and the multiplicity of occupation it has caused us in preparing for the funeral, the mail closing at ten o'clock … and the body having just left the house for the deposit, leaves no more time than to inform you that immediately after the interment [we] will proceed to take an inventory of the money, documents and other valuable property that may be in the house … We shall anxiously wait for your advice and instruction that everything may be done satisfactory to you.'[6]

John James was buried on 14 November in the south-east corner of the Protestant cemetery. 'When the soul is departed,' he had written in his will:

'how detestable is the body, but in consideration of its having been the fair receptacle and abode of a mild and placid spirit, I recommend to my successors to have the corpse decently interred in the same grave with my much revered brother and partner, William Stephens, showing by this union in death our intellectual harmony during life.'

Coda

The Legacy

As soon as James Bowness's letter reached London, Charles Lyne wrote a death notice for insertion in the major newspapers:

> 'Died at Lisbon on the 12th November 1826, John James Stephens Esq., a member of the British Factory of that city, in the 79th year of his age. His memory will be long revered by a very numerous circle of acquaintances of all nations, having always been conspicuous for many of the best qualities which most adorn the human mind, for integrity, charity, hospitality, placidity and equanimity of temper, great affability and good understanding.'[1]

He proved the will on 13 December and, 'in grateful and affectionate regard for the memory of his kinsman from whom he derives considerable property', he obtained royal licence to add the name Stephens to his own, a licence which also allowed him to create a Lyne Stephens coat of arms. To add to his own considerable wealth, he had inherited assets in Portugal described by the British consul in Lisbon as a 'princely fortune of above £700,000' (about £70 million in today's values), as well as most of John James's investments in London.

The first legacy he fulfilled was the bequest of £500 to Nelson's daughter Horatia, the wife of a clergyman in Norfolk. A few hours after Horatia gave birth to her fourth child on 13 February 1827, her husband took the infant to church and baptised him John James Stephens in gratitude to their benefactor in Lisbon. Eight days later, Charles attended a committee meeting at Christ's Hospital to inform the members that he had transferred the £3,000 East India Stock. This had, the committee noted, appreciated to £7,200 and Charles was thanked for his 'prompt and kind attention to the interests of this Institution'.[2]

On 4 March, he sailed for Lisbon to negotiate the transfer of the factory to the state. He stayed in the Largo do Stephens and, when the door to William's office was unlocked for the first time in twenty-four years, he found letters, bills and money orders which had remained on the desk untouched since the spring of 1803. John James had left instructions that 'the usual hospitality of this house be continued twelve months after my decease', so every day a collection of elderly merchants arrived in the Largo do Stephens, sat on the dilapidated chairs in the reception room, and followed the butler to the dinner table.

After visiting John James's grave in the Protestant cemetery, Charles instructed the stonemasons to copy the enormous oak-garlanded sarcophagus erected in 1795 over the adjacent grave of Lewis Stephens. The inscription he chose included many of the adjectives he had used for the death notice in the newspapers:

> 'To the memory of John James Stephens Esq ... always unostentatious but ever conspicuous for honour and integrity, benevolence, hospitality and affability. And for a most extraordinary equanimity and placidity of temper. For these he may be equalled. He cannot be excelled. This token of love and esteem was erected by his devoted and grateful cousin and companion for many years, Charles Lyne Stephens.'

He had forgotten that John James had asked to be interred in the same grave as William, the headstone having been removed four months earlier when the grave was opened. There was so much for him to do in Lisbon, so much for him to think about. Perhaps it is not surprising that he failed to remember his cousin's burial instructions, as well as that spring day in 1803 when he stood on the same spot, watching William's body descend into the ground while John James stood beside him, inconsolable with grief.

The masons took time to carve the memorial and it was not until several months later that it was taken to the cemetery and assembled above the double grave, close to the monument from which it was copied. John James had lived his life in William's shadow; now the memorial which extolled his virtues had erased the name of the brother he worshipped, the brother whose death he had never truly acknowledged.

...

This was a time of turmoil and danger in Portugal as the country edged towards civil war. Since their return from Brazil, Carlota and her younger son Miguel had rebelled against the constitution, masterminding two plots to restore the absolute power of monarchy. After the failure of the second plot in 1824, Miguel was exiled to Vienna and his mother imprisoned in the palace at Queluz. Meanwhile, her elder son Pedro had declared himself emperor of an independent Brazil, so when João VI died in Lisbon in March 1826, the regency of Portugal was given to his 21-year-old daughter Isabel.

It was she who, with the advice of the government, made decisions about the transfer of the glassworks to the state. Unwilling to subsidise the high running costs, they considered the options of selling the factory or closing it down, but both ran counter to the specific wording of John James's will. In April 1827, a lease was advertised for public auction but no bidders came forward, no entrepreneur was willing to pay rent for such an unprofitable concern. In May, it was decided to rescind Maria's decree of 1780 and offer the lease rent-free; this allowed a consortium of businessmen to take over the administration in early June.

The Stephens brothers had owned the factory for almost sixty years; the state would own it for more than one and a half centuries. In 1941, the workers paid for a bust of William to be erected in the main square of Marinha Grande – almost 150 years after his death, they still revered him. The factory remained in production until the spring of 1992 when the older buildings (William's mansion house, the great workshop rebuilt after the French invasion, the courtyard strung with 2,000 lights in honour of Maria's visit) were transferred to the town council of Marinha Grande, to be converted into a glass museum and a library.

A photographer came to record the workers on the last day of the Stephens factory. Many of them were descendants of the families that William knew. All of them were despondent; some of them were in tears. These elegiac black-and-white images (published in the newspaper *Expresso* on 13 June 1992) are a tribute to William's achievements in Marinha Grande, achievements which transformed the village and enriched the lives of its people for two and a quarter centuries.

Down the generations, the touching relationship between the reigning queen of Portugal and the low-born Englishman was forgotten. The characters who shared three glorious days in the summer of 1788 had left the stage and Philadelphia's account of the royal visit was lost amongst the Cogan family papers in England. But William's legacy lives on. Marinha Grande today is the centre of glass production in Portugal. It is also one of the wealthiest areas in the country.

Appendix

Account of the royal visit to Marinha Grande

Philadelphia Stephens

Marinha Grande, 25 July 1788

On Monday the 30th ult. at four o'clock in the afternoon, Her Majesty and all the Royal Family arrived here accompanied by their Donas, Açafatas, Confessors, Physician, Secretary of State,[1] Camaristas, Guardaroupas, Chaplains, Surgeons, Reposteiros, Moças da Prata, etc., with numberless other People belonging to their Suite. The Royal Family drove straight to the Church, where they spent a few minutes in Prayers, when they got into their Carriages again and came to our House. Our Praça on this Occasion made a very Brilliant Appearance. On each side of the House, the Soldiers were drawn up in form belonging to the Guard and opposite, before the Door of the Fabrick, all the Artificers belonging to the Manufactory in their Working Dress which does not admit of either Coat or Waistcoat. Their Hair was dressed and powdered, their Shirts clean and ironed with the Sleeves tied round the Middle of the Arm with Red Ribbons, Black breeches and clean white Stockings which altogether gave them a very neat Uniform Appearance.

On the Carriages entering the Gate, the Royal Family were saluted with three Vivas from the People of the Fabrick and on alighting at the Door of the House were received by the Archbishop (the Queen's Confessor),[2] my Brother William, my Brothers Lewis and Jedediah, the Visconde de Ponte de Lima, and Camaristas. Your Humble Servant had the Honour of kissing Her Majesty's Hand on her Entrance and received a Gracious Smile in return. The same Ceremony was repeated with the Princess[3] and each of the Infantas.[4] On the Arrival of the Donas and Açafatas, the Archbishop introduced me to them and recommended them to my particular care. Madame Arriaga is a very clever,

---

1 Viscount de Ponte de Lima, secretary of state for home affairs and acting first minister
2 Inácio de São Caetano, Archbishop of Thessalonica
3 Benedita, Princess of Brazil, sister of Maria I and wife to Prince José
4 Mariana (sister of Maria I) and Carlota Joaquina (wife of Prince João)

agreeable, well-bred Lady.[5] She is a widow and a great favourite of the Queen's. I describe her in particular supposing you have often heard her name mentioned.

The Royal Family immediately went up Stairs and, after viewing their own Apartment on the principal Floor, Her Majesty went up to the Attic Storey to see the Accommodations of her Female Attendants with which she expressed great satisfaction. When she had done looking at the Apartments, she intimated a desire of seeing the Fabrick. Accordingly a Procession of the Royal Family and Attendants walked across the Praça from the House to the Fabrick amidst a vast concourse of people. On their entrance into the Fabrick, they were again saluted by the Manufacturers with *Viva Rainha, Viva toda a Família Real* repeated three times. The Royal Family took their seats in a Varanta prepared for the purpose covered with green baize and crimson taffety where they spent about half an hour amusing themselves with seeing the People at work.

The Princess, afraid of being so near the Glass Furnace on account of the Heat so soon after finishing her Baths at the Caldas, immediately on entering the Fabrick called me to her and desired I would shew her the way up Stairs to the Packing Warehouse. Accordingly I ordered a Chair to be placed for her by the Window where she amused herself in admiring the Prospect and talking to me and to D. José Lobo, her Camarista, in a very agreeable familiar style during the time the Queen remained down in the Varanta. Her Majesty, after satisfying her Curiosity of seeing the People at work and applauding them all very much, came up Stairs and examined everything very attentively.

After spending a little time here, they took a view of the other Departments belonging to the Fabrick. In the Cutting and Flowering Room,[6] they sat some time admiring the work, the Queen and Princess both asking me a number of questions about our Craftsmen etc. After taking a view of everything belonging to the Fabrick, they walked into the Garden where Chairs were placed in different situations for them to rest themselves. Here they diverted themselves till Ave Marias, when they retired to the House and drank Tea.

Immediately on finishing tea, they went to the Theatre where the Gallery was elegantly prepared for their reception, the whole being hung round with Crimson Damask and the front ornamented with Crimson Damask Curtains trimmed with Gold Lace and hung in Festoons, the Rails covered with Crimson Velvet ornamented with a Deep Gold Fringe. On the right hand of the Royal Gallery was a side Gallery for the Archbishop and, opposite on the left hand side, a similar Gallery for the Donas and Açafatas, behind which was sufficient room for all the rest of the Female Attendants to see the play. The Pit was allotted

---

5 Mariana de Arriaga, a senior *açafata*, Maria's favourite lady-in-waiting
6 Workshop where finished glass was cut, engraved and painted with flowers

for such People belonging to the Suite as were not Camaristas or in immediate waiting, as also for the Gentlemen of this Neighbourhood and the Ministros of the City of Leiria. There was also a Private Box under the Royal Gallery for the Principal Ladies of Leiria who were here to see the entertainments.

Immediately on Her Majesty's entrance in the Gallery, the Orchestra, which consisted of four Violins, two French Horns and two Violoncellos, began the Overture, during the performance of which the Royal Family admired the design and painting of the Curtain. It represents a Lady sitting upon a large Tree with the Arms of Portugal by her side and a Youth in a light Gardener's Dress emptying a Cornucopia in her Lap as the Emblem of Plenty and Industry. The expulsion of Indolence is represented by a Beggar who is a healthy, stout, hearty looking Fellow covered with Rags, his Pockets stuffed with Bread, and a Staff in his hand pointed with Iron serves as an offensive or defensive Weapon as best suits his purpose. He is going off with a look of contempt on Industry. The explanation at the bottom is in the following words – Lusitania pelas Artes recebe da Industria Abundancia e desterra a Mendicidade[7]. Over the front of the Stage, two female figures representing Tragedy and Comedy are supporting a Target with the following Label – Vinde e descansai porque trabalhistas,[8] alluding to the motives for which the Theatre was built.

On finishing the Overture, the Curtain was drawn up and the Tragedy of Sésostris commenced.[9] This Play was by particular desire of Her Majesty and I must do our Young People the justice to say that, although they had not a fortnight to study it, they performed their parts exceedingly well. Between the Acts, there were different Dances and Pantomimes, during which the Royal Family were served with Ice of different sorts[10] and other Refreshments. After the Play, the farce of Esganarello was performed with great applause.

As soon as the Theatrical Amusements finished, the Royal Family returned to the House where they found Supper on the Table and the Praça illuminated with about two thousand lights, disposed on frames hung in the following manner [diagram], which covered all the Walls of the Buildings between the Windows, an Obelisk in the middle of the Praça crowned with a Sphere at the top. Two Triumphal Cars with Musick were drawn round the Square and played under the Windows during the time of Supper and, as soon as the Royal Family got up from Table, some pretty fireworks were displayed off which amused

---

7 Portugal receives Abundance from Industry and Indigence is exiled
8 Come and rest from your labours
9 *Sésostris*, written by Hilaire Bernard de Longpierre in 1695, was translated into Portuguese in 1785
10 Ice creams and sorbets

them about a quarter of an hour, when they all retired to their Apartments and a total Silence commenced for the night.

The Royal Family supped together in our large Room at a Table twenty-two palmos long and eleven wide. The Queen sat in the centre on one side of the Table, with the Princess on her right hand side and the Infanta Dona Carlota on the left, the Infanta Dona Mariana at the left hand of Dona Carlota. On the opposite side of the Table fronting the Princess sat the Prince[11] with his Brother Dom João at his right hand opposite Dona Carlota. Their usual custom at Lisbon and the Caldas is to sup and dine each in their different Apartments; in travelling they in general eat together and, on this occasion, they seemed to be very happy in each other's company.

The Table and Sideboards were hung round with pink coloured Nobreza; in the Centre of the large Table was a very elegant Glass ornament made here, representing a Temple. The design was given by the Marquis of Marialva's Copeiro who had the direction of all the Confectionery with the assistance of the Queen's Confectioner who undertook mostly the Management of the Ice, of which there was a great variety and exceeding good. The Custom is to put everything on the Table at once, Meat, Fruit, Sweetmeats etc. All the Dishes from the Kitchen is served up by the direction of Her Majesty's Chief Cook, who had three and twenty Cooks to work under him.

When the Royal Family arose from Table, the Donas and Açafatas and your Humble Servant sat down. It is the usual Custom in Journeys for the Camaristas and Noblemen to sit down at the Table after the Royal Family. It is then called Mesa do Estado, but on this occasion it was judged most expedient for the Ladies to remain up Stairs and the Mesa do Estado for the Camaristas and Secretary of State was placed in our dining Room on the ground floor. This Table was a little smaller than the Royal one. It had a Pyramid of Glass Salvers in the Middle decorated with Sweetmeats and the Table hung round with blue Nobreza. The Archbishop had a Separate Table in his Apartment for himself and Companion Padre Rocha, the late Provincial of the Order of St. Domingos,[12] as had also some others belonging to different departments.

At the upper end of our great Walk in the Garden was erected a wooden barraca, eighty palmos long and thirty wide, hung with Tapestry and covered with Sailcloth. In this Room was a Table containing about fifty or sixty people, where my Brother entertained the Cavalheiros da Província, Ministers and Câmara de Leiria and all such Company as could not be admitted at the other tables.

---

11 José, Prince of Brazil, elder son of Maria I
12 Father Rocha, Dominican friar, confessor and companion to Inácio de São Caetano

The Royal Family and their Female Attendants were all lodged in our House which, on this occasion, was called the Paço or Palace, the Archbishop in the house on the right hand side of the gate, and the Camaristas and Secretary of State etc. at the best house in the place, where we had very excellent Beds made for them. The Livery Servants, Coachmen and Soldiers with their Beasts were all well accommodated under the Wood Sheds, where they had their Kitchen and Dining Rooms according to their several degrees, with a plentiful supply of the best Beef, Rice and Bread that could be got in this Country and as much Aljubarrota wine as they chose to drink. Notwithstanding this, for their honour, I must not omit saying that there was not one got Drunk, nor the least disturbance happened during the whole time they were here, and as a remarkable proof of their Honesty, I can assure you that on this, and the former Occasion of their being here, we lost nothing but two dessert spoons which I suppose to be mislaid or thrown out with the dirt of the Kitchen, it being not an object to be stolen where there was an opportunity of stealing things of a much greater value.

You may guess a little more or less of the number of People belonging to Her Majesty's Suite when I tell you that we had Stables provided with Straw and Barley for six hundred Beasts exclusive of the Troops. Besides the People belonging to the Court, there was a vast concourse from all the Country round this Neighbourhood which Curiosity had brought together to see their Sovereign, with whom they seemed mightily pleased.

On Tuesday morning, the first inst., the Infante Dom João got up at four o'clock and took a Ride with a few Attendants to see his Estates at Monte Real, the Camp of Leiria, and the Works at the Foz da Vieira two leagues distant.[13] He examined the whole very minutely and returned very well pleased with his Excursion between eight and nine o'clock. By this time, the Queen and all the Royal Family were up and dressed. They breakfasted in their different Apartments on Tea and Toast à Inglesa. Breakfast being over, their Travelling Altar was erected in the Queen's Dressing Room, where Mass was celebrated by one of Her Majesty's Chaplains in the presence of the Royal Family and a few of their Attendants. This being over, they amused themselves in walking about the House and conversing very affable with any persons who came in their way.

Between one and two o'clock, Dinner was served up in the same manner as the preceding Supper. During Coffee, the Carriages were got ready, when they took a Ride with a few Attendants to see the famous and ancient City of Leiria. After passing under a Triumphant Arch erected by the Câmara or Chamber

---

13 Foz da Vieira, mouth of the River Liz, where engineers were removing sandbanks which narrowed the entrance channel

at the entrance of the City, they drove straight to the Cathedral Church where they were received with the usual Ceremonies by the Bishop. On their first going to any Church, it is the custom for the Bishop or the Principal Priest belonging to the Church to receive the Queen at the Door under the Canopy which they carry over the Sacrament. In this manner, she walks with the Royal Family up to the High Altar where velvet cushions are placed for them to kneel on. During their private prayers, a short Te Deum is sung, accompanied by such Musick as the Church affords. This being finished, they retire in the same manner they entered.

After viewing the Cathedral, they went in their Carriage to the Bishop's Palace, which is very spacious and well furnished. It is situated on an Eminence and commands a most beautiful prospect of the City. The Ruins of an old Moorish Castle, the River and the Country adjacent, they saw the whole with great pleasure and, after partaking of an elegant Merenda, they left the Palace and went to the Convent of Nuns of the Dominican order. After seeing the Church, they went into the Convent and examined every corner of it with satisfaction. They left the poor Nuns highly impressed with Gratitude, not only for the Honour of the Visit, but also for Her Majesty's Gracious Bounty of twenty Moydores which she left for their support. Thirty Moydores were also ordered to be given to the poor of the City. At the Convent Door, they got into their Carriages vastly delighted with the City of Leiria which, on this occasion, made a great figure, the houses being all whitewashed, the streets covered with sand, and the windows hung with curtains the same as on Grand Procession days. At Ave Marias, they all arrived here again safe.

The Prince and his Brother left Leiria some time before the Queen. They came part of the Road in a Chaise, then mounted their Horses and took a Ride to see the Timber Fabrick and the Forest,[14] which is near our House, but arrived here at the same time with the Queen. After drinking Tea, they went again to the Theatre with the same Ceremonies as the preceding night and saw the Comedy of Dom José de Alvarado, Criado de Sigmesmo.[15] It's a laughable piece and was acted with great Humour. At the end of the second Act, a Solo was played on the Violoncello by a Young Man of Leiria who is studying Physic at Coimbra, as a Curioso. He plays very well, the Royal Family applauded much his performance. Between the other Acts were different Dances and Pantomimes, the whole concluded with the Farce of the Letrado Avarento.[16]

---

14 The state-owned sawmill and royal pine forest of Leiria
15 *Dom José de Alvarado, Servant of Himself*
16 *The Miserly Scholar*

The Theatre was illuminated with Wax and the Dresses on each night new according to the Characters. The Performers acquitted themselves with Honour and received universal Applause, not only from the Royal Family but from all the Audience who thought it impossible that a rude Country Place like this could have produced such good Actors. Their Surprise was greatly increased on finding that the greatest part of them had never been more than two or three leagues from this Parish, and that they all worked in the Fabrick. They perform only for their Amusement, which you must allow is very different from the Public Theatres where the Actors have no other Employment than studying their parts and their whole subsistence depends upon the favourable Opinion of the Public.

The Amusements of the Theatre being finished, the Royal Family returned to the House where Supper, Illuminations, Triumphal Cars and Fireworks concluded the diversions in the same manner as on the preceding night.

The next morning, Wednesday the 2nd inst., the Royal Family arose early, dressed, breakfasted and heard Mass in the same manner as before mentioned, during which everything was got ready for their departure between eight and nine o'clock. The Prince and Princess[17] got into their Carriage and drove straight through to the Caldas, being afraid to stop and dine at Nazaré on account of the Smallpox which raged there, it being doubtful whether the Prince [has] had this disorder or not. On taking leave of Her Royal Highness, I kissed her hand and thanked her for the Honour she had done us in this Visit and wished her a good Journey. In return she gave me an Abraço, thanked me for the Hospitable Entertainments she had received, and wished me Health and Happiness. My Brother took leave of the Prince in the same manner and attended him to the Door of the Carriage. On driving out of the Gate, they were again saluted with three Vivas.

Her Majesty and the rest of the Royal Family remained near an hour after the Prince and Princess were gone. On the Queen's leaving her Apartment, I kissed her hand when she thanked me for the Entertainment we had given her, with a Countenance that indicated she was pleased with everything she had seen. I then took leave of the Infantas Dona Mariana and Dona Carlota. The former gave me an Abraço and repeated her thanks in the same manner as the Queen and Princess.

At the bottom of the Stairs, the Administrator of the Fabrick, with the two Book-keepers and Paymaster, were introduced and kissed Her Majesty's Hand who received them very graciously and applauded very much the Industry of our People, the good order and management of the Fabrick, and the Harmony which subsisted between the People belonging to the Manufactory. They then

---

17 José and Benedita, Prince and Princess of Brazil

went through the same Ceremony with the Infante Dom João and the two Infantas, who also received them very graciously. In the Hall were the Bishop of Leiria with his Attendants and the Ministros and Câmara of Leiria who took leave in the same manner.

My Brother attended Her Majesty to the Door of the Carriage where she again repeated her thanks for his Hospitality and drove away amidst the Acclamations of a great number of people who remained penetrated with love and respect for their Sovereign and all the Royal Family for their pleasing and affable deportment during their stay in this place. From our House they went to the Church. After a few minutes in prayer there, they went to the borders of the Forest and, from thence, to Nazaré where they paid their usual devotions to Nossa Senhora,[18] dined, went to the Praia to see some Nets drawn with Fish, and from thence to the Caldas where they slept that night and rested the next day, Thursday. On Friday the 4th inst., they returned to Lisbon where they speak with high encomiums of the Entertainment they received here.

In short, my Brother has attained what nobody else in the Kingdom can boast of, which is the honour of entertaining the Royal Family and all the Court for two days, and given universal satisfaction to everybody from the Queen down to the Scullions and Stable Boys. The first time of Her Majesty's coming here was not so surprising, as curiosity to see the Glass Fabrick was supposed to be the motive, but that she should come a second time and sleep two Nights in the house of a private person, an Englishman and a Protestant, is a thing that never entered the Idea of the Portuguese and has struck all those Country People with amazement. Her Majesty liked her Situation so well that she regretted leaving it, and would have stayed longer had it not been for the unavoidable necessity of returning so soon to Lisbon. The Orders were already passed for the change of Beasts on the Road and everything to be got ready for their reception at the Praça de Comércio[19] and it was now too late to recede. She left one hundred Moydores to be distributed among the People of the Fabrick and twenty Moydores for the poor of the Parish.

Immediately on Her Majesty's leaving us, our House was open for every person who chose to see it. We had a large Company from Leiria and the Neighbourhood who dined with us at the Royal Table; at night, the same Illuminations were repeated. The Tragedy of Sésostris, with the same new Dresses, Dances and Pantomimes as on the first night, were performed with universal applause to a numerous Audience, free admittance being granted (as is our usual custom to every person of all Ranks and Denominations). After the

18 Nossa Senhora de Nazaré, Chapel of Our Lady of Nazaré
19 A reception to welcome the Queen when the royal barge arrived in the city

Play, our Company supped with us at the Royal Table, drank Her Majesty's health, and concluded our three days Festival with no small satisfaction to ourselves and all our Neighbours, it being altogether such a sight as they had never seen before.

A few days previous to Her Majesty's arrival here, the Chief Director of the Household came with the Armador who brought five Beds for the Royal Family and Curtains for the Doors and Windows of the Principal Rooms. They were of Crimson Damask trimmed with Gold Lace and Valance of Crimson Velvet with a Deep Gold Fringe.

The Prince and Princess's Bed was very large and elegant. The Stands were Iron Gilt, the Boards painted white. Over them was a Crimson Buckram Covering with Crimson Damask Valance fastened to it. The Head Board was covered with Crimson Damask, over which was a Case of a most Beautiful fine Muslin worked with small spots of Silver, the edges trimmed with an elegant Silver Blond Lace plaited on pretty thick. The first Mattress was of a very fine new Pano de Linho which they brought empty and filled here with Rye straw. Over this was two Mattresses of very fine Irish Linen stuffed with Wool. These were covered with a very good Pano de Linho Sheet which four men pulled with all their strength and tucked in under the Straw Mattress. Next was a fine Irish Linen Sheet tucked in in the same manner. Two flat Bolsters were then laid on each other, Stuffed with Wool and Quilted in the same manner as the Mattresses. The Bolster Cases were plain but of finer Linen than the Sheets. The Upper Sheet of fine Irish Linen was then put on with a Crimson Damask Coverlid, the part of the Sheet which turns down being tucked to the Coverlid. Over this, instead of a Blanket, was an Orange Colour broad Cloth Covering bound with Ribbon of the same Colour. This Covering was to be taken off, or put on, at pleasure. Upon this was another Crimson Damask Coverlid which was also tucked in very tight under the Straw Mattress, and the whole was covered with the same Elegant Silver spotted Muslin as the Head Board, with a deep full flounce that reached from the Upper Mattress to the Floor, the whole trimmed with Silver Blond lace. The State round Bolster was then laid on the Bed in a Case of the same Muslin trimmed in the same manner as the Coverlid and the ends tied with large knots of the best English white Ribbon. A Crimson Taffety Covering was then thrown lightly over the whole to keep off the Dust.

The Queen's Bedstead was the same as the Princess's but smaller and the Mattresses, flat Bolsters and Sheets the same as has been already described. Instead of an Orange Colour Broad Cloth Covering, hers was white. The Head Board was covered with Crimson Damask, the same as the Coverlid and Valance, without any other ornament than being bound with Silk Lace of the same Colour.

The Infantas Dona Mariana, Dona Carlota and the Infante Dom João's Bedsteads were all three of Brazil Wood, the Mattresses, Bolsters and Covering the same as the Queen's, except the Infanta Dona Carlota, whose Bed was made in the English style. The Sheets which she brought from Spain were remarkably fine but plain. The Bolster was round with a Cambric Case bordered at each end with a fine flowered Muslin. The Coverlid was White Satin Quilted à Inglesa, over which was thrown a Crimson Taffety Covering to preserve it from Dust. The Bedstead had posts and Mosquito Nets.

The Queen's and Princess's had Testers and Curtains belonging to them. But Her Majesty, most graciously recollecting that our Rooms being elegantly furnished with Stucco, the Testers could not be fastened without driving Hooks into the Ceiling, for which reason she gave positive orders for the Beds to be made without Curtains as she would not consent by any means for the most trifling thing to be done to injure the House which she often admired for its neatness. She very politely took every opportunity of praising everything. After Dinner, she told me she had eaten very hearty, everything being exceeding good.

The Marquis de Pombal[20] was the only person who brought his Bed, except the five of the Royal Family. All the rest were provided by us, which altogether amounted to some hundreds which we got from Leiria and its Neighbourhood, it being impossible to collect so great a number in this place. The Livery Servants and Soldiers were delighted to find they had got decent Beds to sleep in. It was a Luxury they enjoyed for the first time since leaving Lisbon on the 3rd of May. During the whole time of their being at the Caldas, they were obliged to sleep on loose straw in the Stables, on the Ground, or wheresoever they could find a place to lay themselves down, such is the Hardship these poor fellows endure when Travelling with the Court and is probably the reason of their committing many Outrages, but I must again repeat that their good behaviour here entitled them to every Indulgence.

The Royal Family are waited upon at Table by their Camaristas and Reposteiros. On the Queen's entering the Dining Room, she is presented by her Camarista on his knee with Water and a Towel to wash her hands, which being done she takes her Seat and the Camarista stands behind her Chair. The same Ceremony is observed with all the rest of the Royal Family. The Camarista then carves such Dishes as they choose to eat of, and when anything is required from the Side Boards, the Reposteiros reach it to the Camarista who puts it on the Table. When water or wine is required, the Reposteiro draws the Cork and brings the Bottle and Glass on a Salver to the Camarista who, on his knee, pours out the liquor and presents it to the Queen, remaining in the same attitude to

---

20 2nd Marquis of Pombal, gentleman of the bedchamber

receive the Glass when she has done drinking. When Dinner is over, they again wash their hands and retire to drink Coffee.

They are very particular with respect to the water they drink which is all brought in flasks from Lisbon, some from the Chafariz da Praia[21] and some from the Ajuda. One of the Reposteiros who was Provedor das Aguas I observed had nothing else to do but to keep the Key of the Water Chests and take care that there was always a Bottle full of water ready on the Side Board and on a Table in each of the Apartments. Her Majesty's Bottle was distinguished by having a bit of narrow White Ribbon tied round the Neck. Claret is the wine chiefly made use of, and that only a very small quantity.

Her Majesty I found greatly improved in her looks since she was here in the year 1786, being now fatter, of a better colour and more cheerful countenance. The Princess is somewhat thinner but still retains a pleasant agreeable aspect. The Infanta Dona Mariana is fatter and, although not handsome, has something agreeable and Majestick in her appearance. The Infanta Dona Carlota appears just the same as when she was here last, lively but very short, nor does her Countenance indicate that she will ever grow much taller. I have seen children as Lusty at nine years of age; she is now in her fourteenth.

The Queen, Princess and Infantas were dressed in Silk Riding Habits, every day a different one. Her Majesty wears her Hair twined up before in a plain tight Toupet, behind in a Bag like the Gentlemen or in a Queue. She makes use of a little old-fashioned Cocked Hat which she generally carries in her hand or under her arm. It's seldom she puts it on her Head but when she rides on Horseback. The Princess had her Hair frizzed before and tied in a Club behind. She wore a large Hat in the English fashion, round the Crown of which was a Ribbon with a Knot on one side ornamented with Steel Bows. The two Infantas were also nearly in the same style with the Princess. They all wore Broad Black Velvet Girdles round the waist, fastened before with two monstrous large Medallions, set and ornamented with steel, which I believe were English.

The Donas and Açafatas are not allowed to wear either Riding Dresses or Hats, let the Journey be ever so long and the Wind, Sun and Dust ever so troublesome. They are obliged to travel through it in Chaises dressed in the same manner as we English people commonly do on Friday nights when we go to the Long Room.[22] No person is allowed to sit in the presence of any of the Royal Family, except the Archbishop who is the Queen's Confessor. The Camaristas, when tired of standing, may rest themselves by kneeling on one

---

21 One of the highly decorated fountains in Lisbon which supplied water to the people
22 Ballroom of the British Assembly Rooms in Lisbon

knee whilst talking or playing at cards. The Donas and Açafatas have sometimes leave to sit on the floor.

The Expense of this Entertainment was about a fifth part of what is computed by People in general, notwithstanding my Brother amply rewarded the Cooks and Copeiros for their trouble. Previous to their coming, everything was provided for them so that, on their arrival, they had nothing to do but begin their Work. We required nothing from Her Majesty's Household but the Damask Hangings for the Doors and Windows and the large Coppers for the use of the Kitchen. China, Damask, Table and Plate we have sufficient for the service of all the different Tables. Having had some reason to expect this visit last year, we got a large supply of silver hafted knives and forks and spoons from England, of the best quality and newest fashion, all which is carefully preserved for the next occasion, which probably will be next year as the Royal Family have some thoughts of going to Coimbra.

A little Anecdote happened which is scarcely worth mention only as a proof of Her Majesty's determined resolution to be pleased with everything she met with. The Queen and Princess have each a particular Teapot and Cup and Saucer which they always make use of. The Princess brought hers. The Female Servant who packed it up enquired of the Queen if she would have hers packed up also, to which Her Majesty said *No*, that she knew very well Stephens had provided everything that was requisite and she was determined to make use of nothing but what belonged to his House.

Glossary

(Portuguese words in italics)

A/O	The
Abraço	Embrace or hug
Açafata	Junior lady-in-waiting. Maria I had several dozen *açafatas* in attendance
Ague/aguish	Cold fit with shivering (sometimes a symptom of malaria)
à Inglesa	In the English style
Aljubarrota	Village near Marinha Grande; wine from this locality
Armador	Royal servant who assembled furniture, hung curtains and oversaw the decorations when the royal family moved from one residence to another
Artificer	Craftsman; workman with skill
Ave Marias	Phrase used to denote time of day (often refers to six o'clock in the evening)
Bacalhau	Dried and salted fish
Bag	Silken pouch to contain hair at the back of the head (eighteenth-century usage)
Barraca	Wooden barrack; marquee
Beija-mão	Ceremony involving the kissing of hands
Bergantim	Barge
Câmara	Chamber; town council
Camarista	Lord of the bedchamber
Cavalheiros	Gentlemen
Cavalheiros da Província	Gentlemen of the province
Chafariz	Fountain
Chafariz de Praia	One of the highly decorated fountains in Lisbon which supplied water to the people
Chaise	Two-wheeled carriage
Club	Club-shaped knot or bun of hair worn at the top or back of the head (fashionable in the late eighteenth century)
Comércio	Business; commerce

Conto	Unit of currency representing one thousand *milreis* (a million *reis*)
Copeiro	Household official in charge of drinks and confectionery
Corregidor	Magistrate
Cruzado	Coin worth 400 *reis*
Curioso	Curiosity
Dom	Title given to men of royal birth
Dona	Title given to women of royal birth; senior lady-in-waiting of noble birth
Dropsy	Archaic medical term for oedema (fluid retention in bodily tissues)
e	and
Estado	State; kingdom
Fabrick	Factory
Factory	Trade organisation of merchants
Família	Family
Foz	Mouth of a river
Guardaroupa	Servant in charge of the royal wardrobe
Infanta	Princess
Infante	Prince
Inglesa	English
Junta	Council
Junta do Comércio	Board of Trade; Chamber of Commerce
Largo	Small square
League	Measurement of distance (1 league = 3 miles)
Louco/Louca	Mad; insane
Manufactory	Factory; industrial enterprise
Merenda	Light meal; collation
Mesa	Table
Mesa do Estado	Table of State
Milreis	Unit of currency: one thousand *reis*
Ministros	Men with official positions in a town or city
Moças da Prata	Servants in charge of the royal silver
Moydore (moidore)	Coin worth 4000 *reis* (4 *milreis*)
Nobreza	Nobility; rich silk cloth used by the nobility
Nossa Senhora	Our Lady
O/A	The
Paço	Palace

Palmo	Measurement of the long side of the hand (one *palmo* = about 8 inches)
Pano de linho	Fine linen cloth
Praça	Square; courtyard
Praia	Beach
Príncipe	Prince
Provedor	Comptroller; superintendent of office
Provedor das aguas	*Reposteiro* in charge of drinking water
Província	Province; neighbourhood
Queue	Long plait of hair hanging down from the back of the head
Quinta	Country house; estate
Rainha	Queen
Rei	King
Reposteiro	Footman
Real	Royal; basic unit of currency
Real Barraca	Royal palace built of wood on the hill of Ajuda near Belém
Real bergantim	Royal barge
Reis	Currency, plural of *real*
Taffety	Taffeta
Terreiro	Square; place of
Terremoto	Earthquake
Tester	Canopy over a bed
Todo/toda	All
Toupet (toupee)	Hair at the front of the head combed back from the forehead over a pad (eighteenth-century usage)
Varanta	Veranda; pavilion
Vivas	Cheers
Viva Rainha	Long live the Queen
Viva Rei	Long live the King

Reference Notes

Correspondence of British envoys and consuls in Lisbon is not referenced in the text. This can be found in the National Archives, Kew (Series SP 89 for years up to and including 1780, series FO 63 thereafter).

The same applies to official correspondence on the limekilns in Alcântara and the glass factory in Marinha Grande. This can be found in two publications: *Real Fábrica de Vidros da Marinha Grande, II Centenário 1769–1969* by Carlos Vitorino da Silva Barros; and *O Período Stephens: Na Real Fábrica de Vidros da Marinha Grande* by Emília Margarida Marques. See bibliography.

Introduction

1 Philadelphia Stephens, 25 July 1788 (WSRO, Add MS 8123)
2 Southey, *Journals*, pp. 19–20, footnote
3 Withering, I, pp. 314–5
4 Hawkey, p. 142

Prelude: The Catalyst

1 Macaulay, *They Went to Portugal*, pp. 273–4

1. A Young Merchant

1 Baretti, p. 63
2 *Gentleman's Magazine*, vol. 16 (1746), pp. 473–4

2. The Most Opulent City

1 Beirão, *Cartas*, pp. 129–30
2 Baretti, p. 107
3 Whitefield, pp. 12–14
4 Carrère, pp. 75–7
5 Wraxall, I, p. 11
6 Ibid, I, pp. 15–16
7 A. Hervey, *Journal*, p. 179
8 Beckford, *Journal*, p. 262

3. The Rise of Pombal

1 Cheke, *Dictator*, p. 50
2 Ibid, p. 33
3 Walford, *The British Factory*, pp. 55–6
4 'Publicus', pp. 11–14

4. Catastrophe

1 *An Account by an Eye-witness*, pp. 6–12, 18
2 *Gentleman's Magazine*, vol. 26 (1756), pp. 67–8
3 Ibid, vol. 83, II (1813), pp. 316–7
4 Ibid, vol. 25 (1755), p. 561
5 Ibid, vol. 25 (1755), p. 592
6 Shrady, pp. 21–2
7 Wraxall, I, p. 17

5. Retribution

1 Kendrick, pp. 137–8
2 Cheke, *Dictator*, p. 110
3 C. Hervey, I, p. 17
4 Ibid, I, p. 115
5 Baretti, p. 180

6. A Quiet Wedding

1 Baretti, pp. 96–7
2 Wraxall, I, p. 35
3 Baretti, p. 256
4 Cormatin, I, p. 132
5 Baretti, pp. 87, 92–3
6 Ibid, pp. 106, 109–11
7 Wraxall, I, p. 36

7. Alcântara

1 Hay to Sir Thomas Stepney, 18 June 1757 (National Library of Wales, Cilymaenllwyn, 261)
2 Advertising leaflet for Alcântara lime, 1759 (British Library, 9181.e.4)
3 Paice, p. 209

4 Christ's Hospital, presentation papers (GL)
5 Ibid, children's registers (GL)
6 W. Stephens to Lord Loudoun, June 1761 (British Library, Add MS 44070, Vol. VIII, f.245)
7 Baillie, II, p. 5

8. An Unfortunate Muleteer

1 Hobart, 5 July 1767 (NRO)
2 Ibid, April 1769 (NRO)

9. Marinha Grande

1 *Gentleman's Magazine*, vol. 19 (1749), p. 512
2 Balsemão, V, ch. III, para. 4

10. A Miniature Welfare State

1 Custódio, pp. 259–61
2 Wraxall, I, p. 64
3 Cheke, *Dictator*, p. 77
4 Vasconcellos e Sá, *Diário da Jornada* (ANP)
5 Stephens to Pombal, 7 April 1778 (BN, PBA 704)
6 Nicolau Luís da Silva, c.1786 (Barros, p. 24)
7 A. Gibbs, 10 December 1798 (GL, 11021/5)

11. The Succession

1 Beckford, *Journal*, p. 43
2 Cheke, *Dictator*, pp. 237–8
3 Ibid, p. 249

12. Absolute Power

1 Cheke, *Dictator*, p. 221
2 Ibid, p. 254
3 Cormatin, I, pp. 29–30
4 Frederick Robinson, Thomas Robinson, July–August 1778 (Bedfordshire Archives, L/30/15/54; L/30/17/2)

13. A Time of Uncertainty

1 Cormatin, I, pp. 174–5, footnote
2 Stephens to Pombal, 12, 17, 25 September 1777 (BN, PBA 704)
3 Smith, II, pp. 322–3
4 Stephens to Pombal, 14 February 1778 (BN, PBA 691)
5 Stephens to Pombal, 7 April 1778 (BN, PBA 704)
6 Ibid, 17 September 1778 (BN, PBA 704)

14. The Trial of Pombal

1 Cheke, *Dictator*, p. 283
2 West, p. 10
3 Ibid, pp. 10–11
4 Cheke, *Dictator*, p. 289
5 Maria I to Charles III, 16 January 1781 (Beirão, *Dona Maria*, pp. 428–9)
6 Smith, II, pp. 352–4
7 Barros, pp. 23, 26

15. The Double Marriage

1 Maria I to Maria Josefa de Bourbon, 20 January, 16 February 1783 (Beirão, *Dona Maria*, pp. 439–40)
2 Maria I to Charles III, 8 May 1785 (Beirão, *Dona Maria*, p. 436)
3 João to Mariana, 30 May 1785 (Pereira, I, pp. 45–6)
4 Ibid, 17 June 1785 (Pereira, I, pp. 50–5)
5 Ibid, 4, 19 December 1786 (Pereira, I, p. 48)

16. English Comfort

1 João to Mariana, 14, 24, 28 March 1786 (Pereira, I, p. 48)
2 Ibid, 28 July 1786 (Pereira, I, pp. 19–21)
3 Beckford, *Italy*, II, p. 73
4 Bombelles, p. 185
5 *Gazeta de Lisboa*, no. 44, 31 October 1786
6 Bombelles, pp. 55, 71
7 Beckford, *Journal*, p. 242
8 Ibid, pp. 263–4
9 Pinto, I, pp. 216–7

17. The Great Occasion

18. A String of Tragedies

1 Philadelphia Stephens, 25 July 1788 (WRSO, Add MS 8123)
2 Charles III to Maria I, 2, 6 November 1788 (Beirão, *Dona Maria*, p. 366)
3 Beckford, *Italy*, II, p. 101

19. A Fragile Mind

1 Winslow, II, p. 175, footnote
2 Maria I to Queen Maria Luísa, 23 March 1790 (Beirão, *Dona Maria*, p. 447)
3 Pinto, 4 February 1792 (Beirão, *Dona Maria*, pp. 411–2)

20. The Hat-Trick

1 Custódio, pp. 259–61
2 Ratton, p. 138
3 *The Lisbon Guide*, p. 58
4 Withering, I, p. 314
5 Withering to Banks, 31 October 1797 (NHM)
6 Watt to Banks, 5 November 1797 (NHM)
7 Banks to Withering, 23 December 1797, 18 May 1798 (NHM)
8 A. Gibbs, 10 December 1798 (GL, 11021/5)

21. The Gathering Storm

1 Link, p. 240
2 Jervis, 28 December 1796 (Tucker, I, pp. 278–9)
3 Southey, *Journals*, p. 151
4 Ibid, *Life*, II, p. 137
5 Baillie, II, pp. 203–4
6 St. Vincent, 24 August 1806 (Tucker, II, p. 293)
7 Ibid, 10 October 1806 (Tucker, II, pp. 302–3)
8 Wilcken, pp. 22–3

22. Exile

1 Santos, I, pp. 219, 220

2 Mello Moraes, II, p. 160
3 Luccock, pp. 96–7
4 Ibid, p. 570
5 Baillie, I, pp. 30–1
6 Baillie, II, pp. 76–81
7 Ibid, p. 81

23. Invasion

1 Hipwell, pp. 187–9
2 Thiébault, II, p. 199
3 *Progresso Industrial*, p. 10
4 Ibid, p. 11
5 Vassall, pp. 243–5
6 Stewart, p. 247
7 Sherer, pp. 45–7

24. Devastation

1 Sherer, pp.158–9
2 Stewart, pp. 434–5
3 Pelet, p. 246
4 Broughton, p. 113
5 Robinson, I, pp. 403–4, footnote
6 Trant, pp. 8–9

25. Aftermath

1 J.J. Stephens to Sousa, 17, 21 April 1824 (CM)
2 A. Gibbs, 4 November 1801 (GL, 11021/6)
3 Lyne, pp. 156–7
4 Ibid, pp. 152–5
5 Christ's Hospital, presentation papers (GL)
6 James Bowness, 13 November 1826 (WSRO, Add MS 8127)

Coda: The Legacy

1 *Morning Post*, 6 December 1826
2 Christ's Hospital, committee minutes, 21 February 1827 (GL)

Bibliography

Manuscript Sources

Arquivos Nacionais, Torre de Tombo, Lisbon (ANP)
> João Christiano de Faria e Sousa de Vasconcellos e Sá, *Diário da Jornada do Marquês de Pombal para Coimbra neste anno de 1772* (Ministeiro do Reino, livro 436, 1720)

Biblioteca Nacional, Lisbon (BN)
> Transfer of glassworks to the state, transcription of documents, 1826–7 (F 2852)
> William Stephens, letters to Marquis de Pombal, 1777–9 (PBA 691, 704)

Biblioteca Pública de Évora (BPE)
> William Stephens, letter to Cenáculo Vilas Boas, 1793

Câmara Municipal da Marinha Grande (CM)
> John James Stephens, letters to José de Sousa e Oliveira, 1811–26
> Stephens brothers, accounts book, 1786–1802

Guildhall Library, Corporation of London (GL)
> Anglican chaplaincy registers, Lisbon
> Antony Gibbs & Sons: archives (MS 11021–5)
> Christ's Hospital:
>> Children's registers (MS 12818)
>> Presentation papers (MS 12818A)
>> Committee minutes (MS 12811/17)

National Archives, Kew (NA)
> Foreign Office papers, Portugal (FO 63)
> Lisbon Factory book, 1811–24
> State papers, Portugal (SP 89)
> Treasury Solicitor's papers (TS 25/18)

Natural History Museum, London (NHM)
> Banks Project: Correspondence of Sir Joseph Banks, Carter transcription, 1797–8

Norfolk Record Office (NRO)
  Journal of tours by Henry Hobart in Portugal and Spain (COL 13/27)

Private collection (PC)
  William Stephens: 'Memórias sobre a Cultura da Lucerna' (MS transcription,
  1803)

West Sussex Record Office (WSRO)
  Documents relating to the families of Stephens and Cogan (Add MS 8123,
  8127)

Published Sources

An Account by an Eye-witness of the Lisbon Earthquake of November 1, 1755
  (Lisbon, 1985).

BAILLIE, Marianne, *Lisbon in the Years 1821, 1822 and 1823,* 2 vols. (London,
  1825).

BALSEMÃO, Visconde de, 'Memória sobre a Descripção Física e Econômica
  do Lugar da Marinha Grande e suas Visinhanças', *Memórias Econômicas da
  Academia Real das Sciências de Lisboa,* V (Lisbon, 1815).

BARETTI, Joseph, *A Journey from London to Genoa, through England, Portugal,
  Spain and France* (facsimile reprint, London, 1970).

BARROS, Carlos Vitorino da Silva, *Real Fábrica de Vidros da Marinha
  Grande, II Centenário 1769–1969* (Lisbon, 1969).

BECKFORD, William, *Italy, with Sketches of Spain and Portugal,* 2 vols.
  (London, 1834).

BECKFORD, William, *The Journal of William Beckford in Portugal and Spain
  1787–1788,* ed. Boyd Alexander (London, 1954).

BECKFORD, William, *Recollections of an Excursion to the Monasteries of
  Alcobaça and Batalha,* ed. Boyd Alexander (Arundel, 1972).

BEIRÃO, Caetano Maria de Abreu, *Cartas da Rainha D. Mariana Vitória
  para a sua Família de Espanha* (Lisbon, 1936).

BEIRÃO, Caetano Maria de Abreu, *Dona Maria I, 1777–1792* (2nd edn,
  Lisbon, 1944).

BOMBELLES, Marc Marie, Marquis de, *Journal d'un Ambassadeur de
  France au Portugal, 1786–1788,* ed. Roger Kann (Paris, 1979).

BOXER, C.R., 'Pombal's Dictatorship and the Great Lisbon Earthquake 1755', *History Today*, vol. 5/11 (November 1955).

BRITO, Manuel Carlos de, *Opera in Portugal in the Eighteenth Century* (Cambridge, 1989).

BROUGHTON, S.D., *Letters from Portugal, Spain and France during the Campaigns of 1812, 1813 and 1814* (London, 1815).

BUSH, R.J.E., *Exeter Free Grammar School* (Exeter, 1962).

CARRÈRE, J.B.F., *A Picture of Lisbon taken on the spot ... by a Gentleman many years resident at Lisbon* (London, 1809).

CHEKE, Marcus, *Dictator of Portugal: A Life of the Marquis of Pombal* (London, 1938).

CHEKE, Marcus, *Carlota Joaquina: Queen of Portugal* (London, 1947).

CORMATIN, P.M.F.D., Duke du Châtelet, *Travels of the Duke du Châtelet in Portugal*, ed. J.-F. Bourgoing, trans. J.J. Stockdale, 2 vols. (London, 1809).

CUSTÓDIO, Jorge, *A Real Fábrica de Vidros de Coina (1719–1747) e o Vidro em Portugal nos Séculos XVII e XVIII* (Lisbon, 2002).

Expresso: photographs by Luiz Carvalho (13 June 1992).

FERRÃO, Antonio, *A Reforma Pombalina da Universidade de Coimbra* (Coimbra, 1926).

FERRO, Maria Inês, *Queluz: The Palace and Gardens* (London, 1997).

FOURCROY DE RAMECOURT, Charles René, *Art du Chaufournier* (Paris, 1766).

FRANCIS, David, *Portugal 1715–1808: Joanine, Pombaline and Rococo Portugal as seen by British Diplomats and Traders* (London, 1985).

Gazeta de Lisboa, no. 43 (24 October 1786).

Gentleman's Magazine (London): vol. 16 (1746), vol. 19 (1749), vol. 25 (1755), vol. 26 (1756), vol. 83, I (1813).

GLOVER, Michael, *The Peninsular War 1807–1814* (Newton Abbot, 1974).

GREEN, Vivian, *The Madness of Kings: Personal Trauma and the Fate of Nations* (Stroud, 1993).

HAWKEY, Charlotte, *Neota* (Taunton, 1871).

HERVEY, Augustus, *Augustus Hervey's Journal,* ed. David Erskine (London, 2002).

HERVEY, Christopher, *Letters from Portugal, Spain, Italy and Germany in the years 1759, 1760 and 1761,* 3 vols. (London, 1785).

HIPWELL, H. Hallam, 'Lisbon on the Eve of Invasion, as Seen in Unpublished Letters of a Local Merchant-Banker of 1807', Report of British Historical Society of Portugal (Lisbon, 1939).

ISHAM, Ken, *Lime Kilns and Limeburners in Cornwall* (St Austell, 2000).

KEENE, Sir Benjamin, *The Private Correspondence of Sir Benjamin Keene, KB,* ed. Richard Lodge (London, 2007).

KENDRICK, T.D., *The Lisbon Earthquake* (New York, 1957).

Letters from Portugal on the Late and Present State of that Kingdom (attributed to John Blankett, London, 1777).

LINK, Henry Frederick, *Travels in Portugal and through France and Spain* (London, 1801).

The Lisbon Guide, containing Directions to Invalids who visit Lisbon (London, 1800).

LODGE, Sir Richard, 'The English Factory in Lisbon: Some Chapters in its History', *Royal Historical Society Transactions* (1933).

LUCCOCK, John, *Notes on Rio de Janeiro and the Southern Parts of Brazil taken during a Residence of Ten Years in that Country from 1808 to 1818* (London, 1820).

LYNE, Francis, *A Letter to Father Ignatius on the Death of his Mother* (London, 1878).

MACAULAY, Rose, *They went to Portugal* (London, 1946).

MACAULAY, Rose, *They went to Portugal Too* (Manchester, 1990).

MARQUES, Emília Margarida, *O Período Stephens: Na Real Fábrica de Vidros da Marinha Grande* (Marinha Grande: Santos Barosa, Estudos e Documentos, no. 11, 1999).

MAXWELL, Kenneth, *Pombal, Paradox of the Enlightenment* (Cambridge, 1995).

MELLO MORAES, A.J. de, *Chronica Geral do Brazil,* 2 vols. (Rio de Janeiro, 1886).

MICKLE, William Julius, *Almada Hill: An Epistle from Lisbon* (Oxford, 1781).

NORRIS, A.H., *The British Hospital in Lisbon* (Lisbon, 1973).

NORRIS, A.H. and BREMNER R.W., *The Lines of Torres Vedras* (2nd edn, Lisbon, 1980).

NOZES, Judite (ed.), *The Lisbon Earthquake of 1755: British Accounts* (Lisbon, 1990).

NOZES, Judite (ed.), *The Lisbon Earthquake of 1755: Some British Eye-witness Accounts* (Lisbon, 1987).

O'NEILL, Thomas (Count), *A Concise and Accurate Account of the Proceedings of the Squadron under the Command of Rear-Admiral Sir W. S. Smith, in effecting the Escape and Escorting of the Royal Family of Portugal to the Brazils* (London, 1809).

PAICE, Edward, *Wrath of God: The Great Lisbon Earthquake of 1755* (London, 2008).

PAIVA BOLÉO, Luísa V. de, *D. Maria I: A Rainha Louca* (Lisbon, 2009).

PELET, Jean-Jacques, *The French Campaign in Portugal 1810–1811*, trans. and ed. Donald D. Horward (Minneapolis, 1973).

PEPYS, Samuel, *The Diary of Samuel Pepys* (www.pepysdiary.com)

PEREIRA, Angelo, *D. João VI, Príncipe e Rei*, 4 vols. (Lisbon, 1953–8).

PETERS, Timothy J. and WILLIS, Clive, 'Mad Monarchs: Comparison of the Nature, Causes and Consequences of the Mental Ill-Health of Maria I of Portugal and George III of Great Britain', *The Court Historian* (14 May 2015).

PETERS, Timothy J. and WILLIS, Clive, 'Mental Health Issues of Maria I of Portugal and her Sisters: the Contributions of the Willis family to the Development of Psychiatry', *History of Psychiatry*, vol. 24, no. 3 (2013).

PINTO, A. Arala, *O Pinhal do Rei – Subsídios*, 2 vols. (Alcobaça, 1938–9).

Progresso Industrial, 'A Real Fábrica da Marinha Grande e a Invasão Franceza', Issue 1 (15 February 1896).

'PUBLICUS', *A Letter to the Merchants of the Portugal Committee from a Lisbon Trader* (London, 1754).

RATTON, Jacome, *Recordações: Sobre Occurrências do seu Tempo em Portugal*, ed. J. M. Teixeira de Carvalho (Coimbra, 1920).

ROBERTS, Jenifer, *Glass: The Strange History of the Lyne Stephens Fortune* (Chippenham, 2003).

ROBERTS, Jenifer, *The Madness of Queen Maria* (Chippenham, 2009).

ROBINSON, H.B., *Memoirs of Sir Thomas Picton*, 2 vols. (London, 1836).

SANTOS, Luiz Gonçalves dos (Padre Perereca), *Memórias para servir à História do Reino de Brasil*, 2 vols. (Rio de Janeiro, 1943).

SCHAUMANN, A.L.F., *On the Road with Wellington: The Diary of a War Commissary in the Peninsular Campaign*, trans. and ed. A.M. Ludovici (London, 1924).

SHAW, L.M.E., *The Anglo-Portuguese Alliance and the English Merchants in Portugal 1645–1810* (Aldershot, 1998).

SHERER, Joseph Moyle, *Recollections of the Peninsula* (London, 1825).

SHRADY, Nicholas, *The Last Day: Wrath, Ruin & Reason in the Great Lisbon Earthquake of 1755* (New York, 2008).

SMITH, J.A. (Count de Carnota), *Memoirs of the Marquis of Pombal*, 2 vols. (London, 1843).

SOUTHEY, C.C., *Life and Correspondence of Robert Southey*, 6 vols. (London, 1849–50).

SOUTHEY, Robert, *Journals of a Residence in Portugal 1800–1801 and a Visit to France 1838*, ed. Adolfo Cabral (Oxford, 1960).

SOUTHEY, Robert, *Letters written during a Short Residence in Spain and Portugal* (2nd edn, Bristol, 1799).

STEWART (afterwards Vane), Charles William, Marquis of Londonderry, *Narrative of the Peninsular War from 1808 to 1813* (London, 1828).

TEIXEIRA, José, *O Paço Ducal de Vila Viçosa* (Lisbon, 1983).

THIÉBAULT, Baron de, *The Memoirs of Baron Thiébault, late Lieutenant-General in the French Army*, trans. and ed. J.A. Butler, 2 vols. (London, 1896).

TRANT, Clarissa, *The Journal of Clarissa Trant*, ed. C.G. Luard (London, 1925).

TUCKER, Jedediah Stephens, *Memoirs of Admiral the Right Hon. the Earl of St Vincent*, 2 vols. (London, 1844).

TYRRELL, Stephen, *Pentillie Castle* (Falmouth, 2009).

VASSALL, Elizabeth, *The Spanish Journal of Elizabeth, Lady Holland*, ed. Lord Ilchester (London, 1910).

WALFORD, A.R., 'The British Community in Lisbon, 1755', Report of British Historical Society of Portugal (Lisbon, 1946–50).

WALFORD, A.R., *The British Factory in Lisbon* (Lisbon, 1940).

WEST, S. George, *The Visit to Portugal in 1779–80 of William Julius Mickle* (Lisbon, 1972).

WHITEFIELD, George, *A Brief Account of some Lent and Other Extraordinary Proceedings and Ecclesiastical Entertainments seen last year at Lisbon, in four letters to an English friend* (London, 1755).

WILCKEN, Patrick, *Empire Adrift: The Portuguese Court in Rio de Janeiro 1808–1821* (London, 2004).

WINSLOW, F.B., *Physic & Physicians: A Medical Sketch Book*, 2 vols. (London, 1839).

WITHERING, Dr William, *The Miscellaneous Tracts of the Late William Withering MD FRS, written by his son*, 2 vols. (London, 1822).

WRAXALL, Sir Nathaniel William, *Historical Memoirs of my Own Time*, 2 vols. (London, 1815).

Index